# Shiva Sutra: The Beginning of the Shiva Sutra

Shiva Sutras

Published by Shiva Sutras, 2024.

SHIVA SUTRA: THE BEGINNING OF THE SHIVA SUTRA

**First edition. May 12, 2024.**

Copyright © 2024 Shiva Sutras.

ISBN: 979-8224972708

Written by Shiva Sutras.

# Table of Contents

# The darkness within

*Om! I bow to Lord Shiva, the one who enlightens himself, delighting in his own being.*

*And now, the beginning of the Shiva sutra.*

*Consciousness is atman, the soul; knowledge is bondage. The body is the union of raman, nature, and raman, the ego, the doer. Spiritual effort is raman. He who applies his total energy, for him the world no longer exists.*

There are two ways of searching for truth. One is that of the male: aggression, violence, the struggle for power. The other is that of the feminine: surrender, withdrawal. Science is the masculine, aggressive way; religion is the feminine, yielding, submissive way. Make this distinction very clearly.

All the scriptures of the East begin with a greeting to God. This greeting is not a mere formality, it is not simply following tradition or convention. The greeting is indicative that the road ahead is one of surrender. Only the humble will reach it. The aggressive and ego-filled, those who wish to attain even truth by clinging to it, those who have the attitude of conquering nature, will be defeated. They may possess the trivial, but that which is so immense, so vast, can never be theirs.

They may be able to seize what is worthless, but nothing meaningful can become part of them.

Hence a scientist discovers all that is not essential, but misses the essential. He manages to gather details about soil, stones, matter, but misses the understanding of the soul and of God. It is like attacking a passing woman. You may succeed in raping her, you may even have her body under your control, but you can never have her soul; you can never win her love.

Thus, those who approach God aggressively are the rapists. They may bring God's physical body under their control; they may dissect and analyse the nature that manifests itself around them, they may discover some of its secrets, but the discovery will be as trivial as that of someone who attacks and rapes a woman.

The man can get the woman's body, but such an achievement is not worth a straw, for he will not even be able to touch her soul. And if the soul has remained intact, the possibility of love that is hidden in it, the hidden seed of her love can never sprout. His love will never be able to spill out upon it.

Science is an act of rape. It is an assault on nature, as if nature were some kind of enemy, as if it had to be conquered, defeated. That's why science believes in cutting things to pieces. Analysis, destruction; it believes in dissection.

If you were to say to a scientist: "The flower is beautiful", he would immediately sit down and start tearing the flower to pieces, dissecting it, analysing it. He has no idea that in the very tearing into pieces, the beauty of the flower disappears. The flower looked beautiful in its entirety, but when it was divided into parts, it lost its beauty. Of course, by doing the analysis, the scientist can find out what chemical elements the flower contains; he can show the substance, the minerals of which the flower is made.

You can put them in different bottles and label them accordingly. But you will not be able to say: "Here is a bottle containing the beauty that was once present in the flower", because the beauty will be gone. When you raid the flower, you will only come across its body, not the soul.

This is why science does not believe in the soul, how could it? Even after trying so hard, not even a glimpse of the soul comes within the grasp of science - it never can.... not because there is no soul, but because the scientist has chosen the wrong method. The method he uses is not the way to discover the soul. The very means applied to its discovery is the good means of finding the trivial. That which is of great value cannot be attained by aggression.

You can only find the mystery of life if you enter through the door of surrender. If you bow, if you pray, you can reach the centre of love. Courting God is almost as good as courting a woman. You have to approach Him with a heart full of love, gratitude and humility. And do not be in a hurry. Any hurry on your part, and you will fail. Much patience is required. Your haste... and His heart will close. Even to rush is an act of aggression.

Hence, for those who set out in search of God, their way of life is contained in two words: prayer and patience. Thus, the scriptures begin with prayer and end with waiting. The search, therefore, begins with prayer.

The first line of this scripture reads:

***Om! I bow to Lord Shiva, the one who enlightens himself, delighting in his own being.***

And now, the beginning of the Shiva Sutra.

Let this greeting penetrate deep inside you, because if you don't get to the door, you won't be able to understand me when I start describing the palace to you. Let go of the macho in you a little. Let go a little of your aggressive attitude. This understanding will not come from your intellect, it will come from your heart. This understanding will not depend on your logic, it will depend on how much love is inside you.

You will be able to understand this writing; but this understanding will not be the same as following a mathematical problem. The understanding will be similar to the understanding you have in appreciating poetry. You don't pounce on poetry. You enjoy poetry slowly, sip by sip, just as you enjoy drinking tea. You don't gulp it down, as if it were a bitter medicine. Rather, you savour its taste little by little; you let its flavour slowly dissolve.

To appreciate even a single poem you need to read it over and over again... which is not the case with a mathematical problem. You don't need to come back to it once you have understood and solved it: then the problem is solved. Poetry never ends, because the heart has no limits. The more you love, the more it unfolds.

That is why in the East we do not study the scriptures, but read them over and over again. Anyway, the scriptures cannot be studied. Studying means: once you have understood, you throw the book away. Now that you have understood it, what need is there to go over it again? Then you feel you are done with it.

Patha, reading over and over again means that you will have to go through this scripture savouring it unhurriedly, reading and re-reading. Who knows how many times, but knowingly or unknowingly, you will have to repeat it in your different moods, in different states of mind. Sometimes, when the sun is on the horizon, or when the night covers everything under its darkness, when the mind is happy, or sometimes when the mind is sad. You will have to enter into this scripture at different times, in different conditions, and only then will its facets become evident to you. And yet it will remain inexhaustible.

No writing can ever be exhausted. The more you seem to have found what you were looking for, the more you will realise that there is so much more to discover. The more you immerse yourself in it, the deeper it will go. No reader can ever exhaust a piece of writing. Patha means reading again and again, many times.

Westerners don't understand. They cannot understand why people have been reading the Geeta for thousands of years. They wonder: "the same man reads the same Geeta every morning, has he gone mad or something? They have no idea that the whole technique of patha, of reading and rereading, is about letting the scripture penetrate the heart. It has more to do with enjoying its flavour than understanding it.

It is not remotely related to logic and calculus. Its main purpose is to dissolve the distance between the reader and the text. The idea is that, over time, the text of the Geeta and its reader merge into each other. That no distinction remains between the Geeta and her reader. This is the feminine state. This is the path of surrender. Keep this in mind.

So these Shiva sutras can be understood if we follow the path of humility. Let them sink into you.

Do not rush to the conclusion whether they are right or wrong. As far as these sutras are concerned, be clear about one thing: it is not for you to decide on their rightness or wrongness.

How can it do so? He who lives in darkness, what judgement can he pass on the light? And he who has never known what it is to be healthy, who has always been confined to a sickbed, how can he understand what it means to be healthy?

He who has never been moved by the feeling of love - who has all the time lived a life of hatred, jealousy, enmity - can, of course, read love poems, because he will follow the words with ease: however, that which is hidden in the words, which is woven into the words, access to that will always remain closed to him. So don't be in a hurry to judge what is right and what is wrong.

Just soak in these sutras - I am not saying that you understand them - just drink them, soak in them, absorb all their flavour. And if this taste can help you to unveil the secrets hidden within you, and if by savouring these sutras a new flower can blossom within you, releasing its fragrance and making you realise if only for a moment that your stinking life has disappeared for ever, and if with the lighting of a lamp within you, you can come to recognise that you are not the darkness and if the sutras can create the impact of a lightning bolt within you offering just a glimpse - then this alone will bring forth understanding, it will not come through your intellect or reasoning. Even a flash of experience will be enough to bring forth understanding in you. Hence I tell you to treat these sutras with humility.

Secondly, a sutra means: the most concise, the quintessential, the telegraphic. Each and every word of a sutra is highly condensed. A sutra is never long and elaborate, it is crystallised, encapsulated, very small like a seed. Even if you wanted to see, you could not find the tree inside the seed. You need penetrating eyes - the kind of eyes that can see the tree inside the seed, that can see in the present what the future will be like, that can see today what will be tomorrow, that can discover the invisible in the visible - you need very keen eyes indeed.

You don't have such sharp eyes yet. At this moment you will only see the seed. You will only be able to see the tree if you plant the seed. Only when the tree opens and sprouts, you will be able to see the tree growing. These sutras are the seeds. You will have to sow them in your heart.

So withhold your judgement, because, if you come to a premature conclusion about these seeds, you can throw them away like rubbish.

In reality, there is not much difference between a seed and a rock. In fact, sometimes rocks are more colourful, shiny, beautiful and precious than seeds. And yet, there is a difference between the most expensive diamond kohinoor and a seed. Nothing will sprout if you sow the kohinoor. Regardless of how expensive the kohinoor is, the diamond is dead. No matter what price the fools assign to it, the stone has no life, it is just a corpse.

However ugly a seed may look, it may not cost a penny, but it contains life. If you sow it, it can produce a huge tree, and a single seed can create millions of seeds. One little seed can give birth to this whole universe, because one seed brings forth millions of seeds, and again one of these millions of seeds can create millions of other seeds. One small seed can contain the whole universe within it.

So the sutra is the seed: you cannot be impatient with it. Only when you have sown the seed in your heart and it has sprouted and blossomed can you know. Only then can you come to a conclusion.

The third thing - before going to the sutras - is that, religion is a great revolution. Whatever you have learnt in the name of religion has almost nothing to do with religion in reality. Therefore, the Shiva Sutras will surely startle you. You will be frightened, you will be frightened also because your religions will be shaken. Your temples, your mosques, your churches will simply collapse if you understand these sutras.

Don't try to save them because, even if they are saved, you won't get anything out of them.

You breathe in these places and yet you are as good as dead. The temples are very festively decorated, but there is not a ray of festivity in your life. There is a lot of light in the temples, but it does not eradicate the darkness in your life. So don't be afraid of these sutras, though they will surely put you in difficulties. Because Shiva is not a kind of priest. The language of a priest always seems satisfactory to you. The priest is basically interested in exploiting you, not in transforming you. His interest lies in keeping you as you are. His business is to see to it that you remain as you are: sick, sick.

I heard. A doctor's son came home after finishing his studies. The father had never been on holiday before, so he said to his son: "I want to go on holiday for three months. In the meantime, go on with my practice. I have spent my whole life earning money without a break. So now you take over the business for a while.

After completing a world tour, he returned after three months. He asked his son how things were going, and he replied: "Everything is going very well. You'll be surprised, but the patients you couldn't cure in your whole life, I cured in three months". The father could not believe his ears. He said, "You idiot! They gave us the business. I could have cured them too, but then how could I have paid for your education? Those patients made it possible. I could also have helped with the schooling of other children. You have ruined everything.

The priest likes you to be the way you are: sickly, unhealthy. That's what helps them run their business. Shiva is not a priest. He is a teerthankara. Shiva is an avatara. He is the seer, the paigambara. His words are like fire. Approach him only if you are willing to burn; accept his invitation only if you are willing to disappear as you are. For the new will be born only when you cease to be as you are. Only when you have turned to ashes will the new life emerge. So, keeping these things in mind, now try to understand each sutra.

The first sutra is:

**Consciousness is the atman, the soul.**

Although we are all conscious, we never come to know the soul. If consciousness is really the soul, then we should all have knowledge of it. We all possess consciousness, but what is the real meaning of "consciousness is the soul"?

The first meaning is: in this world, only consciousness is yours. The word atman means: that which is yours. As much as the rest may seem to you to be your own, it is alien. Everything you otherwise claim as yours - friends, loved ones, family, wealth, fame, high position, a great empire - is all a delusion. For one day death will take it all away from you. So death is the criterion for determining who is yours and who is not. That from which death can separate you, know that it did not belong to you, and that from which it cannot, was really yours.

So atman means: one's own. But the moment we think in terms of "mine", the other comes in.

"Mine" in itself means: "Someone who belongs to me". It never occurs to you that, except for your own self, there is no one who can be yours. And the longer you remain influenced by the idea that the other belongs to you, the greater the waste of time on your part, the more you have wasted that much of your life. So much time you gave up for dreaming. You could have awakened in the meantime, you could have attained moksha. But during all that time you only accumulated rubbish.

So this is the first sutra: you are everything by yourself; that is to say, there is nothing, either by relationship or possession, that you can claim as your own. No one and nothing but yourself really belongs to you. This is indeed a very revolutionary sutra. It goes against the very nature of society.

Because society exists on the very premise that others are the mind: caste people are mine, compatriots are mine. A whole series of possessive attitudes are deployed: my country, my caste, my religion, my family. Society survives on the concept of "mine". Religion is essentially antithetical to society: it is a freedom from society, a freedom from the "other".

According to religion, there is no one you can claim as "mine" except your own self. On the surface, this statement seems selfish. Because, if I am only for myself, it is immediately assumed to be a selfish attitude. But there is nothing selfish about it. The truth is that this feeling alone will bring about the attitude of altruism and universal goodness in your life. For he who has not yet become aware that, in essence, his being alone is his own, cannot follow altruism. You exploit them. Your "mine" is but a part of your exploitation of them. Whoever you identify as "mine", you make that person a slave. You make that person one of your possessions. You say: "my wife, my husband, my son, my father...", what happens behind the backdrop of this "my-ness"? What is the basis of your relationship that becomes evident when you call someone as yours? You exploit the other, you take advantage of the other, you tease the other. And if this is what you call altruism, then you have a misconception.

An emperor had three sons. As he grew older, he began to worry about which of the three sons would be worthy to inherit his kingdom. For all three were equally capable and equally qualified, and that made the choice very difficult. One day he called his sons together and said: "Tell me the greatest deed you have done in the whole of the past year.

The eldest son recounted: "Before leaving for a pilgrimage, the richest man in this city left his precious diamonds and jewellery, worth millions of rupees, with me without counting them or listing them with his signature. He asked me to keep them until his return. If I had wanted to, I could have taken possession of his entire treasure, for the man had made no documents and there were no witnesses to prove that the treasure belonged to him. As the man had kept no account, he could easily have kept at least a few diamonds for me. But instead, I handed him the bag intact".

The father said: "You did well, but let me ask you something, wouldn't you have been plagued by guilt, shame and embarrassment if you had kept some of the diamonds for yourself? The son replied: "Of course I would have.

Then the father said, "You can't call this an altruistic act. What you did was nothing more than saving yourself from your own sense of shame and guilt. What good did it do you? Since saving the diamonds would have pricked your conscience, you preferred to return them to their owner. It was a kind act, but there was no altruism in it. You were only being kind to yourself.

Hearing all this, the second son became a little worried. He said: "Once I was passing by a lake. It was night and there was no one there. I heard someone drowning. I could have easily ignored his cries and walked away, but instead I immediately jumped into the lake and saved the man at the risk of my own life."

The emperor said: "You did the right thing, but if you had left without rescuing the man, wouldn't the man's death have haunted you for the rest of your life? Outwardly you might have ignored him, but inwardly his cries would have continued to echo, don't you think his ghost would have haunted you forever? It was out of this fear that you jumped into the lake and risked your life. But this should not give you the excuse to be burdened with the misunderstanding that you did some altruistic act".

The third son narrated: "Once, as I was going through a forest, I saw a man asleep on the cliff of a mountain. One turn on his side and he would have been finished, for on the other side was a great chasm. I approached him to see who he was and discovered that he was none other than my sworn enemy. Having recognised him, I could calmly go on my way. Even if I had passed him slowly, mounted on my horse, perhaps my own step - without my doing anything - might have caused him to turn sideways and fall into the valley. But instead, I approached him very stealthily, creeping along the ground so that he would not fall with my approaching noise. I knew full well that he was a wicked man; that despite saving his life he would still curse me. Nevertheless, I shook him gently and woke him up. And the same man now blames me all over the place. He says: "I went to commit suicide, but this man followed me there. He won't let me live in peace, of course, but he won't let me die either'".

The emperor said: "You are better than the other two; but what you did was not altruism either. Why?

Because you are full of ego, as if you have achieved something great. The glint in your eye. All your behaviour is boastful and egotistical. And any act that creates ego can no longer be an altruistic act. You have used very subtle means to feed that ego. You think you have acted like a religious person, that you have done something good. I can only say that you are simply better than the other two, but I will have to look for someone else, the fourth person who can become the ruler of my kingdom.

When you think you are serving others, you are not. How can you serve others when you don't even know who you are? Serving the poor, caring for the sick in the hospital, gives you the idea that you are doing some kind of service. But if you analyse everything very closely, you will find somewhere in these acts the realisation of your ego. And if it is your ego that ultimately feeds on such acts of service, then this service is also exploitation. Until one has attained self-awareness one cannot be altruistic; for it is only after knowing oneself that such a great transformation can take place.

I heard that Mulla Nasruddin's wife was quarrelling with him. She said to Mulla: "This matter must be settled once and for all. Why do you hate all my relatives? Mulla said, "This is totally false, the facts do not support your accusation. I have the proof of it, and the proof is that I love your mother-in-law more than my mind".

This is how the ego gets its way. Superficially it looks like you are doing a service to others, but deep down it is your ego that is being served by you. And the more subtle the ego's path becomes, the more it slips out of its grasp. Others are unable to gauge it, of course, but even you yourself cannot master it. Others are deceived by you, of course, but even you yourself become a victim of your own deception. Even you get lost in the riddle, the puzzle, that you create for others. We have created our respective labyrinths with the intention and purpose of deceiving others, not realising that one day we ourselves may be deceived by it, and in fact we already are.

So remember one thing: no one belongs to you except your own being. The moment this remembrance crystallises in you that consciousness is being, that except for consciousness nothing else is mine - everything else is alien, disparate - the first ray of transformation enters your life. With it, a rift appears between you and society, between you and your relationships. But man does not want to look at himself. It is difficult to talk about this gaze because it requires one to go through a process that is extremely arduous.

A Marwari businessman fell in love with a film actress. It was indeed an unusual event: a Marwari businessman in love! Normally, such people always stay away from love. But sometimes the impossible happens. He fell in love, of course, but his mind was very suspicious, so he hired a detective to keep an eye on the actress and find out if she was a loose character. He wanted to be sure before he proposed to her.

The detective went ahead and did a lot of research. After a week he sent his report. The report said: "The woman is absolutely clean, innocent and blameless. There is no trace of any evidence to cast doubt on her character, except that in the last few days she has been seen moving around with a suspicious looking marwari". The businessman himself was that suspicious-looking marwari.

The eye sees the other. The hands touch the other. The mind thinks of the other. But you always remain in darkness. Your situation is similar to that of a lamp, whose light reaches everywhere except underneath, except itself. This is how you function. By the light of your own lamp, by the light of your consciousness, you wander and look in all directions; only one remains unknown, invisible, and that is none other than yourself.

So the first sutra is:

***Consciousness is the soul.*** Let this sutra penetrate deep into your heart. Your journey into the whole world is meaningless if you remain unconscious of your own self. If you gain knowledge of everything else but remain ignorant of yourself, even the sum total of that knowledge will amount to nothing.

You may have seen the whole universe, scrutinised the moons and the stars, but if you have not seen yourself you are still a stranger among all. For only he who has seen himself can claim to have eyes; only he who has known himself can claim to have attained knowledge. Only he is purified who has cleansed himself in self-luminous consciousness. Only consciousness is holy, purifying. Except for consciousness, there is no other holy place of pilgrimage.

Consciousness is your innate nature. You have not strayed from it for a moment. But the fact is that underneath the lamp it is dark. You cannot move too far away from the lamp, from the illuminating consciousness, even if you wanted to. You can, of course, have the illusion that you have moved too far away from it; you can be in a dream world. But a dream cannot be reality. Consciousness is your inherent nature and that is the only reality that exists.

Consciousness is being. And, therefore, the first thing is: no one, nothing is mine except consciousness. If this feeling crystallises in you, it will give rise to sannyas. Because, essentially, samsara means to carry the feeling that someone other than me can be mine.

Hence the first sutra is tremendously radical; it can trigger a revolution in your life. It is a provocation to realise for the first time the truth that you alone belong to yourself: there is no one else for you. This realisation will naturally depress your mind; for you have built great relationships, you have stored up lofty dreams around other people. You carry a lot of hope for them.

A mother has high expectations of her child. A father has high hopes for his child. They are completely lost in their hopes. Your father, for example, died carrying similar hopes. What did he gain from you? The same will happen to you; you too will meet death and gain nothing from your child.

And your son will continue with the same stupidity: he will maintain his son's expectations.

No, this will not help you. Look at yourself: not at someone who follows you, not at anyone who has gone before you. No one is yours. No child can ever fulfil you. No relationship can ever replace your soul. You alone are your own friend. Realising all this creates fear, because it makes you feel as if you are left to yourself.

The man is so afraid of being lonely that, even when he passes through a deserted alley, he starts to sing aloud. Just by listening to his own voice he feels that he is not alone. The fact is that he is listening to his own voice, there is no one else around him. In the same way, when the father builds his dreams around his son, the son does not participate in them. He is the father whistling alone in a deserted alley. He is doomed to unhappiness, because all his life he did nothing but weave dreams on the assumption that his son also had the same dreams. He is wrong. The son is caught up in his own dreams, the father in his own, his father cherished other dreams, but they are nowhere to be found.

All parents die unhappy. What could be the reason? Because, the fact is, whatever dreams you create, they all fall apart. Besides, here everyone must see his own dreams, not yours. And if you want to achieve an ideal situation, a fulfilment, then never create your dreams around someone else; otherwise you are sure to lose yourself.

Samsara simply means: the boat of your dreams is tied to others. Sannyas means that you have awakened; and that you have accepted one fact - however painful, however hurtful, however terribly tormenting it may seem at first - that you are alone. That all relationships, all companionship is pseudo. This does not mean, however, that you should flee to the Himalayas.

For he who goes to the Himalayas shows that he still considers his relationships, his ties, to be real, that they have not yet become false and meaningless for him.

Once it becomes clear that something is false, there is no point in running away from it. After waking up in the morning and realising that the dream was false, one does not start running away from home. Once the falsity of the dream is recognised, that's the end of the matter: what is there to run away from? And yet we find a man running away from his wife and children. His own flight shows that he has just learnt that the dream is false: he himself has not realised it. Until yesterday he was running towards his wife, now he is running away from her - in any case, the woman remains crucial.

A Jaina monk - Ganeshvarni - had renounced his wife for years. Twenty years after becoming a monk, he received the news of his wife's death. The words he uttered on hearing the news are noteworthy. He said, "Fare thee well!". His disciples interpreted these words as meaning non-attachment.

But if you were to reflect a little, it would be clear that this is not non-attachment. Because the very idea of getting rid of the wife shows that she was still considered a nuisance even after twenty years.

The arithmetic is quite clear. The woman he left twenty years ago must have followed him like a shadow. She must have been haunting him all the time, weighing him down. Not even after twenty years had he been able to free himself from her thoughts. His mind must have been debating all the time whether what he had done was right or wrong. The words "Fare thee well" at the time of the wife's death say nothing about the wife, they speak for the husband. Although this man ran away from his wife, he could not leave her.

And Ganeshvarni was a holy man. So beware, holy men can also live in great delusion. Indeed, he was a man of impeccable character: blameless, virtuous, upright. And yet something went wrong, he took the same trouble with him when he left for the Himalayas.

There is something else in this respect that also needs to be understood. The fact that in the face of his wife's death the first thing that came to his mind was "good riddance" shows that, consciously or unconsciously, the wish for her death must have been lurking somewhere in the unconscious. This needs to be explored further.

On some level he must have wished that she was dead, finished forever; but this shows violence. Every word we utter does not come out of nowhere, for no reason. Every word comes from deep within us. And in those moments when the news of the wife's death has just come, you don't react through the normal everyday state of mindfulness. After an hour or so you realise it and then you start to rationalise what you have said, you patch it up. But all that would be a falsehood.

At that very moment, Ganeshvarni received the news, which he missed. In an instant he forgot all the façade of sanctity he had created around himself for the last twenty years. If this could happen to Ganeshvarni, it can easily happen to you too.

Running away won't do any good. No one has ever been able to escape by simply running away from something. But the disciples can never recognise this. Believing that the words uttered by Ganeshvarni showed what a detached man he was, they consider them to be of great importance in the whole story.

You can hardly know what "non-attachment" means. Because you live in the world of attachments, you only understand what renunciation is. You understand when someone does something contrary to what you do. You know very well that you cannot give up your wife, whatever this man did: it is obvious that you find him greater than you. The man is certainly opposite to you, but not different from you. You are standing while he is standing on his head, but there is not an iota of difference between his mind and yours. Look for yourself. You all think that the wife is a trouble. Can you find a single husband who can say that the wife is not a trouble? But please don't ask him in front of his wife, ask him when he is alone, confidentially.

Mulla Nasruddin told me: "Once I too was a happy man. But I found out later, after I got married. By then it was too late, happiness had already slipped through my fingers".

If you dig deep enough, you will hardly find a single husband who has not thought of killing his wife, who has not dreamt of killing his wife. He may even wonder in the morning what a ridiculous dream he had, but in the depths of his unconscious his desire was indeed that. It is simple logic, the mind wants to destroy the cause of the problem. But the truth is that the other is never the cause of the problem.

Who can stop you if the wife was really the cause of your troubles? If it were, you would all have escaped to the Himalayas by now. The wife is not the cause of your problems. Because even in the Himalayas you will find a wife for you. The problem is within you. You cannot live alone. You need the other. You are afraid when you are left alone, but when there is another person around, you feel secure and confident. Why? The presence of the other makes you feel secure that in time of need there will be someone, in life or in death there will be someone you can trust. But the fact is that loneliness is the nature of the self. And he who has realised that only the soul belongs to him, has really experienced his loneliness.

So there is no need to run away. Once you stop running away, the problem disappears by itself.

Stay where you are, there is no need to make the slightest change. But be alone within yourself. Experience loneliness within yourself; feel that you are alone, without any friend or companion. But please don't repeat this, there is no need to repeat every morning: "I am alone, I have no friends and no companions". This will not help you at all. Such repetition will only show that you have not yet succeeded. Please understand this.

You are alone is a fact. The problem is to understand it: that is the real tapascharya, the real spiritual practice. It does not mean to remain under the burning sun. Except for man, all other animals and birds live under the sun; none of them are on the way to moksha. Moreover, spiritual practice does not mean abstaining from food, fasting; as it is, half the world is starving.

Fasting does not lead anyone to moksha. Nothing will come out of tormenting, torturing the body: it is self-destruction and the greatest of sins. Only the stupid commit such sins. Those who possess even a little conscience would not do such stupidities.

If forcing another to starve is wrong, how can starving oneself be right? If torturing another is violent, how can self-torture be non-violent? The violence is in the act of torture itself: it doesn't matter who the victim is. Those who are brave inflict pain on the other; while those who are weak hurt themselves. Causing pain to the other is risky, you can take revenge.

There is no such risk in inflicting pain on oneself: who will avenge it? Hence the weak torture themselves.

Has it ever occurred to you that when the man gets angry he beats his wife, but when the woman gets angry she beats herself? The wife symbolises the monks. So the defenceless one hurts himself, what else can he do? The powerful one hurts the other. The one who is powerless always faces the danger of how the other might react, of what the other might do to him. The weak is self-destructive, while the powerful is destructive to others. A religious person is not destructive: he neither hurts the other nor hurts himself. The idea of hurting and torturing is meaningless.

Tapascharya, the spiritual practice, means: to accept the truth that you are alone; that it is impossible to have a friend, a companion. No matter how much you long for them, no matter how much you close your eyes and dream of them, you are still alone. For lifetimes you built a home, formed a family, and then lost it - and in all that you have always remained alone. Your loneliness has not been affected even slightly. So the one who has known, the one who has accepted that he is alone, for him there is an indication in this sutra: *consciousness is the self.* Only the self is yours, nothing else.

Secondly, the sutra says: *this being is consciousness.*

Your being, your soul, is not a doctrine that you can read in a scripture and believe in.

It is not something like a theory of gravitation. The soul is not a matter of theory, it is an experience.

And the experience is that of the intensity of consciousness. Therefore, the more conscious you become, the more you come to know the soul. The more you become unconscious, the more you cease to know yourself, and you are almost unconscious.

The one who wants to realise his own being does not need to go through any philosophical treatise, but he needs to know the technique to awaken his consciousness. He needs a method that helps him to become more conscious. For example, when you dig in the ashes, when you remove the dust from the ashes, the hot coal begins to glow. Similarly, you need to have some kind of technique that can dust the ash and allow your amber to glow. Because only in the glow of that amber will you be able to recognise that you are a consciousness.

And the more conscious you are, the more centred you will be. The day you discover that you are the supreme consciousness, you will have attained divinity. The very degree to which your awareness grows will be the degree to which you will have realised your being. Yet, right now, you are almost unconscious. You are almost in a state of intoxication. You walk, you move, you work, but all as if you were asleep: you are not conscious.

Has it ever happened to you that, while reading a book, after having read the whole page, you realise: "Gosh, I've read the whole page and I can't remember a single word, how could that happen?

Indeed, you can read a book in a dream state. While reading, your mind wanders. After turning the page, you become aware. You realise that you have read the whole page in vain.

In the same way, you walk up and down the street without being aware that you are walking. You go about your work without being aware that you are working.

Although your consciousness is the self, yet you still live in unconsciousness. And then you ask: "What is being, what is the soul? You want someone to give you conclusive proof, or at least someone to rationally explain its existence. Otherwise, you may become an atheist. Atheism is a natural consequence of unconsciousness; theism is the result of consciousness. As your consciousness increases, you will have no need to believe in the soul.

Many fools believe in the soul, but it doesn't do any good. In this country everybody believes in the soul, so what's the difference? It doesn't bring any transformation to your life. Maybe you believe that way because that belief has been repeated for thousands of years. Your ears have gone sour when you hear it. You have completely forgotten that you need to think about it. Hearing the same thing over and over again hypnotises you. Hearing the same thing you forget that it is subject to doubt, that it needs to be thought about.

To hear that there is a soul gives you great satisfaction. You know very well that the body will die; it gives you great courage when you are told that the soul will not die. You find great comfort in hearing, "The soul will never die; fire cannot burn it, weapons cannot pierce it, death can do it no harm". But such consolation is not the truth. Neither can the soul be accepted as a theory, nor can it be hypnotised by the repeated assertion of its existence. Only those who are able to raise their consciousness can know what the soul is.

So live in such a way that the ash does not accumulate in you. Live so that the amber in you continues to burn, to glow. Live a life where you are not unconscious, where you are aware in every moment.

A boy was born to Mulla Nasruddin. It was his first child. He was immensely happy. He invited his friend to celebrate the happy occasion and they both went to a tavern. He knows only one way to celebrate happiness: to become unconscious.

This is very strange. Shiva, Mahavira, Buddha keep proclaiming: "There is only one joy in the world".

The pleasure of being conscious. And you know only one kind of pleasure: the pleasure of being unconscious.

Either you are right or they are right, both cannot be.

So instead of going to the hospital first to see his newborn son, Mulla Nasruddin went straight to the bar. He thought to have fun first, after all a long cherished dream had come true. They both drank a lot. When they arrived at the hospital and Mulla looked at his son through the glass window, he began to cry. When his friend asked him why he was crying, Mulla said: "The first thing is that he doesn't look like me. He didn't know who he really was, he didn't even recognise his own face, but he was quick to say that the son didn't look like him. "Secondly," he said, "the child looks very small to me, what will I do with such a small child, do you think he will survive?"

Mulla's friend said: "Don't worry, when I was born I also weighed one kilo. Nasruddin said: "Did you survive? The friend thought for a while, he too was unconscious, and said, "I can't tell you for sure".

Man is unconscious. His whole outlook on life is full of unconsciousness, his whole vision is blurred. He cannot see anything well. And he knows only one pleasure and that is to forget himself, whether it is watching a film, listening to music or through sex. Wherever it is that helps you forget yourself, you feel that this is where you have found pleasure. You call forgetting yourself pleasure. There is a reason for that. Because whenever you become aware, you find nothing but misery in your life. Even a little alertness on your part shows the extent to which you are surrounded by pain, misery and ugliness.

I have a friend who became single. I asked him: "What happened, how did you fail? He replied, "There was a big problem. Any woman I fell in love with seemed beautiful to me when I was drunk. At that time I would be willing to marry her, but she would refuse. When I was sober and conscious, she would be willing to marry me, but I would refuse. That's how I lost my way. What to do, there was no way out.

When you open your eyes, you will find only ugliness and misery all around you.

Everything seems to be fine when you are in an unconscious state. This is why it is difficult for you to conceive: ***consciousness is being.*** You say, "Impossible!". That is why you have to go through pain. That is called tapascharya, spiritual practice. Whenever you start to become conscious, you have to go through suffering first. For lifetimes you have created misery around you, who else would go through it if not you? That is what we have called karma.

Karma simply means: the misery created around you by you for life after life. Knowingly or unknowingly, you have sown the seeds of misery, and now who will reap the harvest? So whenever you return to your consciousness, you will see the harvest far and wide. You will have to go through this farm.

But you sit there out of fear. Looking at the field and realising how annoying it is, you close your eyes and get drunk. But the more you get drunk, the more the harvest grows. Every birth of yours adds something to the chain of your karmas, it doesn't reduce anything. It takes you deeper and deeper into a pit, hell comes closer and closer.

As soon as you become conscious, the first thing that will happen is that you will begin to see the misery, the hell that surrounds you. Because it is you who have created it. However, if you remain courageous and go through the misery consciously, you will have cut the harvest. You will not have to go through the same miseries again. Once you have gone through this chain of miseries - the chain of karmas, the chain tied around your soul - ..... If you could go through it without losing your consciousness, bravely, unworried; if you could determine, "Whatever misery I have created, I will go through it, I will go to the end of it. I want to get to that initial moment when I was innocent and had not yet begun the journey of suffering, when my soul was absolutely pure and had not accumulated any misery - I am determined to penetrate to that point regardless of any consequences, pain or sorrow."

If you could show so much courage, sooner or later you will break through your misery and come to the point where this Shiva sutra, CONSCIOUSNESS IS BEING, will become clear to you. And once you have centred yourself in your consciousness, no misery will ever be caused by you. Only an unconscious man creates misery around him.

Have you ever seen a drunk walking down the street staggering? That's your life. You take a step in one direction and your foot lands in another. You set out to go one place, but you get somewhere else. You leave the house to talk about one thing, but end up talking about something else. You see this happen every day and yet you don't understand why it is so. You go out to apologise to someone, but you come home having quarrelled some more. Are you in your right mind? You start with loving talk, but end with hostility.

A man, drunk, was walking down the street looking up at the sky. A car passed by him. The driver barely managed to avoid the accident. He stopped the car and said to the man: "Sir, if you don't look in the direction you want to go, you may end up going where you are looking now". And we are all....

You have no idea where you are going, why you are going, where you are looking, why you are looking. You are in constant movement, because there is a restlessness inside you that doesn't allow you to sit still. The energy inside keeps you moving. So whatever you do, it produces the opposite results.

People come to see me and say: "We never did any bad deeds, we were always good to others but we received evil from them in return". But it is not possible for you to do good and receive evil from them in return. It is impossible for you to sow the seed of a mango tree and the tree gives you the bitter fruit of a neem tree in return. This is impossible. The only possible thing is that in your unconscious state instead of sowing the seed of the mango you have sown the seed of the neem tree. Because why would the tree lie? You must have sown the wrong seeds by mistake.

Therefore, even if you do good, your intention is never the same.

Even when you tell the truth, you do it to hurt the other person. You tell the truth to insult the other person. You tell the truth as if you are going to use it as a kind of deadly weapon. Your truths are bitter.

The truth doesn't have to be bitter too. But you find pleasure in making the truth sound bitter. In fact, you are not interested in the truth itself. Your lie is always sweet; your truth is always bitter. What is it? Is bitterness the nature of truth? Is sweetness part of the lie?

No, the fact is that you want your lie to be passable, so you make it sound sweet. You know very well that it won't work otherwise. You know that a lie is difficult to promote in the first place if it is not accompanied by sweetness. It works like giving a child a bitter but sugar-coated pill.

He swallows it, taking the pill for a piece of candy. Before you can feel the bitterness, the pill is already inside.

You make the lie sound sweet because you want to promote the lie. You make the truth sound bitter because you are not interested in promoting the truth, but in using it to harm others.

You only tell the truth when you want to use it in a way that is even worse than a lie.

You are unconscious. You are totally unaware of your actions. You have to look at yourself a little more carefully. Did you say what you meant to say, or was it something else? Was what you said really in your mind?

Mark Twain came home one night. His wife asked him: "How did your speech go? He replied: "Which one? The one I had prepared or the one I delivered? Or the one I had wished to deliver?

The speech you prepare and the speech you deliver are always very different. Moreover, when you go home, the speech you think you should have made is totally different.

Are you in your right mind? You keep missing all the targets; have you ever hit a single target in your life? Even a blindfolded man can sometimes hit the bull's-eye with his arrow, but not you.

I have heard it said that even a stopped watch gives the right time twice in twenty-four hours, but you can spend your whole life without getting it right twice. Are you worse than a stopped watch?

A man can hit his target one day even if he keeps shooting his arrows in the dark.

You shoot your arrows with your eyes open, into the light, and yet you never hit the target. What could be the reason?

Mulla Nasruddin was fond of hunting deer. When he arrived at the hut on his third hunting trip and opened his suitcase, he found a large photograph under which his wife had written: "Mulla, this is what a deer looks like". Mulla loved to hunt, but he had no idea what a deer looked like. His wife wanted to make sure he didn't kill any strange things and bring them home as a deer, hence the photograph.

You have failed at every turn, and that is the cause of your misery. And the only reason you have failed is that you are not conscious. I say to you, therefore, whatever you do, do it with awareness.

Walk with a conscience, talk with a conscience.

Mahavira has said: "Be alert when you walk, when you sit, when you eat your food, when you talk, even when you sleep". When Mahavira was asked who is a sadhu, who is a holy man, he replied: "He who is conscious". When he was asked who is a non-sadhu, he replied, "He who is not conscious". The man who lives as if asleep is the non-sadhu; the one who lives in full consciousness is the sadhu.

This is exactly what Shiva says: ***consciousness is the soul.*** Raise your consciousness and, little by little, you will see a glimpse of the soul in your life.

The second sutra is: ***knowledge is bondage.*** It is a very strange sutra. "Knowledge" has many meanings. One, as long as you are filled with the knowledge that "I am", you will remain in ignorance, because, the very sense of "I", the ego, is ignorance. The day you are filled with the soul, the "I am" will remain, but the "I" will disappear. From the "I am", the "I" will fall away and simply "I am" will remain.

You can experiment with this. Sometimes sit quietly under a tree and look inside yourself, where is the "I"? You will not find it anywhere. The "I" you will find, of course, everywhere in existence, but never the ego. The ego is your creation, it is your own work, it is false, false. There is nothing more false than the ego itself. It pays off.

Although it is necessary in the world, as such it has no place in truth.

So there is this knowledge that "I am", which is the cause of bondage. The consciousness I have of "I am" is pure and unlimited. When you say "I am", can there be any difference between your "I am" and the "I am" of a tree? Would there be any difference between your "am-ness" and my "am-ness"? When you just are, you, the rivers, the mountains and the trees become one.

However, the moment you say "I", you separate yourself altogether. The moment you say "I", you separate yourself, you alienate yourself, you disconnect yourself from existence.

Am-ness is Brahman and "I" is man's state of ignorance. When you simply know that you are, then there is no separate centre within you. Then you become one with existence. Then you become like a wave that is lost in the ocean. Right now you are like the wave that has frozen in the ice, that has become separated from the ocean.

Gyanam bandaha So the first thing is: ***knowledge is bondage***: the knowledge that "I am".

The other kind of bondage is all the knowledge that you have picked up from outside, that you have stolen from the scriptures, the knowledge that you have borrowed from the great Masters, the knowledge that is stored in your memory: all that is bondage. You will not be able to free yourself from it. That is why you cannot find a man more enslaved than punditry.

All kinds of people come to me, all kinds of patients. But no one among them is more afflicted with cancer than the expert, the scholar. There is no cure for him, he is beyond treatment. His problem is that he knows it. Therefore, he can neither listen nor understand. Before you have said anything to him, he has already understood your meaning; before he has listened to you, he has already formed his own theory. A mind full of words is incapable of knowing. It knows much without knowing, because all its knowledge is borrowed.

If knowledge could be attained through the scriptures, the whole world would have attained it. Knowledge is attained when a person has become silent, when he has abandoned all scriptures, when he gives back to the world all the knowledge he has borrowed from others, when he goes in search of that which is his original existence, which he has not obtained from other people.

Try to understand this a little bit. You have received your body from your parents. You have nothing in your body that is really yours. One half of it is a contribution from your father, and the other half from your mother. Also, the body is made up of the food you eat every day. And furthermore, the body contains the five elements: air, fire, etc. You cannot claim any of them as your own.

But your consciousness does not consist of any of these elements, nor did you get it from your parents.

Everything you know, you have learnt in your schools and universities, you have heard it in your scriptures, you have got it from your gurus. But all that is not part of your body, not part of your soul. Your soul is that which you have not got from anybody. So your true nature consists of that which you have not received from any body: not from your mother, not from your father, not from society, not from the guru, not from the scriptures. Until you have discovered that pure element which is innately yours, you cannot realise your true self.

So knowledge is slavery, because it does not allow you to reach your true nature, your true self. It is knowledge that has divided humanity. You call yourself a Hindu or a Mohammedan.

Have you ever thought about why you are a Hindu or a Mohammedan? What is really the difference between a Hindu and a Mohammedan? Can a doctor ever find out, based on a blood test, whether the blood belongs to a Hindu or a Mohammedan? Can anyone determine whether a particular bone has been taken from the body of a Hindu or a Mohammedan? There is no way.

You will know nothing by investigating the bodies, because the bodies of both - the Hindu and the Mohammedan - are made of the same five elements. But if you examine their minds, you will know for sure who is a Hindu and who is a Mohammedan. For the simple reason that their scriptures are different, their principles are different, their words are different. The difference between the two is in the words. Someone is a Hindu because he has received a kind of knowledge that is labelled "Hindu". Someone is a Jaina because he has received a different kind of knowledge which is called Jaina. All the differences between you, all the walls, are the walls of knowledge, and all your knowledge is borrowed.

Raise a Muslim child in a Hindu home, and he will grow up to be a Hindu. He will wear the sacred thread like a Brahmin. He will quote the Vedas and the Upanishads. Similarly, bring up a Hindu child in a Muslim home, and he will start reciting the verses of the Quran.

Knowledge binds you. It creates a wall around you. It makes you fight against your fellowmen and brings malice, enmity into your life. Think for a moment, if you were not brought up as a Hindu, Mohammedan, Jain or Parsi, what would you do? You would grow up as a human being, without walls around you.

There are about three hundred religions in the world: three hundred prisons. Every man is locked up in one prison or another as soon as he is born. And the priests do their utmost to get their control over the child as soon as possible. They call it "religious education", but there is nothing more irreligious than this. The child is taken young, before he is seven years old, because after that it would be more and more difficult to exercise control over him. If the child were to acquire even a little understanding, he would start asking questions. And the experts have absolutely no answers to the child's questions.

The expert can only satisfy idiots. The less intelligent a person is, the quicker the expert satisfies him. He asks a question and is given the answer. You ask an expert: "Who created the world? He answers: "God created the world". You go home happy and satisfied without asking him: "Who created God? The expert would have been angry if you had asked him this second question, because even he does not know the answer. The answer is not given in the book. And it is an annoying question: who created God? You can go on and on asking questions along the same lines endlessly, no matter what the answer is.

If you look closely, you will see that your first question was not answered: the expert merely satisfied your curiosity. Seeing that you are not that smart. Children are innocent. Their reasoning and thinking faculties are not yet developed. They are not in a position to ask questions. Whatever rubbish you pour into their brains, they will accept it. Children are open to everything, because they believe that whatever is given to them must be right. A child cannot ask too many questions. To raise a question requires a certain degree of maturity. That is why all religions grab children and practically strangle their spirits.

This strangulation looks very beautiful, very ornamental. One has the Bible hanging around his neck, another his samayasar, while someone has the Koran around his neck, and another has the Geeta around his neck. These ties are so endearing that it takes tremendous courage to get rid of them. And whenever you try to get rid of them, a danger will present itself to you: to do without these books would mean that you know nothing, for only books contain all knowledge. Hence you are anxious to guard these scriptures with your life. Only in this way will you be able to hide your ignorance.

It would be very simple if one could do away with one's ignorance by simply hiding it. The fact is that ignorance grows more when you hide it. It is like hiding a wound. But hiding a wound will not heal it, but it will grow deeper and deeper inside. And the pus will spread all over the body.

Shiva says: *knowledge is bondage.*

Whatever knowledge - whether learnt from someone or borrowed from somewhere - knowledge is the cause of bondage. Therefore, abandon whatever you have acquired from others. Go in search of that which you have received from no one. Go in search of the face that is truly yours.

There is a wellspring of consciousness hidden within you, which no one has given you. It is your own nature, your own treasure, your very soul.

The third sutra is: *yonivargaha kalashariram* Yoni means nature. That is why we call woman, or the female element, prakriti or nature. The woman gives birth to the body, she represents prakriti. And kala means the will to do. There is only one art, and that is: the art of entering this world. And this comes through the will to do, to be a doer.

Your body is made up of two things: your will-to-do, your ego, and the physical form you have received from prakriti, nature. If the will-to-do is present in you, then nature will continue to provide you with a suitable body. This is how you have been born again and again. Sometimes you were an animal, sometimes a bird, sometimes a tree, sometimes a man. Whatever it was that you wished to achieve, it has happened. Your desire to achieve it becomes reality; thoughts become real things. So be careful when you wish, because all wishes come true, sooner or later.

If you are in the habit of watching birds flying in the sky and you ask yourself: "How free the birds are, I wish I were a bird", you will soon become a bird. You see the dogs mating, and if at that moment a thought arises in you: "How free! What happiness!" - you will soon become a dog. Whatever desire you hold within you, it becomes a seed.

Nature only gives birth to the body. You are the artist, you are your own creator. So the meaning of kala is: you have shaped your own body. No one else gives you the body: it is your own desire that shapes it.

Has it ever occurred to you that the last thought before going to sleep at night becomes the first thought when you wake up in the morning? All night long, while you sleep, the thought remains in you in seed form. And so, what is the last thing at night becomes the first thing in the morning.

At the moment of your death, all your desires will come together and become a seed. That same seed will consequently be the new life in the womb. You will start again from where you left off.

What you are is your own doing. Don't blame others. In fact, there is no one you can blame. It is basically the cumulative effect of your own actions. Whether you are what you are, handsome or ugly, happy or unhappy, male or female, it's all a result of your actions. You are the architect of your life. Don't blame your stars: you are simply fooling yourself. In this way you are offloading the responsibility onto someone else.

You don't need to say that God has sent you, don't dump the responsibility on God. That is just a strategy to avoid your own responsibility. You alone are the cause of being imprisoned in this body. Whoever fully understands that he himself is responsible for being in this world, there is a transformation in his life.

Shiva is saying: the body is a product of nature and your will to do. Nature is but the source, the womb. Your ego functions as a seed in it. Your will to do this or that, to achieve this or that, to become this or that, acts as a seed. And the moment the art of your doing meets the womb of nature, a body is formed.

That is why the buddhas say "Abandon all desires, only then will you be liberated": If you were to desire heaven, you would become an angel, but that would not be liberation either. Because as long as desires persist, there can never be liberation. All desires lead to the formation of bodies.

So, as long as you have not attained the absence of desires, as long as you have not completely renounced them, you will go on being born and wandering in different bodies. And however different the forms of the body may be, its basic condition is always the same. The evils of the body are the same whether it is the body of a bird or of a man. There is no difference in its miseries, because the fundamental misery is only one: the soul being confined in the body, the entry of the soul into the prison of the body. After all, a prison is a prison; whether its walls are circular or angular, it doesn't matter what you think.

A friend of mine is a drawing teacher. He was sentenced to three years in prison. When he got out, I asked him how his stay went. He said: "Everything went well, except that the corners of my cell were not set at right angles". He was the brain of a drawing teacher: it bothered him that the corners were not at ninety degrees. This is what bothered him for the three years he spent in the same cell, day after day, looking at the corners that were not at right angles.

Now, what difference does it make whether the corners were at ninety degrees or not? A prison is a prison. Whether the body is that of a bird or a man is of little consequence. The fact is that you are imprisoned - and that is the misery. You are bound - and that is the pain. Desire binds. Desire is the rope that binds us. And remember, except for you, nobody else is responsible for it.

The fourth sutra is: udyama *is bhairava*. Udyama means the spiritual effort by which you try to get out of this prison. And this effort is bhairava. Bhairava is a technical term:

bha" means that which sustains, that which maintains, "ra" means that which destroys, "va" means that which expands. Thus bhairava means: Brahman, that which sustains and maintains us, that into which we are born and into which we will eventually disappear; that which constitutes the whole expanse and which will eventually shrink; that which is the origin of everything and into which everything will end. Total existence is bhairava.

Shiva says: udyama *is bhairava*. The day you begin your spiritual effort, you begin to become bhairava: you begin to become one with God. Your first rays of effort, and the journey towards the sun has begun; the first thought of liberation, and the destination is not far away. For the first step is almost half the journey.

Spiritual effort is bhairava. It will take time for you to attain it; it will take time before you reach the destination. But as soon as you have started the effort and the seed is sown: "Let me come out of this prison and free myself from this body, let me free myself from all desires, let me not sow any more seeds and increase my involvement in this world, let me not desire any more births". As soon as the feeling of overcoming your unconsciousness intensifies in you, you begin to become bhairava, you begin to become one with Brahman. In fact, you are already one with Brahman, you just need to remember it. You are basically that: a current of the same ocean, a ray of the same sun, a small part of the same vast sky. Once you begin to remember this and the prison walls begin to crumble, you become one with infinite space.

*Udyama is bhairava*: very intense effort is needed. The sleep is very deep. Only constant hammering can break it. So being lazy will not help. You can destroy the dream today, but create a new one tomorrow. Then you will go on wandering from one birth to another. It would be of no use if you break the dream on one side and go on creating a new one on the other: all your effort would be in vain. So, udyama means that you should try your best.

People come to me and say: "We make an effort, but nothing happens". I look them in the face and realise that either they don't make any effort at all, or even when they do make an effort it is always so half-hearted. Their efforts lack spirit, so nothing happens. But they come to me complaining as if they are doing God a favour and yet nothing happens. They feel that something is wrong, otherwise why do things happen to others but never happen to them? They think it's unfair.

There is never injustice in this universe. Everything that happens is always just and right, for there is no human being sitting up there who does justice or injustice. The universe is governed by certain laws, and these laws constitute religion. If you walk around in a daze, you are bound to fall down and break your leg. In that case you can't blame it on the law of gravitation in court.

Gravity is neither interested in making you fall, nor in preventing you from falling. When you walk upright, it protects you from falling; when you don't, it makes you fall. As such, gravity has no self-interest in either seeing you fall, or in saving you from falling.

Universal law is always neutral. Religion is the name of this neutral law. Hindus call it "rita": it is the supreme law. It shows no favouritism: it brings someone down, lifts someone up, nothing like that. When you walk right, the law protects you; when you want to fall, it helps you fall. The law works in all conditions. The law is always available. You can use it as you like, its doors are always open to you. If you want to bang your head against the closed door, it won't stop you. If you want to walk through the door, it will allow you to do so. The law is absolutely neutral.

So udyama *is bhairava*. It needs a great effort. udyama means: an intense effort. An effort that requires you to involve your whole being is udyama. So, to become bhairava will not take too much time.

The fifth sutra is: **the one who applies his total energy, for him the world no longer exists.**

And if you have made the right effort, if you have channelled all your energy into the search for truth, for God or for the soul, then the circuit of your energy is complete. Right now it is not complete, it is torn and divided.

Scientists say that even the most intelligent person in the world uses no more than fifteen per cent of his intellect: the remaining eighty-five per cent rots away. If this is true in the case of the genius, imagine what it must be like in the case of a fool. He may never use his intellect at all. Even our physical energy we do not use more than five per cent. So if you live an apathetic and spiritless life, whose fault is it? You never live fully. You are afraid that the flame of life may engulf you. So you live in apprehension, in fear, so that the energy circuit within you is never completed.

Your life is like a car that moves sometimes with jolts caused by the dirt in the petrol, as if it had hiccups. That's how you normally live: bit by bit. Your energy moves in fits and starts, little by little, never coming to an integrated whole. It's about using all your energy, in anything. For example, if you are a painter and you devote all your energy to painting a picture, without holding back one iota, you will attain liberation at that very moment. Such application of total energy is udyama. As soon as the circuit is completed, you become a bhairava. If you are a sculptor and you have poured into your sculpture all that you have - so much so that only the sculpture remains, you disappear - the energy circuit is completed. So when you put all your energy into any work, it becomes meditation. Then the bhairava is near, the temple is near.

The fifth sutra says: *he who applies all his energy, for him the world no longer exists.*

When the circuit of your energy becomes complete, whole - not broken into pieces, but whole - at that very moment the world ceases to exist for you. You become God. You become Bhairava. You become free. Then there is no bondage for you: no body, no samsara.

So remember, you have to apply all your energy. If you put all your energy into practice in this meditation field, if you don't meditate superficially, but give all your energy, you will experience at that very moment, suddenly, that the world has disappeared and you are in front of God.

Transformation takes place the moment you apply your energy totally. Then you turn your back on the world and face God. One glimpse of this experience and you will never be the same. Just a glimpse of it is enough to set your life on that journey.

So remember, drown yourself here completely: only then will something happen. If you restrain yourself even a little, all your effort will be futile. Until the effort becomes udyama - total effort - you cannot attain bhairava.

Enough for today.

# The reflected stars

*Jagratswapuasushuptbhede turyabhog samvita gyanam jagrat swapnovikalpaha aviveko mayasowshuptam.*

*Tritiya bhokta vireshaha.*

*Knowing wakefulness, sleep and deep sleep - each separately - leads to the fourth state.*

*The constancy of knowledge is the waking state.*

*Choosing is the dream state.*

*Unconsciousness and lack of self-awareness create the illusion of deep sleep.*

*The one who is aware of all three is the supreme hero.*

*Knowing waking, dreaming and deep sleep - each separately - one attains turiya, the fourth state.*

Turiya, the fourth state, means supreme knowledge. The fourth state means that there is no darkness of any kind within. The entire inner landscape is illuminated; no area of darkness remains.

Nothing of ourselves, inside or outside, is unknown to us. The light of wakefulness makes everything visible.

As we are now, we are either awake or dreaming or in deep sleep. We have no idea of the fourth state. When we are awake we see the outside world, but we ourselves are in darkness. Objects become visible, but we have no knowledge of our inner self. The world is illuminated, but not the soul.

This is the state of semi-awakening, of half-awakening.

What we call waking up in the morning is nothing more than this half-awake state. This is not really worthwhile, because what is seen is the useless; the useful remains hidden. We see the rubbish, but the diamonds remain in the dark. We cannot see ourselves, though the whole world becomes visible to us.

The second state is the dream state. In sleep we lose not only ourselves, but also the outside world. All we see are images floating in the mind, reflections of the outside world. We see these reflections as we would see the moon or the stars reflected in a lake. When we are awake, we see things clearly; in dreams, we see them as reflections.

The third state we know is deep sleep. In this state, first the outside world, the world of objects, is lost to us; then reflections fade, dreams disappear and we are left in total darkness. This is known as deep sleep. In this state we have no knowledge of either the outer world or the inner world.

In the waking state we have knowledge of the external world. In the dream state, which is between wakefulness and deep sleep, we only have knowledge of the reflexes formed in the waking state, but not of external objects.

The fourth state is turiya. This state is the goal that we strive to reach. All meditations, all yoga, are efforts to reach the fourth state. The fourth state means the knowledge of both what is inside and what is outside: complete wakefulness; there is no darkness inside or outside. It is what is known as Buddhahood. Mahavir called this enlightened state, jinatva. Light spreads everywhere, within and without; and in this light we know objects and we also know ourselves. These sutras show how the fourth state is attained.

The first sutra says

***Knowing wakefulness, sleep and deep sleep - each separately - one attains turiya, the fourth state.***

We know, but we do not know that we know, each of these states. When we dream, we do not know that we are dreaming; we are completely identified with the dream. It is only when we wake up in the morning that we realise that we were dreaming; but by the time we realise it, the state has long since disappeared. While we are in this state we are not conscious of it, apart from it, because we are identified with it. In the dream world we become the dream. When we realise that it was a dream, we have already identified with the waking state.

You will say: I am awake. You have forgotten that again, that very night, you will abandon your identity with this state and become one with your dreams. You become one with everything that appears before your eyes, but the truth is that you are separate from all of them.

It is like when the rains come, you feel you are the monsoon; when the summer comes you feel you are the summer, when the winter comes you are the winter. The three seasons are all around you; you are totally separate from them. In childhood you thought you were a child; in youth you think you are young; when old age comes you will think you have become old. But you are beyond all three.

If not, how could the child become a youth? There is something within you that could leave childhood behind and continue into youth. That something is separate, apart from childhood and youth.

You are lost when you dream. When you wake up, you know the dream was false. There is an element of consciousness within you that is the traveller; waking, dreaming and deep sleep are only stops on the way. As soon as you become aware that you are alone and separate from them, the fourth state is born in you. This separation, this detachment, is the fourth state.

Mahavir has coined a beautiful word for this state. He calls it the science of discrimination. He says that the whole science consists in carefully discriminating the spiritual secrets. And this is also what the Shiv-Sutra aims at: to make you realise that each of these states is separate. As soon as you attain this understanding, you will also know your separate identity. You will have learnt the art of making distinctions. Right now your state of mind is such that you identify yourself with whatever appears before you.

Someone abuses you: you get angry. In that moment you are one with the anger. You completely forget that a moment ago there was no anger, but you; and in a moment the anger will disappear, but you will remain. So anger is the smoke that envelops you momentarily; it is not your nature.

In anxiety, the cloud of apprehension overcomes you; the sun hides behind it; you completely forget that you are separate. In happiness you dance with joy; when sadness comes, you weep. Whatever happens, you are one with it. You are not aware of your separation. You must begin to learn to separate it little by little. At each stage you have to disidentify. While eating you must know that it is the body that feels the hunger, not you. You are only the knower. Consciousness does not feel hunger. When you feel hot and perspire, make sure you realise that it is the body that perspires.

This does not mean that you should sit in the sun and get drenched in sweat. Let the body be comfortable, but keep the awareness that the comfort is being provided by the body, you are only the knower.

Little by little, detach yourself from everything that is going on around you. It is very difficult; the gap is small and hard to see, the boundaries unclear. For millions of lifetimes you have learned to identify. You never learned to disidentify. You learned to identify with every situation. You have totally forgotten the art of disidentification, and this is your unconsciousness: that you have learned to identify.

One morning he found Mulla Nasruddin at the bedside of his friend who was in hospital. The patient opened his eyes and said: "What happened, Nasruddin? I have no idea.

"You drank too much last night," said the Mulla. "Then you leaned out of the window and said you could fly. You tried to fly out of the third-floor window. And this is the result: your bones are broken!".

The friend was surprised. "But you were with me, Mulla, why did you let it happen? What kind of a friend are you?"

"Let's not talk about it," Nasruddin said. "At the time I was convinced you could do it. If my pyjama drawstring hadn't broken, I would have taken off with you. But how could I keep my pyjamas on while flying? That was the only thing holding me back. You weren't the only one who was drunk".

The meaning of unconsciousness is to be one with whatever comes to mind. If the drunkard thinks he can fly, he cannot discriminate. He has no capacity left to discriminate. He becomes one with the thought.

Your life is exactly like that. OK, you don't fly out of the window and break a bone and land in the hospital, but if you look very, very carefully you will find that you are in the hospital with all your bones broken. Your whole life is one long illness, which gives you nothing but pain and suffering. At every step you fall. At every step you have fallen. At every step you hurt yourself, and behind all this devastation there is only one reason: your unconsciousness. You fail to create a distance between you and your surroundings.

Step back a little. Take it one step at a time. It is a long journey, because what has been built over millions of lifetimes cannot be destroyed so easily. However, it can be done. Whatever you have created is false. The Hindus call it maya. Maya means: the world in which you are trapped is false. Actually, this does not mean that the sun and the stars, the mountains and the trees are false. It only means that your identification with your perception of them is false. You live with this identification. That is your world!

How can you break this association? First, start with your waking state. Because only in the waking state is there a slight glimmer of consciousness. How can you start with dreams? It would be very difficult. And you don't know deep sleep at all, because there all consciousness is lost. Start with the waking state, that is where your spiritual path begins. That is the first step. The second step is the dream state, and the third step is deep sleep. The day you complete all three steps you will have naturally entered the fourth step: turiya, the state of self-realisation.

It begins with the waking state. That is the way; that is why it is called wakefulness. Otherwise it is not wakefulness. What kind of wakefulness can it be when you are lost in objects and have no awareness of yourself? This is wakefulness in name. But it has been called a waking state.

Actually, we have called the buddhas "the awakened ones".

However, it is a waking state in the sense that there is some possibility of waking up in this state.

So start with the waking state. When you are hungry eat, but always remember that it is the body that is hungry, not you. If you hurt your leg, wash and clean the wound, apply medication, but always remember that it is the body that is hurt, not you. With this remembrance, you will find that ninety-nine percent of the pain is gone. This slight knowledge, this small awareness, eliminates much of your suffering. The one percent will remain because the knowledge is not total.

When knowledge becomes total, all suffering disappears.

Buddha said that an awakened person is beyond suffering. You can cut off the limbs of such a person, you can throw him into the fire, you can kill him, but you cannot make him suffer, because he remains aloof from everything that happens around him.

So start with the waking state. Walk on the road, but remember that you are not walking: the body is walking. You have never walked. How could you? The soul has no feet to walk. The soul has no stomach, how can it be hungry? The soul has no desires; all desires are of the body. The soul has no desires, so it does not walk. It simply cannot walk. It is only your body that walks. Try to maintain this awareness as long as possible. In the end you will get a joyful experience: walking on the road with full awareness that it is the body that walks and not you, you will suddenly feel that you are divided into two parts. One part walks; the other part does not walk. One part eats; the other does not.

The Upanishads say Two birds are sitting on the same tree. The one on the upper branch is quiet.

It neither moves, nor cries, nor flies; it neither comes nor goes, it just sits serenely. The one on the lower branch is very restless. It moves from branch to branch. It jumps from one fruit to another. It is very restless. Both birds are inside you. You are the tree. The bird that is serene is called a witness.

Jesus says that you sleep in one bed, but you are two: one is dead and the other is eternal.

You are the bed. When you sleep at night, inside you is both a lifeless corpse and an eternal consciousness. Differentiate between the two; keep your distance. It means hard work.

Start with the day. With the first glimmer of awareness when you wake up in the morning, the experiment begins. After a thousand attempts, perhaps one will succeed, but even if one attempt succeeds, you will realise that the thousands of attempts have been worthwhile. If, even for a moment, you come to experience that the one who walks is not you, but that you are the motionless one; that the one who is full of desires is not you, but that you are the eternal desireless one; that the perishable is not you, but that you are the source of the eternal nectar; if you become Mahavira or Buddha even for a moment or attain the state of Shiva, if this knowledge comes to you even for a moment, you will have opened the gates of the supreme treasure. After that, the journey becomes easy. After the taste, the journey is easy. All difficulty comes before the taste!

Start with the day, and little by little you will be able to carry it through to the dream. Gurdjieff used to teach his disciples to practice mindfulness during the day, and then tell them that just before going to bed they should remember: "This is a dream. You are still awake. There is no dream yet, but you have to keep repeating to yourself: "Everything I see is a dream". Touch the bed and intensify the feeling: "Everything I touch is a dream". Touch one hand with the other and experience: "Everything I touch is a dream". Fall asleep sinking deeply into this sensation. There will be a constant stream of sensation moving within you.

After a few days you will discover that, in the middle of a dream, you will suddenly become aware that it is a dream. As soon as you remember that it is a dream, the dream will break, because the dream only works in the absence of consciousness. Then you will be filled with a bliss such as you have never known before. Your dream will vanish, dreams will disappear and a deep light will surround you. The dreams of an enlightened person disappear, because in the dream he also remembers that they are dreams.

Shankara Vedanta proposes the concept that the universe is an illusion. This philosophy is an experiment of the same kind.

The sannyasin has to constantly remember that everything that happens is a dream. As he gets up in the morning, walking along the road, in the middle of the market, he has to remember:

"It's all a dream. Why? Because this is the method. It is a process. If you experience constantly for eight hours, this remembrance will penetrate so deeply that you will remember it even in the middle of sleep; you will remember that it is a dream.

At the moment you are unable to remember. Actually, you are doing it even now, but in reverse order. During all your waking hours you feel and understand that everything you see is real. And that's why dreams seem real at night, because the feeling is so strong.

What could be more false than dreams? How many times have you woken up and realised their falsity, their uselessness? Yet every night you make the same mistake. Why? There must be a very deep reason behind this madness. The reason is: in your waking state you take everything for true. If you believe that everything you see is real, how is it possible that the dreams you see at night seem illusory to you?

You take them as real.

The Mayan experiment is just the opposite. Whatever you see during the day, remember that it is unreal. You forget it again and again, but once again you pull yourself together. You remind yourself that everything you see is nothing more than a great drama in which you are only a spectator. You are not the actor, not the doer, but only a witness.

If you nurture this feeling, it becomes a constant flow within you. Eventually the dream disappears in the night, and this is a great achievement. If the dream is shattered, you are ready to take the third step.

If sleep is broken, you can take the third step of retaining consciousness in deep sleep. But now this is difficult for you. It is not possible to do it all at once; you must proceed step by step.

When sleep is broken, there is nothing to see. But in the daytime, when your eyes are open, objects are very visible. No matter how much you think it is illusory, the objects will still exist. As much as Shankara says the world is an illusion, you must use a door to get out, you cannot go through the walls. Even though everything is an illusion, you will eat food and not pebbles. No matter how much you maintain that everything is an illusion, your presence is required to utter these words. If you do not exist, who will utter them?

So no matter how much you reinforce the feeling that the outside world is an illusion, the world of objects will remain. If someone hits you on the head with a rock, you will bleed. You may not feel it, you may not complain, you may say it's maya, but the incident has happened anyway.

But dreams have a singularity: they are all illusions. So an extraordinary experiment is carried out with dreams. The moment you come to know that dreams are illusory, they are lost; there is nothing to see. When the seen is lost, the seer becomes visible. As long as there is something to see, you look out because the scene attracts. When the scene no longer exists and the screen is empty, when even the screen is not there, you are left alone. That's why people meditate with their eyes closed. Calling the Mayan world, illusion, is a method.

The world is real. It does not depend on what you think. Even if it is a dream, it is Brahman's dream, and not yours. But there are your personal dreams which take shape in the night; therefore, when you shatter your own dreams, something very revolutionary happens: space then becomes empty. There is nothing to see. The play is over and it's time to go home. Now, what are you going to do sitting there? This is the moment when the eyes suddenly turn inwards, because there is nothing left outside. So the energy that was flowing outwards, towards the objects, now turns inwards, towards the observer.

Meditation is energy turning inwards. And the moment the energy turns inwards you can be conscious, even in sushupti, deep sleep. Because in deep sleep you exist, but the world doesn't exist, dreams don't exist. Your attention was entangled in observing the world and your dreams; you remained unconscious in deep sleep. Now this entanglement is uprooted. You have no connection with the seen and you can be without it. When the lamp burns, it doesn't care whether someone passes through its light or not. Now your consciousness will turn inwards and you will be awake even in deep sleep.

The experiment you have to do after waking up from the dream is that you should not open your eyes when the dream disappears, because once you open your eyes, the world of objects is present everywhere. The "seen" returns. So, when you wake up from the dream, do not open your eyes.

He continues to stare intently into the emptiness within. The dream has vanished. There is nothing anymore. Keep looking intently at the emptiness. In doing so, you will find that your consciousness has turned inwards.

So you are awake even in deep sleep. This is what Krishna means when he says in the Gita that the yogi is awake even when everyone else is asleep. What is sleep to others is not sleep to the yogi.

It is awake even in deep sleep.

So, when you see each of these states separately, you invariably enter the fourth state. Turiya" means "the fourth", just that! There is no need to give it any other meaning. It is enough to refer to it as "the fourth", because all meanings bind; all words are bindings. A gesture is enough. Because it is unlimited and infinite.

As soon as you come out of the three states, you become God. As you have entered the three, you are constricted. It is as if from an open space you enter a tunnel and it gets narrower and narrower. When you come to the five senses, it has become very narrow. Now you have to go backwards. As you go further and further back, your space increases. The day you find yourself outside the three, you will be the great expanse of space. Then you are God Himself.

Give another example: You look at the sky through a telescope. Through a very small aperture you focus your attention on something outside, and become one with it. When you look away from the telescope, you realise that you are not the telescope. In the same way, you are not the eyes, but you have concentrated on the eyes in millions of lifetimes. You are not the ears, but you have been listening through them for infinite lifetimes. You are not the hands, but you are so used to touching with your hands. You are tied to your telescope! You are like the scientist who carries his telescope everywhere and refuses to see without it. He moves everywhere with his telescope fixed on his eyes. You keep telling him, "Throw away this telescope. You are not that. But he can only see through a telescope and does not know that he can see otherwise. This is the state of forgetfulness.

The method to destroy this forgetfulness is: start from the waking state and let it culminate in the state of deep sleep.

***The waking state, the dream state and deep sleep: knowing these three states separately, the fourth state is known.***

Start with the first and proceed gradually. The day you realise that you are fully conscious in deep sleep, then there will be no difference between you and Mahavir or Buddha or Shiva.

Right now you are doing just the opposite: even in your waking state you are not fully awake. How are you going to be awake in deep sleep? You have the illusion that you are awake, but you are only awake in name. You manage to go about your daily activities. You ride your bicycle or drive your car and you think you are awake.

But have you ever noticed how automatic your actions have become? The cyclist doesn't even have to think: now I have to turn left, now right. He can be completely absorbed in his thoughts and the bicycle wheel turns automatically, out of pure habit. The bike turns left, then right and you're home! There is no need to be conscious while cycling. Everything has become mechanical, a habit. You are destined to get home. The driver of a car is still driving. He doesn't have to pay attention to the car.

Our lives are ordinarily very routine. We follow the beaten path. We are no better than the oxen in the oil mill. We tread the same path day after day. At most, the paths may be a little wider for one and a little narrower for others; a little ugly for one and a little beautiful for another, but they are paths all the same. Your life goes round and round like an ox in an oil mill. You get up in the morning and begin the journey; in the evening you complete the circle. You get up again in the morning... and the same routine! So regular is the repetition that you no longer need to be conscious of your activities. Everything happens like in a trance. At the appointed time you feel hungry; at the appointed time you feel sleepy; you go shopping at the appointed time. In this way you go through your life in a fixed course without any awareness.

When will you wake up, when will you shake yourself, when will you leave the beaten path, when will you declare: "I will not follow this monotonous circle"? The day you consider stepping out of it, you will have begun the journey to God.

Going to temples does not make you religious. That is also part of the same routine. You go there because you have always gone there; because your parents have always gone there, and their parents have also visited the same temple! You read the scriptures simply because your ancestors used to read them. Again the same routine. Have you ever gone to a temple with full awareness? If you do, there is no need to go to a temple anymore; because wherever there is awareness, you will find His temple.

Consciousness is the temple. We see the Christian going regularly to church, the Sikh to the gurudwara, the Hindu to the temple. All are bound by their bondage. No one can break this state of numbness of yours except yourself.

It is important for you to know that your waking state is only a stupor, while the deep sleep of a yogi is a fully awake state. You are a yogi, upside down! The day you become the opposite of what you are today, the quintessence of life will be within your grasp. Know the three stages separately, and the knower will be separated from the three stages; you are pure knowledge, nothing else. You are pure awareness, but only when you separate yourself from the three stages.

I was reading about a Sufi fakir, Junnaid. When a person abused him, he would say: "I will answer you tomorrow. And the next day he would say: "You don't need to answer.

The man who had abused him would ask him: "I abused you yesterday, why didn't you answer yesterday?

You are very strange. Nobody waits a second when you insult him. He retorts immediately.

Junnaid replied: "My master taught me not to rush into anything. Take your time. I must wait a little when someone insults me. If I were to give an immediate reply, the heat of the event would seize me; the smoke would blind my eyes. So I must wait and let the cloud pass.

When twenty-four hours have passed and the skies are clear again, then I will be able to give my answer with full awareness. Now I realise what a cheat my guru was. Because since then I have never been able to answer my opponents.

Is it possible to sustain anger for twenty-four hours? It is impossible to hold it for twenty-four minutes or even twenty-four seconds. The truth is that even if you hold back and watch for a single second, the anger disappears.

But you don't wait a moment. One person abuses you, as if someone pushes the button and the fan starts whirring. There is not the slightest space between the two of you, there is no distance, and you take pride in your alertness! You have no control over yourself. How can an unconscious person be in control of himself? Anyone can push the button and incite you to action. Someone comes and compliments you, and you are filled with joy; you are happy. If someone insults you, you are filled with tears.

Are you your own master or can anyone manipulate you? You are the slave of slaves. And those who manipulate are not their own masters either! And the irony is that they are all experts at manipulating others and none of them are aware of it. What greater insult can there be to your soul than the fact that anyone can affect you?

Mulla Nasruddin worked in an office. Everyone was unhappy with his work. Most of the time he dozed or was fast asleep. Everyone in the office was fed up with him. They started scolding him. The boss also called him and scolded him for his behaviour. Finally, because of the annoyance and humiliation, the Mulla thought it best to resign, because it was easier to resign than to change his ways.

Many people who flee the world and embrace sannyas are actually renouncing the world for this very reason. Transformation is difficult, renunciation is easier. Everyone in the office was relieved to hear the news. However, as he had been there for a long time and was leaving of his own free will, they decided to give him a farewell party. They were very worried about him and could not get rid of him. He had become a burden. So they were very happy. They made elaborate preparations, with sweets and refreshments. Each colleague said a few words of praise for the Mulla. After all, he was leaving. The Mulla was so moved that tears came to his eyes. When it was his turn to speak, he stood up and said: "Friends, I am really touched by your love and affection. I didn't know how much you cared for me. Now I cannot leave you. I withdraw my resignation.

We are being manipulated. Often, everywhere, the whole world is manipulating each and every person. And the climate keeps changing. There are thousands of types of people. As a result, there is a deep confusion within you. This is inevitable, because you are not motivated by any one person. Only the one who is awakened inwardly is motivated by one. In the life of such a man there is clarity, transparency. His life is clear and purposeful; he has a direction.

There is no direction in your life. There can't be. You behave as if you are in a crowd that pushes you where it wants you to go. A person like that has to keep moving. He can't stand still for a moment.

Someone pushes him to the right, he goes to the right; someone pushes him to the left, he goes to the left. Your whole life goes like this, pushed by the crowd. Reflect on this and you will come to understand it.

Someone says something; you do it. Then someone else says something else and you do it. And then you are filled with a series of contradictions.

One of my acquaintances fell off a rickshaw and hurt himself. Then he was discharged from the hospital. Six months passed. When he fully recovered, he was still using crutches. When I asked him if he still had difficulty walking, he said, "No".

"Then why don't you get rid of the crutches?" I asked.

"You see," he said, "the doctor says I don't need them anymore, but my lawyers say I do, at least until the court case is resolved. So you see my dilemma.

Your lawyer says one thing and your doctor says another; the wife says one thing and the husband says another; the son says one thing, the father says another - all around you there are millions of teachers pushing you. There are infinite teachers, but you are alone! You listen to one and listen to another. You listen to whoever holds you back. And your personality fractures into a thousand pieces. Until you start listening to the inner voice, you cannot be an integrated whole.

I call him a sannyasin who has begun to listen to the inner voice and is willing to stake everything on it.

But you cannot hear the inner voice while you are unconscious. Until then, what you take for the inner voice will not be the inner voice, but an outer voice. The unconscious man knows nothing of this voice. Otherwise, all the politicians sitting in Delhi would have spoken of this inner voice: Indira, Giri: the voice of the soul! How can a sleeping person know it? How can he know what the inner voice is? The voice that satisfies you is the voice of your desires, but you call it your inner voice.

Only the awakened person has an inner voice. Once this voice comes within earshot, all that is sinful, all that is impure and unclean, all the chaos and confusion within you, will cease at once. Then you will realise what a collection of personalities you have been. You were not one, but many, like a crowd in a market or a stock exchange. You are the Delhi stock exchange: it is all nonsense! Nothing can be understood. An outsider will not be able to understand what you are. There are all kinds of voices. And in the midst of all that din your own voice is completely lost.

The fourth state means to recognise the soul. Only when you break with the first three states will you be able to recognise the soul. Start with very small experiments. When anger arises, stop! What is your hurry? When you feel hatred, wait! There must be some interval. Respond only when you are fully conscious, not until then. You will find that all that is sinful in life is gone from you; all that is wrong is banished forever. Suddenly you will find that there is no need to respond to anger.

Maybe you feel like thanking the man who insults you. Because he has forced you. He has given you the chance to wake up.

Kabir has said to stay close to the one who criticises you. Take care of him and serve the one who criticises you because it is he who gives you the opportunity to awaken.

All the occasions that drown you in unconsciousness can become stepping stones to consciousness if you want them to. Life is like a huge rock in the middle of the road. The foolish see the rock as a barrier and turn back. For them, the road is closed. Those who are clever, climb on the rock and use it as a stepping stone. And the moment they turn it into a stepping stone, greater heights are available to them.

A seeker has only one factor to keep in mind, and that is: to use every moment to awaken consciousness. So, whether it is hunger or anger or lust or greed, every state can be used towards awareness. If you build up awareness little by little, you will eventually have a good reserve of fuel within you. In the flame that creates this fuel, you will discover that you are neither awake, nor dreaming, nor in a deep sleep; you are beyond and apart from all three.

*The constancy of awareness is the waking state. Being aware of everything around you is the waking state.*

*Choosing is the dream state.* The thought network of the mind, the extension of imagination and fantasy is the dream state.

*Unconsciousness and lack of self-awareness create the illusion of deep sleep.*

These are the three states. When we pass through the first state, we are one with it. When we reach the second, we are one with it. When we reach the third state, we become one with it.

Therefore, we cannot see these three separately. To see, we need some distance, a perspective.

There must be some space between you and the object. If you stand right up against a mirror, you will not be able to see your reflection. A small distance is necessary. But you are so close to the waking, dreaming and sleep states that you actually become one with them. You are coloured by them.

This habit of becoming one with others is so ingrained that we are not even aware of it, and this habit is being exploited.

If you are a Hindu and you are told to set fire to a mosque, you will think a thousand times whether it is right to do so, because the mosque is dedicated to the same God to whom your temple is dedicated. The mode of dedication may be different, the method may be different, the form may be different... but the destination is the same. And yet we find a Hindu mob setting fire to a mosque. If you are one of them, you don't wait to think. You become one with the mob and help burn the mosque. If you are questioned later, you ask yourself how you could have done it. Alone you would never do it, but in a crowd you would. Why? Because in a crowd you tend to get lost; it's an old habit.

No Muslim is as evil and vicious on his own as when he is in a mob. No single Hindu is as wicked and wicked as when he is in a mob. No man alone has ever committed such sins as have been committed by crowds. Why? Because a crowd colours you. If the crowd is angry, you feel anger welling up inside you.

If the crowd weeps and shouts, you too start weeping and shouting. If the crowd is happy, you forget all your sorrows and rejoice with the crowd.

Now watch: you go to a home where someone has died. Many people are crying. Suddenly you realise that you too feel like crying. You may think that you are a very compassionate person, full of love and pity, or you may think that the tears are due to compassion. You are wrong. Reflect: you were at home when the news came that the man had died. When you were alone, you did not feel love and compassion for the bereaved family. It is more likely that you were upset:

so he's dead, what's so special about that? Life and death happen all the time. But now I'm expected to go to his house to pay my condolences, as if I have nothing better to do! And why did he have to die today, when I'm so busy?

That's what you would have thought. But when you arrive at his house and find yourself in the mourning crowd, you discover that your feelings have changed. You too will feel the same as the crowd.

But this feeling is worthless; in fact, it is dangerous. It is the crowd that affects you.

Beware of this feeling of sympathy that does not come from your heart.

You have probably seen people who are normally unhappy and burdened by sadness dancing with joy at holi, the festival of colours. They dance, they sing, they throw coloured powder at each other. What happens to these people who do not know what joy is in their ordinary lives? These same people, who normally move like zombies, have taken to dancing. What has happened to them? Once again, it is the colour of the crowd.

The seeker must beware of the crowd. Seek your own voice, your own melody. The crowd has always pushed and shoved you. It can mould you in any way it wishes.

Why does this happen? It happens because you don't feel your separateness, and whenever you have the opportunity you quickly lose your separateness. You are always ready to lose it. If sleep comes, you lose yourself in sleep; if you are awake, you lose yourself in wakefulness; if dreams come, you lose yourself in dreams. If those around you are happy, you are happy; if they are sad, you are sad.

Do you exist as a separate entity or are you just a centre that is lost in its surroundings? Do you have an existence, a centre? Truly you do, and that is the soul.

Awaken your being! Save yourself from drowning! That is why all religions are against alcohol - which in itself is not bad - for the simple reason that it is a means of getting lost. All religions are in favour of awakening. Whoever drinks alcohol is drowning. Religion is against all those things that drag you into oblivion, that make you unconscious. As it is, you are almost unconscious. You have a little glimmer of awakening, and you are anxious to lose even that on the slightest pretext.

It is very surprising that you become happy when you lose your conscience. It is impossible to find a bigger fool than you. You lose consciousness and you say, "That was beautiful, that was pure joy!" Why? Because your little ray of consciousness helps you to see the problems of life. It makes you aware of life and fills you with anxieties. It makes you aware of the fact that you are not aware. This little ray of awareness reveals the darkness within you, which is already dense enough. You want to stifle this ray so that you are not reminded of the darkness. So you indulge in alcohol or drugs, or join politics or any other crowd activity: you lose yourself anywhere, in anything, to forget yourself.

In the West, psychologists advise people to forget themselves if they want to stay healthy. In the East, religious teachers tell you that you can only be healthy if you can awaken yourself. These are two contrary concepts, but both make sense. The Western psychologist accepts you as you are; then, in these circumstances, he tries to help you live as well as you can. That is why he is right when he says: "Forget about yourself. Being more conscious is dangerous because you will be filled with anxiety because you will begin to see things as they are. And nothing in life is as it should be; everything is confusion and chaos. So the best thing to do is to close your eyes and forget about it. What is the need to fixate on all the problems?

But the oriental master does not accept you as you are. He says: "You are ill, you are sick, you are confused and bewildered. Even if your anxieties increase and you become more restless, it doesn't matter; this is the way to transformation, to revolution.

It's like this: a man has cancer and there is no cure for it, so they give him morphine to help him forget the pain. But the Eastern masters say that morphine cannot transform life. It awakens the person, only then is transformation possible. Man, as he is, is neither at the initial stage nor at the final stage of his journey. He has not even begun his journey; he is outside the door.

It has not yet entered. There is the possibility of supreme bliss, but not in the state you are in now: drowsy, sleepy.

Understand the difference between happiness and bliss. Happiness is the state in which the faint ray of consciousness awakened within you also goes to sleep. Then you are not conscious of any pain. Ananda, bliss, is the state in which the faint ray of your awareness becomes the vast sun, and darkness is banished completely. Bliss is negative: insensitivity to pain. You get a headache; you take an aspirin. It gives you happiness, not bliss. This pill helps you forget the headache; it makes you insensitive to the headache.

You are sick; you are distressed; life is full of problems. You take to drink and everything seems to fall into place. A troubled man's footsteps lead to the tavern; when he returns there is a song on his lips. Thus you lose your little ray of conscience and acquire so-called happiness. But this will not give you bliss. For happiness is the non-remembrance of sorrow, and bliss is the remembrance of the soul. And this is not forgetfulness, but total remembrance. Kabir calls it surati, which is constant and continuous remembrance.

This sutra will lead you to total remembrance. So be careful! Stay away from anything that makes you drunk or insensitive or unconscious. There are so many easy ways to become unconscious, and we are so completely possessed by them, that we are not even aware of them.

A man goes mad after eating; he goes on eating. It may not have occurred to you, but he is making the same use of food that another makes of alcohol. Overeating causes sleep. The more you eat, the deeper you sleep. The day you fast, you can't sleep well. Food causes drowsiness. So a man who indulges in eating all day long is seeking oblivion through food.

A man's obsession is ambition. He will not rest until he has amassed millions of rupees. Until then he is like a madman. Day and night, dawn or dusk, it doesn't matter, in his mind there is only one calculation: ten million! He is completely dedicated to his calculation. Nothing else worries him. His eyes are focused on the millions. Until the day he reaches his goal, anxiety will take hold of him. Then he will discover that it has all been in vain. He has got his millions. What now?

Three men were locked up in the same cell in an insane asylum. They had been friends before and all went mad at about the same time. It was quite possible that they were affected by each other's company. A psychologist came to study them. He asked the doctor in charge what was wrong with the first one. He was told that he was trying to untie the knot of a rope. He did not succeed and lost his head.

"And the second?"

"He managed to undo the knot, and that's how he went crazy".

"And the third?" asked the psychologist.

"He is the one who tied the knot".

One is concerned with tying the knot, another with untying it. Some succeed, others fail, but this is not the point, because they are all crazy. Why do people engage in such useless activities? To avoid meeting oneself! They are tricks to escape from the self. If you are not ambitious, if you don't want to struggle in elections or crave wealth, how will you avoid meeting your own self? At some point you will have to meet yourself. Everyone fears this encounter. This fear makes you tremble.

There is a lot of talk about knowing the self, the soul. But if you understand yourself, you will realise how many tricks you use to avoid meeting the soul. The Buddhas say When the soul is known, bliss reigns and nectar rains. Kabir says Clouds of nectar thunder and showers of nectar rain down on you. But this happens in the end. In the beginning you have to go through a lot of pain and suffering. You have to destroy every delusion that you have created over infinite lifetimes, and it is difficult to let go of each one of them, because the delusion had given you an illusion of comfort, a sweet drowsiness in which we lose ourselves. And now we have to break it. Shattering it is very painful. Without breaking it you can never get there, where the clouds are filled with nectar and bliss pours out in torrents.

This journey towards the goal is called tapascharya, practice. Start with the waking state. Then take your practice to the dream state and then to deep sleep.

To choose is to dream. When the mind is full of dreams, that is the dream state. Don't think that you only dream at night; you also dream in the daytime. Sitting here and listening to me does not necessarily mean that you are hearing what I say. You hear, but you are also weaving dreams within yourself.

A constant stream of dreams keeps flowing inside you. Even when you are awake, dreams are still swirling inside you. Close your eyes and look inside and you will always find something going on.

It is as if we see the stars at night and they disappear during the day; but it is only the sunlight that hides them. So don't think that they disappear during the day. They are very much present.

If you go down into a deep well and look up you can see them. You need darkness to see the stars. They are not visible because of sunlight.

It is the same with dreams. It is not that dreams are only seen at night, but that at night the eyes are closed, darkness comes and dreams stand out from this darkness. During the day, your eyes are open and all your attention is occupied by a hundred other things. But the dreams are still happening. You just don't see them. Close your eyes and you start daydreaming immediately. There is a constant undercurrent that has to be broken. And only if you manage to break it during the day, you will be able to break it during the night; otherwise it is not possible.

All mantras are devices to break this undercurrent. A person receives a mantra from his guru, who says, "Repeat it within yourself as you go to the market to sell your wares. Let the sound of the chanting resonate within you". So this man goes about his daily business, but at the same time he lets the mantra flow within him. What does this mean? The energy that was previously spent in creating dreams now becomes a Ram-Ram current. So now the chanter creates his own dream within himself. Outwardly he goes about his worldly duties; inwardly he keeps a constant remembrance of Ram-Ram.... This will not lead him to Ram, but it will help him to break the chain of sleep. The day you find that there is an incessant flow of Ram-Ram instead of dreams, you will know that you have succeeded in breaking the chain of dreams during the day.

So the success of the mantra can only be measured in dreams, never during the day. How is this possible? If you repeat the mantra throughout the day, there will be no dreaming at night, the chanting will flow in your sleep. It will be much more intense than you can imagine.

Swami Ram used to repeat this Ram-Ram mantra. Once he was a guest of his friend Sardar Puran Singh. They were alone in a small hut high in the Himalayas. There was not a soul for miles and miles around. One night, Sardar could not sleep well because of the heat and the mosquitoes.

And what did he find? The sound of Ram-Ram floated in the hut. He was a little startled, could there be anyone besides him and his friend asleep in the room? Swami Ram was sleeping soundly. The Sardar got up, took the lamp and looked everywhere, inside and outside. There was no one.

He re-entered the hut and, to his surprise, found that the sound was louder in the room than outside. He raised the lamp and held it over Swami Ram's face: Is he awake and chanting the mantra? He was fast asleep. In fact, he was snoring. And, wonder of wonders, the sound grew louder as he approached the swami. He brought his ear close to Swami Ram and found that every pore of his body was vibrating with the Ram-Ram sound.

This happens when the memory becomes very intense. A lot of energy is spent on creating dreams. You don't get them without a price. Dreams have no value in themselves, but the price you pay is immense because you spend the whole night dreaming. Recently, there has been a lot of research on dreams in the West. Scientists claim that a normal, healthy person dreams eight dreams a night.

Each dream lasts about fifteen minutes. This means that at least two hours are spent dreaming every night. But this is the case of a completely healthy man who has no mental disorder. It is not easy to find such a healthy person. Generally, people dream for six of the eight hours they sleep. The constant flow of dreams consumes a great deal of your energy. It is not free! You acquire it at the cost of your life.

The mantra centralises this energy around Ram, Krishna, Christ, Om or whatever you like. Any word will do. It need not be the name of God. Your own name can be equally useful.

The English poet Tennyson writes in his memoirs that in his childhood he stumbled upon a method.

When he couldn't sleep at night, he would repeat over and over again: "Tennyson, Tennyson, Tennyson..." and fall asleep. As he grew older, he realised that this was a wonderful resource.

When he was restless, he would repeat to himself: "Tennyson, Tennyson, Tennyson..." and his mind would regain peace and balance. Then he would use his own name as a mantra.

Your own name may give the same result, but it won't, because you don't have that much faith in your name. It doesn't matter whether you say Ram or Rahim. It is not about names; the words make no difference. All words are the same, and all names are the name of God, including yours. When any name is repeated like this, it produces a musical note within and the energy of the dream dissolves in it. Mantras serve to destroy dreams. No one has attained God just by repeating a mantra, but destroying dreams is a great step towards attaining God.

The mantra is a method, an instrument, a hammer to smash dreams. And what are dreams? They are also nothing but words, and that is why a hammer of words can break them. It is not necessary to use a real hammer. Dreams are unreal, so a pseudo-hammer will do.

A real medicine is dangerous to pseudo-disease; only an imaginary medicine will help to remove the false disease.

What are dreams? They are thought waves. And what are mantras? They are will power, which is also a form of dream. But dreams are impermanent, changing; whereas the mantra is constant and one. Little by little, the energy of the dream is absorbed by the mantra. The night you discover that there are no dreams and you hear the constant music of the mantra as you sleep, you will know that you have conquered the dream state. The illusion has been shattered and the truth has begun to reveal itself. Then you will be able to enter the state of deep sleep.

But you do just the opposite. You reinforce your thought waves. You are invaded by useless thoughts and you cooperate with them. You are sitting alone, there is nothing to do and you start thinking about fighting the next election. The dream begins! Nothing will please you less than reaching the presidential chair. You have become president in your dream. There are congratulations and you enjoy them to the fullest. You never stop to think: what stupidity is this! What are you doing? You are just giving energy to useless fantasies. Your mind is full of useless illusions of this kind.

If we examine human life in detail, we will find that ninety-nine per cent of life is wasted in fruitless dreams like this one. Some dream of wealth, some of power, some of various conquests. What will you gain even if you achieve them all?

There was a great president of America, Calvin Coolidge; he was a very serene person by nature. It must have been a total accident that he became president, because such serene people can never attain such a turbulent office, which can only be won after a mad career. The craziest beats the least crazy and gets to the top. How Coolidge got there is a miracle. It is said that he was so quiet by nature that he hardly spoke. It is said that there were days when he spoke no more than five or ten words.

At the end of his term, his friends implored him to stand for election again. Everyone was anxious to have him back. He refused. People asked him: "Why? All the countrymen are in your favour". He replied, "The first time was a mistake. What have I gained from it all? I will not waste another five years of my life. And there is nothing ahead of the president. I have already experienced that office. There is nothing else ahead. If there had been anything, my dream would have continued."

You don't realise it, but no man is a bigger failure than the one who has realised his dreams.

For on the very brink of success he discovers that everything he fought for, everything he worked so hard to achieve, had nothing to offer him. But the successful man hides his disappointment and defeat from others who, being equally foolish, struggle to get where he is. If all the successful people in the world were honest and declared the futility of their achievements, many of those mad careers that spring from their dreams would stop instantly. But the successful man cannot do this, because it would hurt his ego to declare that he has achieved nothing after a lifelong struggle. Instead, he exaggerates the pleasures of his achievements. He whose tail is cut off, makes others lose their tails too; otherwise he would be ashamed of himself for being the only one without a tail.

When the stream of sleep begins, stay awake and alert, and observe: What am I doing? All the stories of Sheikh Chilli from the children's books apply to you. Your mind is Sheikh Chilli, and as long as you dream you will remain Sheikh Chilli. The meaning of Sheikh Chilli is one who dreams useless dreams and then takes them for true. God grant that these dreams never come true! They will demand tremendous energy.

If your dreams come true, you will find that you have achieved nothing. Your hands are full of dust. All the successes of the worldly world turn to ashes. By the time you have achieved them, your life is over and there is no way back. And you have no choice but to hide your failures; that your life was not spent in vain, that you have achieved something. Your life was fruitful.

Mental waves are nothing but dreams. Do not strengthen them. When the dream starts running inside you, shake it off and break the dream as fast as you can. Mantras can be helpful. Later we will talk in detail about how they can be tools to break dreams. Mantras definitely break dreams.

***Unconsciousness and lack of self-awareness is deep sleep.***

In it, all is lost. There is no discrimination, no wisdom, no conscience, neither within nor without. You are like a rock, in a deep trance. Think of it, how hectic your life must be! Only when you sleep soundly, you wake up in the morning and say what a pleasant dream you have had. Think of it: what a hell your life must be that you only find happiness in the oblivion of sleep, when you are unconscious. The rest of the time you are full of pain and suffering.

You only feel at ease after a good sleep, and sleep means nothing but unconsciousness. But you are right. For you it is more than enough, because your life is a long history of worries, anxieties, tensions and agitation. You rest for a while and feel fulfilled, but in reality there is nothing to feel fulfilled about.

Sleep means where there is nothing, no inner world and no outer world. Everything is lost in the darkness. Yes, you certainly feel rested, but what good is that rest if the next morning you fall into the same routine? The energy you gain from the night's rest will be used to create new tensions, new anxieties. You will rest every night and create new tensions every day.

If you would only realise this little fact: in unconscious sleep you feel a lot of pleasure, because there is no tension or anxiety there. You forget all your problems when you enter this unconscious state. Imagine how much pleasure and joy you will achieve the day when your worries and confusions disappear and you are filled with awareness. This is what is called moksha, nirvana, brahmananda.

Sleep gives you the feeling of having rested and fills you with pleasure, because in it all chaos and confusion are dissipated. Then, when these actually dissolve and you remain in complete relaxation twenty-four hours a day - the place sometimes reached in deep sleep - imagine what bliss you will experience. It is a state of perpetual serenity! Think of it! For samadhi is like deep sleep with one slight difference: there is consciousness. In sleep there is no consciousness; in samadhi you are fully conscious. The fourth state is like deep sleep, with only one difference: in deep sleep there is darkness, while in the fourth state there is light.

Suppose you are brought into this garden in an unconscious state, on a stretcher. The sun's rays will touch you, because they are not unconscious, because you are unconscious. The breeze will play over you, it will caress you because they are not unconscious, you are unconscious. The flowers will spread their fragrance. The freshness of the early morning dewdrops will touch you because they are not unconscious, you are unconscious.

Everything will be happening around you, but you will not be aware of it; yet when you come to yourself you will say, "What a restful sleep it was. All the factors that contribute to your rest - the rays of the sun, the fragrance of the flowers, the cool breeze - you are not aware of them. Yet you say, "What a restful sleep!

Now consider the other way. Suppose you are sitting in the garden in full awareness. The morning sun sends its welcoming warmth, the flowers fill the air with breathtaking perfumes, the cool breeze creates music in the leaves of the trees as they rustle against each other, the dew glistens on the petals.

In the midst of all this, can you imagine the joy, the bliss ....!

In deep sleep we arrive exactly where Buddha, Mahavir and Shiva arrive in full consciousness. Even from deep sleep you bring the message: What happiness! Even though you cannot clearly express this happiness: how it was, what it was like. You cannot define it, you cannot bring the taste with you. So, after a good night's rest, you wake up refreshed and joyful. You get a little glimpse of buddhahood in the faces of people who sleep very soundly, especially young children, for their minds are not yet filled with tensions. As their worries increase, their sleep decreases. Watch a small child as he is about to get up in the morning. His face bears the freshness of Buddha. Something blissful has happened within him, though he is not aware of it.

All tensions vanish in deep sleep, but there is no wisdom. In samadhi - that is, in the fourth state - all tensions vanish, but wisdom remains. Wisdom plus deep sleep equals samadhi.

**The one who enjoys all three is the supreme hero.**

He who is an experiencer of the three states - waking, dreaming and deep sleep - and who is apart and separate from them; he who passes through them, but does not identify with them; he who goes beyond the three and considers himself different and apart - he is a warrior, a conqueror.

Viresha means the warrior of warriors, the conqueror, the supreme hero. Viresh is one of the names of Shiva. Mahavir also means the great warrior. We have called "Mahavir" only those who attained samadhi. We do not call a person a conqueror just because he has climbed Everest or reached the moon, it is a brave act, but they are not the ultimate heights to reach. We call him a Viresh, a Mahavir, who has attained the soul. What Everest can be higher than God? He who attains the ultimate is a Mahavir, a great warrior. We accept nothing less. What if you have reached the moon? It has simply opened up new vistas for exploration: Mars, Jupiter, and so on and so forth.

The universe has no limits!

We call him Mahavir, who has reached where it is no longer possible to reach. Why do we refer to him as Mahavir? Because there is no act more courageous than the act of reaching the self. There is no journey that demands as much courage and fearlessness as the journey to the self. For the path is full of difficulties that are to be found nowhere else. It requires the utmost austerity.

The journey to the self is the most difficult journey. It is like walking on a razor's edge. Perhaps that is why you run away from the self and devote yourself to worldly things. And perhaps that is why, though the knowledge of the self appeals to the mind, you do not have the courage.

Some fear takes hold of you.

It is very difficult. You will have to walk alone. The most difficult thing is that in this world, everywhere you can go with company. However, there is one place where you will have to go alone.

No wife, no brother, no friend, not even the guru, can accompany you. At most, the guru can show the way. Buddha shows the way. That's all. You must go alone!

We are afraid of being alone. There are so many people around us, so many dreams. Some of these dreams are very nice, very interesting. A few outstanding people break through this web of dreams and set out on the road. Many of them turn back. One in a million continue the journey, for it is an arduous and difficult path. Among them all, perhaps one person will reach it. That is why he is called Viresh, warrior of warriors.

The fourth, which lies hidden beyond the three, and within you, is Everest. That is where you have to get to. And the way to reach it is to be awake in your waking state. Right now you are in a lukewarm state. Become a burning flame of consciousness, so that its heat permeates your own breath.

Stay awake in the dreams so that the dreams are broken. Be so alert in the dream state that a ray of your consciousness passes through the state of deep sleep. The day you enter the deep sleep, with this little flame of consciousness, you will have opened the gates of the state of Viresh; you will have struck your first blow at the door of the temple.

Bliss is infinite, but you will have to cross the middle road. You will have to pay the price. The greater the bliss, the higher the price. There are no bargains.

Many are looking for bargains (compromises?). They look for shortcuts, and find gurus to take advantage of them. The guru tells them to wear this amulet and everything will be fulfilled, or that it is enough to have faith in him, or demands that they give a certain amount to charity, do good deeds or build a temple. These are "bargains" that lead nowhere; they simply deceive you. You must follow the path.

There are some who try even cheaper methods. They take hemp or hashish and believe that they are in samadhi, that they have attained knowledge. There are thousands of sannyasins and sadhus who take drugs like opium and hemp. The West is very much influenced by them, and they have discovered even better drugs, like l.s.d., hashish, marijuana. They also have injections that take you to samadhi. Like instant coffee, now they make instant samadhi.

If only it were that easy! If only someone had attained enlightenment under the influence of drugs, then the world would have become an enlightened place. It is not that easy, but the mind looks for cheaper ways.

The mind wants to bypass the long and arduous path and enter directly into samadhi. That cannot be, for salvation lies in treading the path. The path is not a prefabricated path; it is also your development.

This is the difficulty. In the outside world the journey can be shortened. The plane flies directly from London to Bombay, without intermediate stops, but the man who gets on in London is the same as the man who gets off in Bombay. This man is the same as he was before. He has not grown up during the flight. But this is an outer journey. In the inner journey, you cannot reach the destination without growing from what you were at the starting point. Those who say it is possible are simply deceiving you, because it is not a journey from one place to another place, but a journey from one state of being to another state of being. You have to grow in the process of the journey because it is in that growth that you will be cleansed, purified and transformed. It is in the agony of the process of the journey that you will grow. This pain, this agony is indispensable. If you look for shortcuts, you only cheat yourself.

In the West there is a great search for shortcuts, so people like Mahesh Yogi have a great impact there. The reason for this is that Mahesh Yogi says: "Everything I say is like a jet of speed".

Give a little mantra that the seeker should repeat for fifteen minutes a day. This is all that needs to be done and you get it. You do not need to change your behaviour, your lifestyle, nor do you need to give up anything in the outside world. This is all: relax every day for fifteen minutes and repeat the mantra. The mantra is everything.

The mantra is valuable, but it is not everything. The mantra can destroy dreams, but it cannot give the truth. The destruction of dreams is part of the path to the destination of truth, but if someone thinks that it is enough to repeat the mantra, that it is enough to count beads, he is childish. Such a person is not yet worthy even to speak of the path, let alone to reach the goal.

The path is difficult, but it must be trodden. That is why the sutra says that the path is an enormous effort. It takes willpower to undertake such a mighty effort. You must be willing to stake yourself on the effort. Liberation can only be acquired if you put your all on the line. Nothing less will suffice. If you give anything more, it will not do; you will not have paid the full price. Only when you give completely of yourself is the price enough and you get it.

Enough for today.

# Yoga maxims: Sense of wonder

*The sense of wonder is the basis of yoga. To be established in oneself is the strength. Transcendental logic is a means to self-realisation. Enjoying the bliss of existence is enlightenment.*

*A sense of wonder is the basis of yoga.*

Try to understand this.

In the dictionary, "wonder" means amazement. But there is a basic difference between awe and wonder. If you don't understand this basic difference, you may embark on a totally different journey. Awe is the foundation of science, the sense of wonder is the foundation of yoga.

Awe is extroverted; wonder is introverted. Awe is about the other; wonder is about ourselves. This is the first point.

Wonder is born of what we cannot comprehend, of what leaves us speechless, of what our intellect cannot grasp, of what turns out to be bigger than us, of what we are suddenly dumbfounded by, of what destroys us.

If the same state of wonder - which is born when we are confronted with the illogical, the incomprehensible - is diverted towards external objects, it gives rise to science. When we begin to think about matter, when we begin to contemplate the world and try to investigate that mystery that surrounds us all, science is created. Science is born out of wonder. Astonishment means that it has taken the journey outwards.

There is one more difference between astonishment and wonder: if we are surprised by something, sooner or later we will get fed up with that surprise, because surprise creates tension; hence the effort to destroy what surprises us. Science is born of this surprise. Then it destroys the surprise. It tries to find interpretations, doctrines, formulas, keys, and it does not rest easy until it destroys the mystery, until it is in possession of knowledge, until science can say: "Yes, I have understood!

Science is determined to eradicate the element of wonder from the world. If it succeeds, there will not be a single thing on earth that man cannot boast of not knowing. That is to say, this world will be without God, because God means that which we cannot claim to know even if we have known it. We can know it, but it remains unknowable. We can continue to deepen our knowledge of it, but it cannot be exhausted. We are in a state of eternal wonder about him.

There are some objects that have become known to us. We can call them the known. There are other objects which we do not know, but which we will know. Let us call them the unknown.

And existence also consists of such objects which we have never known and about which we can never know. We will call them the unknowable. God is unknowable. This is the third element. Science does not accept God because it says that there is nothing unknowable in the world. We may not have known it so far, we may not have tried hard enough, but sooner or later we will know it. One day we shall know the world completely; nothing will remain unknown in it.

Science is born out of wonder and then begins to destroy wonder. That's why I call science parricidal: it tries to kill that which created it. Religion is just the opposite. Religion is also born out of a certain awe; this sutra calls it "sense of wonder". The only difference is:

When a religious seeker is filled with wonder, he does not undertake the outer journey, but an inner pilgrimage. When some kind of mystery envelops him, he begins to think about himself:

I must know who I am.

If the mystery becomes introspective, and the search and the journey are directed inwards, the arrow of the search points towards oneself, the attention is totally absorbed by the thirst to know one's own reality... then it is awe.

And the second point to understand is that the sense of wonder is inexhaustible. The more we know, the more it increases. That is why wonder is contradictory. As a rule, the sense of wonder should disappear the moment we come to know something. But Buddha or Krishna or Shiva or Christ do not lose their sense of wonder. When they attain supreme consciousness, their sense of wonder becomes supreme! At that moment they do not say that they have known everything, they say that after knowing everything there remains everything to be known.

The Upanishads have said: "Even if you extract the whole from the whole, the whole remains". Even if you know the whole, the whole remains to be known. Therefore, spiritual knowledge does not feed the ego, scientific knowledge feeds the ego. Spiritual knowledge will never make you a knower; you will always remain humble. And the more you know, the more you will feel: "I know nothing". At the highest peak of knowledge you will be able to say, "I know nothing". At the moment of ultimate knowledge, the whole existence fills you with a feeling of awe.

If science triumphs, the whole world will be known; if religion triumphs, the whole world will be unknown. If science triumphs, you, the knower, will be full of ego and the world will become ordinary, for where there is no sense of wonder, everything becomes prosaic; where there is no wonder, there is no spirit; if there is no possibility of mystery, the process of evolution comes to a dead end. The thirst for knowledge is gone, curiosity is dead.

If science has its way, the world will be filled with a boredom the likes of which it has never experienced before. If Westerners are more bored, science is to blame for it, because people are losing their capacity for wonder. They are not amazed by anything. They have forgotten to wonder. If you give them a problem that has no solution, they will say, "Oh, it can be solved! - because according to science, basically, there is nothing that can remain unknown forever; it can be unravelled.

The religious journey is, however, paradoxical. The more we unveil, the more we discover that the mystery continues to deepen. The closer we get, the more we come to know: it is very difficult to know. And the moment we penetrate to the very core of existence, everything becomes mysterious. For Buddha, the stones and pebbles lying on the ground are as mysterious as the twinkling stars high in the sky: it is not only the enormous that seems mysterious, the smallest event holds the same mystery for him. A seed that sprouts in the earth is as mysterious as the creation of the whole universe.

Then, when the sense of wonder becomes intense, your eyes will become like those of a small child. A child is amazed by everything. Watch a child walking down the street: everything amazes him.

A coloured stone looks like a diamond. You laugh at him because you are the connoisseur; you know it is a coloured stone. You tell him: "Don't be crazy, this is not a diamond". But the boy wants to put it in his pocket. You will say, "Don't carry this burden. After all, it's a dirty stone lying in the mud. Throw it away.

But the boy grips it tighter. You are not able to understand it. It is a marvel for the child. This coloured stone is in no way less valuable than the diamond. The value lies in the sense of wonder.

Stones are worthless. A tiny butterfly can hypnotise the child immensely, but you won't be hypnotised by the almighty himself even if he comes to see you! The child starts chasing the butterfly....

The highest state of awe, of buddhahood, is like the innocence of a small child. One becomes childlike in that state. That is why Jesus has said Those who are like little children will be able to enter the kingdom of God. Jesus is saying the same thing that Shiva has said in this sutra: the sense of wonder is the foundation of yoga. Awe is the first stage of yoga. In that case you have to understand many things.

The more knowledgeable you are, the weaker the foundation of yoga will be. If you are filled with the pride of knowing, the chances of your becoming a yogi are less. If your heart is burdened with scriptures, your sense of wonder will be destroyed. You ask a scholar about God, and he begins to answer as if God is a thing to be answered... as if God can be explained. You ask a scholar and he already has a ready answer. As soon as you ask him, he has already given you the answer. Even God does not leave you speechless. All the formulas are definite, he explains them instantly.

But if you go to the Buddha and ask him about God, he tells you nothing. You may come back thinking that this man remained silent, and the meaning is clear: he doesn't know. But the reason this man remained silent is that this sense of wonder is the gateway to the divine. If you had been a little wiser, you would have stayed with the man who did not respond. And you would have tried to understand him: you would have peered into his eyes; you would have lived in his company, in his proximity, because he has experienced something, and the experience is so immense that words cannot express it; he has seen something that cannot be converted into a response.

Questions and answers are fine for schoolchildren. Your question itself is absurd. You can't ask a question about God. How can you ask a question about infinity? Both the question and the answer fall on their own in the face of infinity. Your question is petty, that is why Buddha has kept silent. But you may come back thinking that if this man had known, he would have answered. He did not answer, that means he did not know. You recognise a scholar because your head is also full of words. You will not be able to understand a scholar because a scholar is full of wonder.

And your sense of wonder is dead.

The greatest calamity in the world is: the destruction of wonder. The day your sense of wonder is destroyed, your possibility of liberation is destroyed. The day your sense of wonder is dead, your childish heart is dead, frozen. You have grown old.

Are you still in awe, does life ask you any questions, are you moved by the chirping of birds, the sound of running streams, the rustling of the wind in the trees, do you feel joy, does this life that surrounds you on all sides leave you speechless? No, because you know that the birds make these sounds and the wind rustles through the trees, you have answers to all the questions. These answers have killed you. You have become a connoisseur before you have attained knowledge.

### A sense of wonder is the basis of yoga.

The sense of wonder becomes a door for those who want to enter yoga. Relive your childhood! Start asking questions again. Awaken your curiosity, your search and the roots of life that have dried up in you will start greening up again. All blockages will melt and the streams will start flowing. Open your eyes and look around you again: all the answers are false, because all your answers are borrowed. You have known nothing. But you are crammed with borrowed knowledge, to the point that you feel you know it.

Awaken your sense of wonder. Your yoga postures and breathing exercises are useless if there is no sense of wonder in you, because all yogic exercises belong to the body. It is true that your body will be purified, healthy, but a purified and healthy body will not help you to attain divinity.

The sense of wonder purifies the heart. Wonder means: the mind is free of all answers. Wonder means: you have eliminated all the rubbish of answers. Your question has become new, rejuvenated; you have understood your ignorance.

Wonder means: I don't know.

Beca means: I know.

The more you know, the more you are wrong. When you are simple enough to say "I don't know" - though this is not enough either - when the realisation of your own ignorance settles deep in your heart, you have taken the first step of yoga. After that, the other steps are very easy. If you skip the first step, you can go on travelling endlessly, but it will not do any good. The one who skips the first step cannot reach the destination. If you get the first step right, you will have covered half the distance.

A sense of wonder is the first step.

Observe carefully, do you possess knowledge? If you look deeply, you will realise that there is no knowledge, only rubbish gleaned from the scriptures, the teachers, the saints, and you have kept it as a priceless possession! It has brought you nothing, it has only killed your sense of wonder. Your sense of wonder writhes, it lies dead. Now you are no longer surprised. Nothing surprises you any more.

There was a Christian mystic, Eckhart. He made a unique statement: he who is surprised by everything is a saint. Everything, very small events surprise him. A pebble falls into the water, it creates noise, the ripples begin to spread: the saint is amazed. It is so wonderful, so mysterious!

Breathe, live, it's amazing.

Every morning, as he prayed to God, Eckhart used to say: "It's another day! The sun has risen again.

Great is your mercy, what would we do if the sun had not risen? The human being is defenceless.

Eckhart used to say: "Today I breathe, tomorrow I may not; what can I do?

You can't draw breath from somewhere. It is not under your control. The breath is so close to you and yet it does not belong to you. If it goes out and does not come back, it will simply return! We do not know or own a thing that is so close to you. And we think we know everything. This "all-knowing" has killed you. Get rid of this rubbish and get rid of it. Immediately, when the blindfold of knowledge is removed from your eyes, your eyes will be filled with mystery.

The inner pilgrimage of this mystery is called wonder; the outer journey, awe.

If you apply those mysteries to objects, you will become a scientist, and if you are able to apply that mystery to your own being, you will become a great yogi. And in both cases the results will be different, because wonder is violent, the sense of wonder is non-violent. Awe, applied anywhere, begins to disintegrate, analysing because awe is restless, wonder is full of interest. Try to understand this difference well. It is not written in the dictionary; it cannot be written because the compiler of the dictionary has no idea what wonder is.

Astonishment is violent, aggressive. When something astonishes you, you get tense.

This tension has to be faced. A certain restlessness will hover over you as long as your enquiry is not complete, as long as you have not known. A scientist is absorbed in his laboratory eighteen hours a day.... for what? He is restless, as if possessed by a ghost. And he will go on investigating until he has solved it.

But the sense of wonder is not aggressive. And the sense of wonder is not restlessness, on the contrary, the sense of wonder is rest. When someone is full of wonder, he is at rest. You don't have to destroy the sense of wonder, you have to drink it, you have to savour it. You have to merge with wonder, you have to become one with it. Wonder participates in destruction, wonder begins to live. Wonder is a way of life, wonder is a violent state of mind.

So science thinks in terms of victory: destroy, smash, win. Religion thinks in terms of surrender: dissolve. When the sense of wonder enters you, it will dissolve in you just as a bucket of salt is dropped into water and all the water becomes salty. On that day you will become salty with wonder. Every fibre will be filled with wonder.

As you walk, as you move, the sense of wonder will throb within you. You will be in a perpetual state of wonder. Every phenomenon will become mysterious. The smallest particle will become part of the vast, because the sense of wonder envelops the small, it becomes vast. Then nothing will remain known, you will be surrounded by mystery.

So every moment is new and every moment is an invitation.

Mulla Nasruddin was standing for election. While on his door-to-door campaign, he went to the local priest. He was drunk at the time. The priest was a gentleman; to say anything directly to him would have been impolite, so he said to Nasruddin: "I want to ask you something. If you give me a satisfactory answer, my vow is all yours. Do you ever drink?" There was no need to ask.

Mulla was puzzled. He said: "Before I answer your question, I would like to ask you something:

Is it a consultation or an invitation?

The sense of wonder is an invitation.

A sense of wonder is an enquiry and a sense of wonder is an invitation. The sense of wonder is an inner call. And as you go inward, you keep diving deeper and deeper. One day you will disappear and only wonder will remain. On that day enlightenment will have taken place. If you follow the path of wonder, one day only you will be left and the wonder will disappear. That is the culmination of science: the ego will remain and wonder will disappear. If you take the path of wonder, you will disappear and wonder will remain, every pore of your being will be filled with its flavour. Your very existence will be a wonder.

Shiva has called it the foundation of yoga. Eliminate knowledge, be filled with wonder. At first it will seem difficult because you think you know.

There was a great thinker, a very valuable and important thinker: D. H. Lawrence. He was walking in the garden with a little boy. The little boy asked him: "Why are the trees green?

A child can only ask questions like that, so fresh! You cannot even think of such questions. You will say: "Trees are green because they are green! What is there to ask? What kind of question is this? This child is stupid. But think again why trees are green. Do you really know the answer?

Perhaps someone with a science background could answer: "It's the chlorophyll that makes them green". But that won't solve the child's question. He will ask again: "Why is there chlorophyll in the tree? Why does it have to be in the tree and not in man? And how did chlorophyll find the trees? The answer "chlorophyll" does not (answer?) any question.

All the answers found by science are of the same category. Those answers just push the question back one step, that's all. If you are a little wise, you can ask the question again. Science cannot answer any "why". That's why science cannot destroy the sense of wonder, it can only create the illusion of destroying it.

But D. H. Lawrence was not a scientist. He was a poet, a novelist. He had an aesthetic sense. He stopped at that moment and thought. He said to the boy, "Give me time. I don't know myself.

Your child will also have asked the same kind of question many times. Have you ever said: "I don't know"? That hurts the ego. Every parent thinks they know. The child asks and the parent gives an answer. And because of these very answers, the parent loses his credibility later on, because one day the child comes to know that you don't know anything. You were giving answers unnecessarily. You are as ignorant as I am. You were a little older, so your ignorance was greater, that's all. But you give answers to the little child. The child also accepts them thinking you might be right. But how long will he believe it?

D.H. Lawrence stood there. He said: "I will think about it. And if you keep on insisting, I can only say that trees are green because they are green. There is no other answer. I myself am overwhelmed by this mystery".

If you pull back the curtain of knowledge, you will find mystery everywhere. It is a mystery that trees are green. It is also mysterious that green trees have red flowers. And is it not mysterious that a small seed contains within it a giant tree? If you preserve a seed and plant it after thousands of years, the tree materialises. Life seems to be eternal. Every moment throbs with mystery.

But you have closed your eyes. You are calm. But this state is your inertia. You don't even doubt, for the simple reason that your ego feels the security that it knows. If it knows, it feels secure; if it doesn't know, all security disappears. You don't really know anything, but it pains you to admit that you don't know. So you cling to anything. A drowning man clutches at a straw, he leans on it. What you're clutching at isn't even a straw. A straw may save someone from drowning, but what you cling to is not even a straw, it is just a dream, empty words.

Someone firmly believes in God. It is absurd to say I definitely know. Definitely" means that you have unravelled the mystery of God. Definitely' means that you have seen through Him, that you have measured Him. Definitely' means: even He can be measured, you have weighed Him in the balance, you have investigated Him in the laboratory. What does 'definitely' mean?

There is another man who definitely knows that God does not exist. Both are stupid and both suffer from the same disease. One calls himself a theist, the other calls himself an atheist; and there is not an iota of difference between the two. Deep down, they both suffer from the same disease. Both think they know and both engage in arguments.

Knowledge creates argument, wonder creates dialogue. When you are full of wonder, your life will have dialogue. If someone comes to Mahavira and asks him, "Does God exist?

If an atheist comes to him and says: "God does not exist", he replies: "No, He does not exist". And if any agnostic comes to him, Mahavira says: "The existence of God is doubtful".

It is very difficult now. We would like you to give direct and clear answers. They may be wrong, but they must be clear. And remember, this existence is so complex that clear answers will be wrong. Here, if the answer is not contradictory, it is bound to be wrong. Here, only the answer that encompasses its opposite will be correct, because existence absorbs its opposite.

There is life and there is death. The path is not clear. Here darkness exists together with light. Good and evil exist together. Here the saint and the sinner are not separate, they live simultaneously.

Both are two aspects of the same coin. God contains both poles within Himself. Existence is vast.

It is not chiselled on the touchstone of logic, it is beyond logic. Duality melts into each other.

One night Junnaid prayed to God: "I want to know who is the biggest sinner in this town, because by studying him, by understanding him, I will try to abstain from sin. I will have the criterion that here is the biggest sinner, I have to avoid this kind of life". A voice said, "Your neighbour. Junnaid was surprised. He had never imagined that his neighbour could be the biggest sinner. He was an ordinary man, running his small shop, how could he be the biggest sinner? He had thought that the greatest sinner would be someone like Ravana [mythological character representing the devil], the greatest sinner would be someone diabolical, a satan. This man runs a tent, he raises his children....

Junnaid was perplexed. He was an ordinary man, no one would call him a sinner.

The next day, while praying, he said: "OK, I accept your decision. Now I want one more criterion: I want to know about the greatest saint, a virtuous man in the village". God said: "The same man, your neighbour".

Junnaid said: "You are confusing me. There is already great confusion in me. Yesterday I was watching the man all day and he did not seem to me to be a sinner. Now this adds to the confusion: he is also a virtuous man!".

The voice said: "In my existence the opposites are intertwined. It is the intellect that divides them in two. Here the greatest saint has a shadow. And here the greatest sinner has a glow on his face.

This same phenomenon makes it possible for a saint to become a sinner and a sinner to become a saint. This transformation is possible so easily because both are hidden in one and the same person.

Darkness and light are not separate. Day and night are interrelated. Logic creates fragments and traces clear paths. Logic is like a well-made garden, clean and cultivated. Life is like a forest; nothing is clear in it. Everything is entangled in it.

Whoever wants to understand life must have the ability to avoid ready-made answers. If you stick to them, you feel safe because they reassure you: Yes, I know! You feel safe and courageous enough to walk the path of life. That's why you are afraid to give up knowledge. It is very painful. If someone steals your wealth, it doesn't matter so much. You can earn it back.

And wealth was dirt. You knew that already. If you lose your position, you can take it easy.

You yourself may give it up one day. But knowledge...

I have observed a very interesting phenomenon. Someone renounces his society, his village, his home, his family, but if he was a Jaina, he remains a Jaina in the Himalayas; if he was a Hindu, he remains a Hindu; if he was a Mohammedan, he remains a Mohammedan. It is the same society which he has renounced, which had given him this Mohammedan conditioning: that the Koran is a true scripture, all other scriptures are false. He renounces everything, but keeps his knowledge even in the Himalayas.

Nothing has changed in this man's life because he still believes in knowledge.

If you drop the knowledge, the Himalayas will appear wherever you are. The Himalayas will appear wherever you are. The Himalayas signify that which is mysterious; where there are high mountain peaks, you will not be able to climb them; and where there are unfathomable valleys, you will not be able to explore them; that which transcends all our measures.

The sense of wonder means: where your intellect fails, where your ego is crippled, where you become impotent. There you can laugh or cry, but you cannot utter a word.

It is said that when Moses came to the mountain Sanai, he wept, he laughed, but he did not speak at all. When he returned, his disciples asked him "What have you done? God was present in person.

He said to you, 'Take off your shoes, for this is holy ground, and I am present here'. And you took off your shoes. You cried, you laughed, but why didn't you say anything? Why did you miss this opportunity? You could have asked whatever you wanted. You could have at least asked for the key that opens all the doors".

Moses replied: "When He was present before me, my mind disappeared; only my heart was beating. I laughed, I wept for pure joy.

And this is the interesting thing about life: happiness can make you cry and happiness can also make you laugh. So don't think that people always cry out of grief. It's a calculation of logic. Life does not believe in logic. The river of life breaks all boundaries and overflows like a total wave. One can cry out of happiness. Then tears have a different quality. Then joy is reflected in tears.

It can also cry! These opposites can express a principle. This is the mystery of life.

Then Moses said: "Not only my heart, but also my intellect. It seems that my conditioning fell off along with my shoes".

And don't just take off your shoes outside the temple, take off your head too! If you take off your head together with your shoes, you can only enter the temple, and shoes and head go very well together!

That's why, when you get angry with someone, you hit him on the head with your shoe. A monk hits his head with his own shoes.

They are the two extremes, the two poles. The head is at one end... you are at the centre. And that central point is a meeting place of all opposites. Your head and your feet meet there. Your heart dwells there.

Then Moses said: "I wept, I laughed because I was filled with wonder. I was speechless. Now I will not be able to sleep. I cannot erase what I have seen. What has happened cannot be erased. The Moses who lived before no longer exists. I am a different man now.

It is a new birth. Hindus call it "dvija": twice-born - when you are born a second time. Not all Brahmins are dwijas. Occasionally a brahmin becomes a dwija. You do not become a dwija by wearing a sacred thread around your neck. Dwija means twice born. Moses said, "Now I am twice born. Now I am a different man. That person is dead.

If you experience wonder, the old will die and the new will be born. And if you remain perpetually in the sense of wonder, every moment the new is born and the old dies. Every moment the old disappears and the new appears. And your flow is eternal. Then you will never grow old; then eternal life throbs within you.

That is why Shiva says that the sense of wonder is the foundation of yoga.

The second maxim: to **establish oneself in oneself is the strength.**

A sense of wonder is the basis. To wonder means an inward enquiry. An inner search for the question: who am I? If you move outside, there is wonder. If you move outwards, there is logic. If you move outwards, there is science. If you move inwards, there is wonder, meditation, gratitude. It is a totally different method.

The sense of wonder will take you inwards because the whole world will seem mysterious. And then only one question will seem important: who am I? This is the foundation of the sense of wonder: who am I? As long as I do not know this "I", this journey to know myself cannot be complete. How can I know these trees, how can I know you, how can I know the other if I do not know myself, if I myself am ignorant; when I do not know who I am.

Therefore, "who am I" is the great mantra. And do not rush into the answer, for the answer is ready within you. "Who am I?", and you answer from within: I am the soul. This answer will not help you. You already know. This has not changed your life. Knowledge is fire; it will burn you. When you ask:

"Who am I?" and an inner voice answers you, it is your mind that is speaking: the hidden scriptures within the mind, the memory. When you say, "I am the soul", it is useless, it has no value because this answer has not transformed you. This is not fire, this is ash. There may once have been an amber in it, for some wise man, but for you it is ash. The person who possessed this amber has departed from this world, now you carry only the ash.

Keep asking: Who am I? And don't give a borrowed answer. Whenever the borrowed answer comes, you say, "This is not my answer. I have not known it, how can it be mine? Only that which I know can belong to me". What you have earned by your own effort is your treasure.

Knowledge cannot be stolen or begged for. You cannot steal it. You can't beg for it. Here you have to create it yourself with your own effort.

The second maxim: to *establish oneself is the strength.*

The moment a sense of wonder is born, move inward, sink inside and try to establish yourself in the self. When you ask: "Who am I?", when will you get an answer? If you want the answer, you will have to establish yourself within. We have called it health: establishing yourself in the self. And one is only able to see when one is established within. If you run away, how will you be able to see?

Your situation is more or less as follows: you are sitting in a speeding car, you happen to see a flower through the window. You have barely asked for it, and the car has sped off. You are going at full speed. And no vehicle is faster than your desire. If you have to get to the moon, even the spaceship takes time. Your desire doesn't even need that much time, it arrives at this very moment. Desire has the fastest speed. And the one who is full of desire shows that there is no depth in him. It is running, running. And its pace is such that even if you ask: who am I, there is no room for an answer.

You will have to give up this race and settle in the Self. You will give up all the desire, all the running around, all the travelling. But the moment one desire is fulfilled, you create several new desires. As soon as you finish one journey, several new avenues open up. And you start running again! You don't know how to sit. You have not stopped for many lifetimes.

I have heard that an emperor employed a very clever man as prime minister. But the prime minister was dishonest and in a short time stole millions of rupees from the empire's treasury.

When the emperor found out, he called the prime minister and said: "I don't want to say anything. What you have done is not right.

I won't say much, but I can only say this: that it is a breach of trust. Don't show your face to me again. Leave this kingdom and go elsewhere. And I wouldn't want rumours to spread everywhere, so I won't say anything to anyone about it and you don't need to utter a word about it.

The prime minister said: "If you order me, I will leave. Certainly, I have stolen millions of rupees. However, I would like to warn you as prime minister that I now have everything:

a big mansion, houses in the mountains and by the sea. I have everything. My future generations don't need to earn anything. You will dismiss me and appoint someone else, who will have to start from scratch". The emperor was intelligent, he understood.

You never reach a point in your life where you can say: I have it all. Your journey will end when that point comes. Otherwise, every moment you will have to start from scratch. Every moment, a new desire takes hold of you, a new thief enters, a new robber comes to steal your treasure. And the thief is not just one, there are innumerable desires. You are running in many directions simultaneously. You have never thought that many of the objects are opposites of each other; you can't have them both. If you get one, you lose another; if you get the second, the first is lost.

Mulla Nasruddin was on his deathbed. He said to his son: Now, before I die, I will tell you two things. Remember them. There are two things: honesty and wisdom. Now you will look after the shop, you will take care of the work. There is a sign in our shop: 'Honesty is the best policy'. Always practice it. Never cheat anyone. Never break a promise. If you make a promise, keep it.

The son said, "OK, what about the other one, what does wisdom mean?"

Nasruddin said: "Never make a promise to anyone!

That's life: divided into polar opposites. One tries to manage both: honesty and wisdom.

Honesty is about keeping a promise. On the one hand you want to be worshipped as a saint and on the other hand you want to enjoy yourself as a sinner. How strange! On the one hand you want your character to be praised like that of Rama and on the other hand you are keen to kidnap someone's wife. You want to do the impossible. You would like to become like Ravana and you want to be worshipped like Rama. Then we find ourselves in a difficult situation. Then you move in two opposite directions and create infinite targets before you. In their pursuit you fragment yourself, you tear yourself to pieces. At the end of your life you will find that the treasure you had brought with you is lost.

There was a great player. His wife, family and friends did everything they could to convince him. He didn't listen. In the end he lost everything. In the end he reached such a point that he had only one rupee left. His wife said to him, "Now wake up! Pull yourself together!"

The husband said, "When you have lost so much and there is only one rupee left, give me one last chance. Who knows, this last rupee may bring luck". A gambler always thinks like that. And he said, "Now that we have lost millions, this is the last rupee, why lament over it? And a rupee is meant to be spent, it cannot be saved. Let me bet it.

His wife also thought: now that all is lost, this is the last one; and one is going to spend it anyway, so let her gamble!"

The gambler went to the joint and was amazed! He started winning every game. One became a thousand, a thousand became ten thousand which in the end became a hundred thousand. At the end he bet that hundred thousand and said: "Now is the last chance".

And he lost everything! He returned home. His wife asked him: "What happened?

He said to me: "I lost the last one, too!

You can only lose what you had brought with you. Why talk of thousands? He said, "I have lost one rupee. It doesn't matter. That bet was unfortunate. But he did not tell him that he had won a hundred thousand. He was right. You cannot lose what does not belong to you. At the moment of death you will find that you have lost the soul you brought with you. You will be deprived of "one". That is all. All your calculations of credits and debits, your losses and gains are worthless. The millions you have earned will be thrown here at the moment of your death. Only "one" will be taken into account; and that one is "YOU". If you settle on the "one", you are a winner. If you return to the "one", establish yourself in it..... Shiva speaks precisely of this phenomenon: to be established in oneself *is the strength.*

You are weak, wretched and miserable, not because you have no money, house or wealth.

You are unhappy and miserable because you are not established in yourself. Being established in oneself is the source of energy. The moment you are established in it, you are flooded with tremendous energy.

Someone asked Jesus "What shall I do? I am very poor, sickly and miserable". Jesus said, "Do nothing else, seek first the Kingdom of God, everything else will come later. If you lose 'one', you lose everything. That 'one' is none other than you, and that alone is your treasure because you had brought it with you. And in the final reckoning you will be asked whether you have been able to save what you brought with you or whether you have lost it too.

*To establish oneself in oneself is strength.* To become grounded in yourself is to become immensely powerful. You already have this immense power within you, but you are like a bucket with a thousand holes in it. If you put the bucket in the well, it looks like it is full. As long as the bucket is submerged in the water, it looks full; the moment you start to pull the bucket and it begins to rise above the water level, the water begins to seep out of thousands of holes. When you pull the bucket completely out of the well, there is nothing left inside.

Your thousands of desires are your holes. Your energy dissipates through them. While you dream, the bucket is full. As you wish, the bucket is full. The moment desire becomes action, you begin to pull the bucket upwards; the moment you try to make the dreams come true, the energy begins to leak out. The moment you pull the bucket out, you find only holes, no water at all. You are still as thirsty as ever. Every time you pull the bucket out, it makes a lot of noise in the well. You feel water coming to you, as if a big storm is coming. But in reality nothing comes. You are left empty-handed. However, the desire is very strange.

A traveller asked a fisherman how many fish he could catch. The sun was about to set, and he had put his fishing rod in the water since morning. This traveller had passed that road several times and had noticed it. When he got lost, he couldn't help himself and asked "How many have you caught?" The fisherman replied "If I catch this one I am trying to catch, and if I am able to catch two more, the total number will be three!". So far he hasn't caught a single one. But he is imagining it:

if I take this one, plus two more, it will be three.

You are perpetually in the state of this fisherman. The one you are trying to catch, and two more you dream of. Not even this one has materialised. But the calculation is three! And you are completely satisfied. Every time you take the bucket out, you find it empty again. And remember that the more you throw it into the well, the wider the holes get. That's why children look very happy. The old people look very sad. Their bucket is full of holes. They have put the bucket into the well and pulled it out countless times. The holes have become bigger, that's all! But they keep hoping against hope: sometime we will be able to draw water because the bucket looks full! Water comes out of the holes.

You have the energy of infinity, but your mind is like a bucket with holes in it.

This maxim means: thou shalt not make a wish trip. When you drop a wish, a hole is cemented. When all desires fall, all holes are cemented. And then you don't need to put the bucket in any hole, you yourself are the hole. You have tremendous energy within you. If only your energy could be prevented from leaking out, you are born with tremendous energy. You don't have to achieve anything. All that is worth getting is within you; be careful not to lose it. It is not about reaching God, you have to avoid losing it. You have already attained Him. How you lose it is the greatest mystery of this world.

The third maxim: ***discrimination and transcendental logic are a means to self-realisation.***

Each and every maxim is like a master key. First: the sense of wonder. The sense of wonder will make you surrender. Second: to be established in yourself in order to be available to tremendous energy. But how will you establish yourself? The key is in the third maxim: Transcendental logic and discrimination are a means to self-realisation.

You have to understand this word: transcendental logic. We know what logic is. It is an instrument of logic. It is a sword that cuts through wonder. Logic cuts, it analyses. Logic moves outwards, transcendental logic moves inwards. It does not fragment, it unites. Logic is analysis, transcendental logic is synthesis.

There was a Sufi monk, Farid. One of his devotees brought him a pair of golden scissors.

It was very valuable, studded with precious stones. And he said: "It has been my family treasure for generations. It cost millions of rupees. It is of no use to me. I give it to you.

Farid said: "Please take it back. If you want to present something, bring a needle and thread, because I don't believe in cutting, I believe in sewing. A pair of scissors cuts. If you want to present something, you better bring a needle and thread".

Logic is like scissors: it cuts. In Hindu mythology, Ganesha is the god of logic; that's why he rides a rat. A rat is a pair of scissors. It cuts, it is a living pair of scissors. It goes on cutting. Ganesha rides it. He is a god of logic. And the Hindus have made him a laughing stock. If his appearance doesn't make you laugh, you are surprised. You don't laugh because you have become accustomed to his appearance, otherwise he is a humorous figure.

If you look closely at the structure of Ganesha, you will see that everything is formless in every way. Even his head does not belong to him, it is borrowed. A logician has a borrowed head. It is big enough, it is the head of an elephant, but it is not his. A borrowed head is useless, even if it belongs to the elephant. It will only make you look ugly. His body is bulky; he rides like a rat. His body is only an ornament; his vehicle is a rat. However great a scholar he may be, his vehicle is a rat: a pair of scissors: logic! Farid rightly said: "If you want to present something, bring a needle and thread, because I believe in sewing".

Transcendental logic is an art of synthesis. The Sanskrit word *"vitarka"* means a special logic.

Common logic analyses, special logic synthesises. Buddha, Mahavir, Shiva, Lao Tzu, all use logic, but it is a specialised logic.

There is another type of logic, which is a logical fallacy. There are three possibilities. Logic fragments, analyses; but its intentions are not bad. You have to resolve the astonishment. It is not interested in analysing. Analysis is the process. It aims to achieve a doctrine that dissolves surprise, things will become crystal clear. The aim of logic is constructive.

When logic has no aim, only scissors, enjoys being destructive, then it is called "KUTARKA" logical fallacy. It is a state of madness of logic. It goes mad, it is bent on destruction. Then there is no other motive, destruction gives pleasure.

Vitatka, special logic is an inner journey of logic. You have come back from your home; your eyes, your vision, your direction were focused on me, towards me. You have turned your back to your home.

When you return home, the road will be the same - how could it be different? - Only the direction will change. You will turn your back to me and look towards home.

Logic and special logic follow the same path; that is why it is called special logic. The path is the same, only the direction has changed. First logic was directed towards the other, towards the object; now logic is directed towards the self, towards the home. Only a change in direction changes the total quality. When it had to move outwards, destruction was the way. If you want to move into the other, you can only do it by analysing, there is no other way.

If you go to medical school, you will see students dissecting. They dissect the frog because they have to know what's inside. There is no other way, you can know the inside of a frog by dissecting it. But if you have to go inside yourself, there is no need to dissect. You are present inside yourself! If you want to know the other, you will have to dissect it, destroy it, because there is no other way to know it. If you want to know yourself, it is not a question of dissecting or destroying, because you are already there! If you want to know yourself, just close your eyes. To close your eyes is to meditate. When attention is withdrawn from the outside and focussed on the inside, logic becomes transcendental.

The other name for vitark is vivek, or conscience. It actually means consciousness. This consciousness is a process of synthesis. As you go within, you begin to integrate. For example: imagine a circle with a wide circumference. Now take two points, far apart on the circumference. Join each of them with the point at the centre of the circle. You will see that, as the lines approach the centre, they get closer and closer to each other, until they are one at the centre. Now, if these two lines extend further outside the circle, they will be further and further apart, until the distance between them is infinite.

In the same way, when you move away from yourself, things start to fall apart, and the further you move away, the greater the difference between them. That's why we find many different branches of science, because the distance is getting bigger and bigger. New theories are born every day, and scientists face a dilemma: one science cannot understand the language of the other. There is no person on earth who can understand all sciences, who can synthesise the different branches of science.

As things stand, it is impossible to know a single branch of science. There is no dearth of knowledge in the world, but we have lost the power of synthesis. Religion is one, no matter how many names you give it, because as soon as a man begins to go within, distances diminish and all things merge into the centre. The centre is the ultimate synthesis.

Vitark or vivek, intelligence or consciousness, discrimination leads to self-realisation. Don't dissect things. Don't go outwards; don't pay attention to "the other". Direct your attention inwards; synthesise! Move slowly towards the centre, where your life force is focused. Establish yourself at this point and a great energy will arise in you.

The light that we see around Mahavir or Buddha, the bliss that we find around Krishna, Meera, Chaitanya... what bliss is that? What bliss is that? What light is it? What does it mean? It means that these people have reached the point which is the source of infinite energy. They are no longer miserable, they are no longer poor. They are emperors in their own right. This is also your potential, but you have to go step by step.

First comes the sense of wonder; then, being centred in the self; then, intelligence as a way of getting to the self.

The fourth sutra:

***To enjoy the bliss of existence is samadhi.***

When you have reached the self and are firmly established in it, you have reached the deepest state of existence. Existence reaches its greatest density at this point, for everything is created from here. Your centre is not only your centre, but the centre of all creation.

We are only separated at the circumference. You" and "I" are separations from the body. As we leave the body and turn inwards, the distance becomes smaller and smaller. The day you know the soul you will also have known God. The day you know your own self you will know the self of all creation, for at the centre all is one. Distances only exist at the periphery.

Shiva says: By attaining this existence within oneself, one attains the joy of samadhi.

Samadhi-sukham, the "bliss of samadhi"; these words must be understood. You have known many joys: the joy of a good dinner, the joy of good health and well-being. When you quench your thirst or enjoy sex, you know fully such bodily joys, but understand well that all these joys carry with them complementary sorrows. If you are not thirsty, water will bring you no joy. If you are willing to suffer the torment of thirst, only then will you enjoy drinking water. The affliction, the agony, comes first and is long; the subsequent joy is only momentary. As soon as water slides down the throat, thirst is quenched. It is the same with food. The more you suffer the pangs of hunger, the tastier the food.

This is the irony of life: people tormented by hunger, who could really enjoy the pleasures of food, have nothing to eat. Those who do not know what hunger is, have plenty to eat, but cannot enjoy their food; on the contrary, it is a source of anguish for them.

As long as there is thirst in you, water can quench it; but you can live a kind of life in which you never feel thirsty; don't go out in the sun, don't do any manual labour, stay at home and relax and you won't feel thirsty. But then you will not find joy in drinking water. He who works all day, enjoys the bliss of a good night's rest. This is ironic: if you want to enjoy the pleasure of a good night's sleep you have to work like a labourer all day long. The problem is that you want to spend your days like an emperor and your nights like a labourer.

In the outer world, in the world of objects, joy and sorrow are intrinsically linked; therefore, the day you acquire a mansion, sleep will leave you. The day you get a feather bed you will find yourself tossing and turning in sleep all night. Look at the labourer; he sleeps under a tree on stones and pebbles. He sleeps like a log. He is bitten by mosquitoes; he is so hot that his body is drenched in sweat, but he is oblivious to it all. He has been through such intense misery all day that he has earned the joy he will have at night.

We have to pay for our joy and comfort with work and trouble in this world. Here, every joy is accompanied by an equal amount of sorrow. And the human being is caught in a dilemma: he wants to keep the joy and get rid of the sorrow. But this is impossible. For thousands of years we have been trying to get rid of sorrow and keep joy. But our efforts have not been successful. Sorrow is certainly eliminated, but at the same time joy is proportionally reduced.

We resent sadness and desire joy. Hence the problem.

What is the meaning of the "joy of samadhi"? That which has no sorrow attached to it. The joy of samadhi is not the quenching of any thirst, it is not the filling of an empty stomach, nor is it the exhaustion after a hard day's work. The bliss of samadhi is not related to pain and toil. This is the difference between spiritual bliss and worldly joys. THE BLISS OF SAMADHI IS THE BLISS OF

SIMPLY EXISTING. It is not related to any desire, longing or craving. It is simply the "joy of being".

That is why Shiva speaks of the "bliss of existence", lokananda. That you are... that in itself is a great bliss! It has nothing to do with desires and pain and so on. Remember that the soul does not hunger and thirst; hence the question of hunger and thirst and the pleasure to be derived from their satiation does not arise. All thirsts and hungers belong to the body, so when a person desires the pleasures of the body he must also be prepared for the pains. The more prepared he is to go through pains and suffering, the more happiness he will attain. The joy of the soul is the purest of joys. There is no place for pain in it. But this is only in the centre. At the circumference is the body.

The body is the periphery. It is the wall that surrounds your vessel; it is not you. It is your outer circle. In the centre you are the soul, and it is here that a whole new kind of joy unfolds.

Here joy is the joy of being, simply being. Here there is no peak of happiness and no abyss of misery: no ups and downs, no gains and losses, no night and day, no work and no rest. There is only you. There you become eternal, and this state of eternal being is full of joy. It is overflowing. Its juice never dries up. That is why the saints call it "eternal", everlasting, ever new.

Kabir says: the juice of nectar flows unceasingly without hindrance, without any variation. It rains in this world too, but the rains must be preceded by warmth.

When the summer heat reaches its peak - when there are cracks in the earth, when the trees begin to wail, when the heat becomes unbearable everywhere - then the rains come. We may ask: Why this absurd law, why can't there be rains without all this suffering? But then we have to understand the whole system of nature, the mathematics of nature. Clouds form only when the heat becomes suffocating, because then the water turns into vapour. There will be no rain if there is no evaporation.

The vapour rises and forms clouds, and when the clouds are oversaturated, so much so that they cannot help but rain, it starts to rain. Thus, unbearable heat is a prerequisite for a good rainy season.

In the world of the soul there are no opposites, no duality. That is why it is called "non-dual" or indivisible. Here there is only one, not two. But then it is difficult for you to understand what kind of joy this is, for you know no joy without its attendant pain.

Someone asked Sigmund Freud for a definition of insanity. How do people go insane?

Freud's response was wonderful and very strange. He said: "Success and insanity have a common definition. The road to success is the road to madness". When you want to succeed, you tense up; when you want to succeed, you struggle. Your days and nights are filled with anxiety. When you want to succeed, each and every moment is shadowed by fear: will you succeed or not? What if you don't? You are not alone. There are thousands of competitors. Night and day you are in a state of acute tension, and this is exactly the recipe for losing your sanity! Look closely at the people you call achievers; you will realise that they live in the same state of constant restlessness, tension and anxiety in which the insane live.

When Khrushchev was in power in Russia, he went to inspect a psychiatric hospital. While he was in the hospital he remembered an important message, so he called his office, but the switchboard girl ignored him. There was a reason why she ignored him, which became clear later.

Finally he had had enough. He shouted: "Young lady, do you know who I am? This is common to all those who are successful, who are in power and have money - inwardly this thought echoes incessantly in his mind: do you know who I am? He may not say it out loud, but inwardly he repeats it over and over again. This is the reason why he has gambled it all away. In the end he could not contain himself and said to the girl: "Do you know who I am? I am Khrushchev, the prime minister.

The girl said: "I don't know who you are, but I know where you are calling from: from the mental hospital".

The fact is that all prime ministers speak from the same place. They have no other place to speak from.

Once Khrushchev went to London, where he was given a very expensive cloth. The cloth was so expensive that he wanted the best tailor in the world to sew it. He asked the best tailor in Moscow.

He wanted to make a coat and trousers, with a waistcoat. The Russian tailor said that the fabric was not enough for a three-piece suit. He could only make a two-piece suit. The material was so expensive that Khrushchev wanted to have three pieces made. He took the cloth to London. There he was told that he could easily get a three-piece suit and that he would have enough fabric left over to make something for his son as well.

Khrushchev was stunned. He asked, how could his own Russian tailor be so dishonest? He said that only two pieces could be made. The London tailor replied, "Don't be angry with him. In Russia you are a very big man. Here in London you are almost nothing.

When a man sets out to surround himself with the pleasures of success and ambition, he will have to endure sufferings and hardships exactly equal to the pleasures he pursues, and these sufferings and hardships break him down completely. Long before he can experience any feeling of success, he will almost have become a failure. In this world no one can succeed because the price of success is terrible madness, insanity. And when success knocks at your door, you are no longer in a position to enjoy it.

The pleasure of samadhi is totally different. You don't have to pay the price for it, because what you set out to find is present now, in this very moment. It is not somewhere in the future, so that you have to go out in search of it and toil and toil. It is present here and now. You already possess it. This treasure is your birthright, you don't have to pay the price of suffering to get it. In that case one wonders, what would it be like?

Any joy you have known cannot compare, or even give you an idea, of this joy, for all your joys are mixed with sorrows. All the nectar you have known is mixed with poison. With the body this is inevitable; birth and death, nectar and poison are side by side. Every worldly joy brings its counterpart of pain. But the soul alone is immortal. There is no death for the soul; it is eternal. There are no opposites; there is only existence, pure existence.

Perhaps, if you could visualise your physical pleasures without their pain and bitterness, leaving only the bitter taste lingering in your mouth, you might be able to imagine this happiness or something like it; but this would be only a glimpse. It cannot give you a clear picture. The circumference can only give you a glimpse. No matter how much you contemplate, you cannot imagine or conceptualise that which you have never experienced. You have to experience it first.

These sutras are invaluable. Be filled with wonder. Turn to yourself. Focus on your being so that the great energy is available to you. Let life be yours: the supreme life. Attain self-knowledge through intelligence - through awareness, supreme awareness - and by breaking your lethargy you will enjoy the bliss of existence. The bliss of samadhi is at your disposal.

One more thing about the bliss of samadhi: worldly bliss depends on so many factors. It depends on your ability and inability, on your education or non-education, on your strength, on your natural gifts, on your relationships, on your connections... it depends on all of these and much more. You are not alone in this. If you are born into a poor home, it will take you longer to achieve your goal, perhaps a lifetime. If you are born into a rich family, it may take less time. If you are smart, clever, intelligent, you will get there soon. If you are clumsy and stupid, you will wander a lot; it is doubtful whether you will get there. If the body is unhealthy or sick, it is difficult; if the body is healthy, you are better equipped. So everything is accidental and depends on a thousand and one things.

The bliss of samadhi is not dependent on anything, it is unconditional. It depends neither on your intellect nor on your body. It does not matter whether you are worthy or unworthy, nor does it depend on your family, your education, your looks, your sex, your castes, your religion or your age. It is an absolutely unconditional joy, because it is your own treasure. It is already within you.

You are born with it. You just haven't paid attention to it; that's all. You've just forgotten it, you haven't lost it. Turn your eyes, look back and look at yourself.

It is not that an intelligent person attains more samadhi bliss and a dull person less. It is not like that at all. Even illiterate people get there. Kabir, who was illiterate, unlettered, reached where Buddha reached. And when they both get there, there is not an iota of difference between the two. The bliss of samadhi is the very nature of existence. Whether you are light or dark in your periphery, ugly or beautiful, wholesome or unwholesome, whether your brain is filled with the words of various doctrines or not, it matters not at all. Your being is enough. That you exist is enough.

Therefore, all meditation is a quest to become pure. When you forget the body, forget the mind, then you will begin to attain the joy of existence, the bliss of samadhi. Just try to do one thing: try to forget the body and the mind for some time. As soon as you forget them, you will begin to remember the soul. As long as you are conscious of the body and the mind you cannot remember the soul. The mind and the body are on the periphery, while the soul is in the centre. You cannot look at both at the same time.

In this meditation field, if you could forget the body and mind for a while, you would get a taste of the bliss of samadhi. Once you taste it, it will be enough. Your life will take a different turn. It is the initial taste that is difficult. Once you know it, once you have turned inwards and seen, then you will know the trick. Then, every time you turn, you will see. All the effort is needed in this initial turning.

Once the key is in your hands, you are the master. Then you can savour this pleasure at will. Now you can roam the world without fear, and no one can steal your treasure. Wherever you are, whether you are a shopkeeper serving your customer, this bliss is with you and you experience it. One thing will begin to happen: you will stop seeking worldly pleasures. When supreme bliss is attained, who cares about trivial pleasures? When diamonds and rubies are in your hands, who will cling to the coloured stones? They will fall of their own accord; you need not give them up.

That is why I always say that a wise person renounces nothing; what is useless, falls by itself. Ignorant people renounce because renunciation is very painful for them. They have no knowledge of what makes sense, and they engage in renunciation of what is meaningless. But the mind clings. The mind says: You are giving up what is in your hands, and how can you trust what is not yet within your grasp? Besides, who even knows whether it exists or not?

That is why I tell you not to give up anything. I only tell you to taste the bliss of samadhi once. This simple taste will become the supreme renunciation of your life. Then you will know for yourself what is useless, and once we know that a thing is useless, we feel no reluctance to part with it. Then it falls by itself.

There was a great saint of Bengal, Yukteshwar Giri. He was known as a great renunciant. Once a wealthy person came to him and said, "You are a great renunciant".

Giri burst out laughing. "Look at him!" he said, pointing to the man. "Look at him! He is a great renouncer himself and he is calling me. Don't try to trap me with your words, my good man."

Everyone was shocked, even his disciples. They begged him to explain, for there was no doubt that Giri was a great renouncer. Giri said, "Suppose there is a heap of diamonds and a heap of pebbles.

This man clings to pebbles, while I cling to diamonds! And he thinks I am a renouncer".

Who has renounced, Mahavir or you, Buddha or you? You have renounced, for you cling to rubbish. You have discarded the bliss of samadhi in favour of the anxiety-laden affairs of the periphery, and what you have got in return for your bliss is so flimsy, so coarse and crude, so stale and filthy!

The worldly man is a great renouncer, but he thinks that the sannyasin is the renouncer. In fact, worldly men look at sannyasins with pity: "Poor things, they have given up everything. They have missed all the pleasures of life".

They revere the sannyasins and deep down they also pity them: "Poor things! They have given up everything without enjoying anything. They should at least have enjoyed a few things". But the worldly man has no idea who he is talking about. The sannyasin has experienced the greatest enjoyment. He has been invited by the vast existence to partake of the greatest enjoyment of all.

I'm not asking you to give up anything. I only ask you to know, to taste. This very taste will gradually displace all that is useless and trivial in your life. The useless simply falls away; it must be renounced.

Enough for today.

# Being Dead Doing Nothing

*Chittam mantrah prayatnaha sadhakash guruh upayah shariram*
*havih gyanamannam vidyasanghara tadutthaswapnadarshanam.*
*The mind is the mantra, the effort is the seeker.*
*The guru is the medium.*
*The body is the offering.*
*Knowledge is food.*
*When knowledge is destroyed, the dream is seen.*
*The mind is the mantra.*

Mantra means that which creates energy through continuous repetition; the repetition itself creates power. If a thought is repeated continuously, it translates into action. The thought that is repeated over and over again begins to manifest in life. What you are is the result of thoughts that have been repeated over and over again.

Much research has been done on hypnosis. Modern psychology has been able to penetrate hypnosis at its deepest levels. The basic principle of hypnosis is: if you want to turn any thought into reality, repeat it as many times as possible. Through repetition a line is first drawn, which gradually becomes a pathway into the mind. It is as if we dig a ditch and the ditch becomes a channel. Very soon the thought begins to materialise.

There was a great French psychologist called Emile Coue, who cured thousands of people with the help of mantra. Thousands of patients from all over the world came to him. His treatment was very simple. He would tell the patient to repeat to himself "I am not sick. I am well. I am getting healthy. He told him to repeat it to himself before going to bed, as soon as he woke up in the morning and as many times as he could remember during the day. He should constantly repeat to himself a single thought "I am healthy! I am getting healthier every day!

It seems like a miracle. People with incurable diseases were cured with this little mantra. People came from all over. But the trick is very small.

Normally, when you heal yourself, psychologists say that ninety percent of the work is done by repetition. Medicine does only ten percent of the work. A patient takes the medicine four times a day, eight times a day. Every time he takes it he feels Now I am going to get better, because I have taken the right medicine.

In homeopathic medicine, pills are not a remedy in themselves, but they still cure people as effectively as allopathic medicines. If a doctor you trust gives you just water, you will be cured. It is not a question of medicine, but of having faith in the doctor. Faith becomes repetition. The doctor who charges higher fees cures more people than the one who charges less, because as your pocket gets lighter, your faith gets stronger. Also, you feel that for someone like you, only the best treatment is good enough.....!

Psychologists have experimented with placebos, fake drugs, but when the doctor prescribes them, he pretends that they are normal drugs. The result of the experiments was astonishing. Patients with the same ailment were divided into two groups. One group was given the usual treatment, while the other was treated entirely with the placebo, plain water. Of course, they didn't know. They assumed it was a drug. At the end of the treatment there were as many cures in the placebo group as in the first group. This means that the water was as effective a cure as the usual medicine. This is why so many people respond to a cure when it is first discovered; they are convinced that the right cure has now been found. Patients from all over the world are influenced. Then, little by little, the drug loses its effectiveness. Occasionally a person is not cured, or a stubborn patient takes the medicine and suffers, thus destroying the faith of others. Then the medicine loses effectiveness. So every year new cures have to be found.

New medicines are only impressive if they are well advertised. That is why all media should be used: radio, newspapers, cinema, magazines, television. Advertising is more effective than the drug itself; it is advertising that hypnotises. It becomes a mantra, a repetition. Open the newspaper...

Aspirin! Turn on the radio... Aspirin! Turn on the television... Aspirin! Billboards by the roadside...

Aspirin! Wherever you look, you are confronted with "Aspirin". It becomes a bigger headache than the headache itself. Only then is it effective in curing the headache.

Repetition creates energy. Mantra means to repeat something over and over again. This sutra says THE MIND ITSELF IS THE MANTRA. The sutra says you don't need any other mantra if you understand the mind The functioning of the mind is nothing but repetition. What does your mind do?

What have you been doing for infinite lifetimes? Just repeating. What do you do every day? What you did yesterday you repeat today, and you will do it again tomorrow if you don't change. And the more you repeat, the more intense the repetition will become and you will become so involved that you will find it difficult to get out of it.

There are people who come to me and say: "I can't stop smoking". Smoking has become a mantra, they have repeated it so many times. If they smoke two packets of cigarettes a day, that means that person is repeating something forty times a day, and they have been doing it for years. Now, if you want to stop, you can't. You can stop smoking. You can stop smoking, but the mind will still want to smoke; then the body will demand: I want to smoke! I want to smoke!

This is what we call addiction. The craving arises when you suddenly want to stop doing what you have been doing repeatedly. Now, this addiction that has become a mantra has to be broken with an alternative mantra.

Pavlov has done a lot of research on this subject. He is perhaps the only person who has cured patients with addictions. If you were addicted to tobacco and wanted to quit, Pavlov would use this method of repetition. He would give you a cigarette. As soon as you hold it in your hand, you get an electric shock. Your whole body feels the tremor and the cigarette falls out of your hands. For seven days you stay in his clinic. Every time you smoke you feel the electric shock. In seven days the mantra is stronger than the impulse, so much so that the very mention of a cigarette makes you tremble. You develop an aversion to smoking.

Pavlov cured thousands of patients in this way. His argument was that unless a person is given an opposing habit, which is stronger than his addiction, he cannot be made to overcome his habit.

The pattern of your life, whatever it is, is the result of your mind. You keep repeating it. Every day you want to get rid of anger, and every day you get angry. The more you repeat anger, the stronger it becomes. How many times you vow not to get angry, but your vows are always broken.

Now the confusion is compounded. It was better not to swear at all, for now the mantra is reinforced; it has become doubly effective. Now you keep repeating, "I will not be angry. I will not be angry...".

knowing full well that your anger is much stronger than your vows. Vows are worthless; they are not worth a penny, no matter how many times you make them. Now this too becomes hypnosis. Now you will swear not to get angry, knowing full well that it will not be effective.

Never make vows you cannot keep. It is better to live with a habit than to make a vow and break it. If you get into the habit of making vows and breaking them, you will be unable to make any resolution in life. The so-called religious teachers have made you very irreligious.

They give you very cheap vows. You go to the temple, to a holy man or a wise man, and he says, "Make a vow." Now you are in a bind. Sitting in the sacred surroundings of a temple you cannot say to the sage, "I am incapable of taking any vows. That would hurt your ego. Instead, you say, "From today I will never smoke again".

I have a friend who is a bit eccentric, but he is much better than you! He went to see a monk - he's a Jain - and the monk said to him: "Take a vow!

"All right, I'll do it," he said.

The monk asked, "What have you sworn?".

He said: "I am committed to smoking from today". He had never smoked before. He was a bit eccentric, but he kept the vow faithfully! And I tell you, this man has gained much more than the man who vows not to smoke and doesn't keep it. He broke his vow, he filled himself with self-condemnation.

This man at least kept his word. He may be eccentric, but he's better than you. He could at least stick to his resolution.

Every time you break a vow, your self-esteem goes down and you are filled with guilt. Each time you fail, your guilt increases and you become more and more miserable. You will lose your soul in this state of wretchedness. To win your soul you need the self-esteem of a king; self-condemnation simply drives you further and further away from yourself.

Understand the nature of your mind and you will understand this sutra. The whole art of the mind, its structure, is based on repetition. The mind is a mantra. Whatever you repeat becomes your habit. Whatever you repeat becomes part of your life. For lifetimes and lifetimes you repeat the same things over and over again and you get it in every lifetime, and you are addicted to the repetition of all that is wrong and false!

So what is to be done? One: don't be in a hurry to destroy the false. The best way to do it is to start doing the right thing instead of fighting the wrong thing. Learn a new mantra! If you smoke, that's OK! Start meditating, and intensify the mantra of meditation every day. The day meditation permeates your being, you will be filled with self-love. When this happens, quitting smoking will be child's play, for you will now have started a positive mantra.

Do not be negative in your approach or you will find yourself in trouble. You will be gripped by remorse and guilt; you will be lost in pain, sorrow and despair. All your holy men sitting in the temples, how sad they are! There is no joy or flowering in their lives; they only use negative mantras. Their quest is centred on denial: to get rid little by little of what is wrong.

I say don't be in a hurry to get rid of your bad habits. Be in a hurry to develop the good ones. The day the good habits become powerful, it will be easy to give up the bad ones. Don't fight your illness; strive for health. That was what Coue used to tell his patients. He would tell them to practice auto-suggestion: "I'm getting better! I'm getting better...".

You can also do the opposite. You have a headache. You can repeat to yourself: "I don't have a headache". Now, as many times as you repeat this to yourself, you are repeating the word "headache". If you have a headache, there is no point in telling yourself that there is no headache. The headache exists! No matter how many times you repeat the opposite, you know that your repetition is a lie. Superficially you can keep saying that there is no headache, but inwardly you know that you have a headache.

You repeat only for Coue. And the headache will be cured by an inner process, not by following Coue's suggestions. Don't use the negative word "no".

Therefore, I say to you, do not be in a hurry to renounce the world; instead, strive to attain God! Therefore, I say to you, do not tread the path of renunciation; seek the ultimate enjoyment! Do not concentrate on what is wrong, because to renounce what is wrong you have to look at it again and again. And the more you look at it, the more the mantra repeats itself. And you are hypnotised by what you constantly look at.

A lot of research is being done on car accidents. Today, the number of people who die in car accidents is higher than the number of people who died in World War II. The number of people who die each year in car accidents is double the number of people who died in the Second World War. This is not a small figure. Something has to be done. In examining this phenomenon, it was found that fifty percent of accidents take place between midnight and three o'clock in the morning. That is the period of sleep, and the mind is the sleepiest. When the mind is drowsy it is hypnotised. The driver is hypnotised by the monotonous purr of the engine and the straight road with no bends for miles and miles.

And psychologists say that thousands of people die because of the white line in the middle of the road. The driver keeps looking at it and is hypnotised. Then he is not in his right mind, he is in a state of drug addiction. The situation is as follows: it is between midnight and three o'clock in the morning; there is the monotonous sound of the engine; the road is long and empty, everything is shrouded in darkness; even the trees and bushes are invisible; the driver sees only the road and the white line in the middle.

You can do a little experiment. Draw a straight white line on a table. Take a chicken and press its head down for some time so that it can see the line. Now release it. It will not move from that spot for hours. It is hypnotised by the line. It will sit there for hours.

Psychologists say that drivers are hypnotised in the same way. They say not to make the road too straight and regular; they suggest changing the sound of the engine from time to time. Any change reduces drowsiness, and many accidents can be avoided.

It can also reduce the number of accidents in your life. One: don't fix your gaze on things that are wrong, because what you see, little by little begins to penetrate you. You are addicted to fix your gaze on what is wrong; you only pay attention to what is wrong inside you. The angry man concentrates on his anger and how to get rid of it. Although he wants to get rid of anger, he actually concentrates on that white line of anger inside him; the more he concentrates, the more hypnotised he is by it.

Sexual people continue to focus on sex.

Mulla Nasruddin reached the age of 100. Journalists rushed to interview him because he was the only centenarian in town. Among the many questions they asked him was: "What do you have to say about the fairer sex?

Nasruddin said: "Don't raise that question. I stopped thinking about women three days ago".

A hundred year old man, and it's only been three days since he stopped thinking about women! Thoughts about women will take over your mind because you want to get rid of them. This has become your negative mantra. You will find that what you are trying to get rid of, traps you even more because it becomes the object of your concentration. If you keep looking at the bad, you will be meditating on it more.

Mahavir said that there are four types of meditation; two are right and two are wrong. No one except Mahavir has suggested that the "wrong" be used as an object of meditation. Psychologists would agree with him. Mahavir says that wrong meditation is also meditation. For example, an angry person becomes a meditator, because when he is filled with anger, nothing exists for him at that moment except his anger. In anger, the mind is completely focused on one point. That is why there is so much power in anger.

Have you noticed? An angry person is capable of lifting someone twice his size. If he had been in his right mind, if he had not been consumed by anger, he would have thought many times before touching that person. Why cause trouble? A man can move a huge boulder when he is enraged, something he could never imagine in his wildest dreams. If a man is angry enough, all his energy reserves are awakened. How does this happen? The energy that is dissipated throughout the body is concentrated in one place. When the rays of the sun are concentrated at one point a flame is produced. Similarly, when in the heat of anger all the attention of the mind is concentrated on one point, an explosion occurs. Mahavir refers to this as "meditation".

Mahavir says that there are two kinds of wrong meditations: one is full of sorrow, the other is full of anger. When a person feels great sorrow, he also goes into meditation. If someone dies, you weep and mourn, and all your attention is concentrated on one point. Beware of the wrong kind of meditation. And you are totally absorbed in the wrong kind of meditation. This is the root of your problems; the basic problem and disease is only one: you have fixed your attention on what is wrong. You have to give it up. You think you are doing it with the intention of avoiding them; but, because of this concentrated effort, you are caught in them.

I say to you Don't worry about the world, fix your attention on God! You are an angry man.

Don't worry, everyone is! Don't focus your eyes on anger, but on compassion.

Concentrate on what is right. As the right becomes more and more energetic, the force of the wrong becomes weaker and weaker. Eventually it will disappear. This happens because energy is one; you cannot use it in two ways. If you have used your energy in becoming peaceful, you will have no energy for restlessness. All your energy has been directed towards peace, and if you have tasted peace and serenity, why bother to become restless? You can only maintain restlessness if you have never known the taste of serenity. You can only immerse yourself in the pleasures of the world if you have not tasted the divine.

Get it right. Avoid the negative; beware of saying "no". Do not be anxious to let go of evil, for then evil will hypnotise you and you will never be able to get rid of it. Whatever you try to get rid of, you will find that you are even more hooked on it.

I have heard: Once, a man was refused accommodation in a hotel even though there was a free room. The manager apologised, but refused to give him the room. "What happens," he explained, "is that the guest in the room downstairs is a troublemaker. If there is the slightest noise he makes a fuss, so we decided never to rent this room when he is here".

"You needn't worry," said the traveller. "I'll be gone all day and won't be back until eleven o'clock at night, and then I have to catch a train at three o'clock in the morning. I'll barely be here three hours.

There will be no possibility of disturbing your guest. There won't be any problem, I will take into account what you have said and I will be very careful".

The man returned at midnight, tired after a day's work. He sat on the bed and took off one shoe, which he dropped. As it fell to the floor, he suddenly remembered the fussy person in the room below, so he carefully placed the other shoe on the floor and went to sleep. After about fifteen minutes there was a knock at the door. He opened the door and saw a man standing there shaking with rage.

The traveller was afraid. He did not know what to do. "Have I done something wrong?" he asked.

"Wrong! I ask you! What happened to the other shoe! I've been waiting fifteen minutes for you to let go of it. You've made it impossible for me to sleep. The other shoe is hanging over my head. I won't be able to rest until I find out about the other shoe.

Everyone sits with the other shoe dangling: the shoe of denial. You have to let go of this, let go of that.

There are so many evils that one life is not enough to eradicate them all. Evil lurks in every corner, in every nook and cranny. Your whole life is full of guilt. Your holy men and priests stuff you with guilt. They tell you, "This is wrong! That is wrong! Everything is wrong!"

They don't give you any information about what is right. They say: "How can you get to the right before you get rid of the wrong! Their argument seems logical. Their argument is that there can be no light as long as there is darkness.

And I say to you that if you listen to them and believe them, no matter how logical their claims may be, you will be trapped for life. It is they who have led you astray. It is not the devil who has led you astray, but the so-called saints, for their argument is very logical: as long as evil is not abandoned, how can good be achieved?

Have you ever tried to get rid of the darkness? If you wait for the darkness to dissipate before you light your lamp, you will never light it. I say to you: light your lamp! Don't worry about the darkness, because as soon as the lamp is lit, the darkness disappears. Bring the light and the darkness disappears. No one in the world has ever succeeded in dispelling darkness by eliminating it. In the same way, you cannot eradicate evil, but you can bring good. You can never give up the world, but you can reach the soul, and as soon as you reach the soul, the world disappears.

We cling to the world simply because we have nothing better in sight. And how can we leave the world if we can't find something better? No matter how much you want to, you can't give it up. You will struggle. You will exhaust yourself; you will even destroy yourself, but you will get nowhere.

Your life will be a meaningless race to nowhere. Then you will come back and take another body, and the vicious circle will continue. The only man who achieves good is the one who gives up concentrating on evil.

The mind is a mantra, whether you use it for good or evil. Repetition becomes energy. If anger arises, accept it! No matter how many times it raises its ugly head, don't feel sorry. Don't fight it either. It is enough for you to act with compassion as often as you get angry. Let others benefit from you as much as they have suffered with you. Savour the taste of compassion. Don't punish yourself for your bad deeds. Give yourself a good deed; don't reproach yourself for your misdeeds. If you have mistreated someone, go sing their praises; make a list of their virtues. You have enjoyed cursing people, now enjoy appreciating the merits of others.

Don't get involved with the thorns; leave them alone and concentrate on the flowers. If you deal with the thorns, you will never get to the flowers. There are so many thorns and you will be so bruised that when you find a flower, it will give you no pleasure. You will be so full of wounds that even the caress of the flowers will not bring you relief. It will hurt!

Don't pay attention to the thorns, concentrate on the flowers. Immerse yourself in the charm and pleasure of the flowers, and you will find that the thorns no longer prick you. Whoever is overwhelmed by the beauty of the flower will not be affected by the thorns. The real thing is to drown in the essence of the flower. Let yourself be impressed by its beauty. Let yourself be enchanted by it. The real thing is to drink in the essence of God, and then the wines of the world will lose their charm; otherwise, you will continue to struggle against worldly pleasures, and you will be defeated by the same pleasures.

He who fights against evil is defeated by evil, for such a mind makes a mantra of evil, for mind is mantra. Try to understand the process of the mind: repeat and repeat and repeat and repeat!

Observe your mind for only seven days. Write down everything the mind repeats. You will see that it moves in a circle. If you observe carefully, you will find that just as night follows day, just as morning, afternoon and evening move in rotation, so do your anger, your love, your sex, your greed; all have their allotted periods. Greed catches you at exactly the appointed time, just as hunger grips you every day at the same hour. You have never carefully observed your mind. You can even make a calendar of your various moods; then you can warn your wife and children: "Watch out for me on Monday mornings! Then they will know to stay out of your way during difficult periods. If you begin to observe yourself during these particular periods, you will be able to locate the points around which the changing moods of your mind revolve. Not only is the body circular, but the mind also moves in a circle.

All the movements of the world are circular. The moon and the stars move in a circle; the earth moves in a circle and so do the seasons. Even the seasons of your mind move in a circle. Scientists have recently discovered that there is a cycle of chemical reactions in the male body that is similar to the menstrual cycle of women. You may have noticed that women tend to become cross, irritable and restless during the menstrual period. The Hindus were very clever. They developed the custom of separating women from the rest of the house during this period. A lot of chemical changes take place in a woman's body at this time, and it is difficult for her to remain alert and self-conscious.

It is exactly the same for men. There is no outward flow of blood, but there is an inward flow from certain glands. If you look closely, you will see that men are also depressed, restless and in a black mood every twenty-eight days.

Watch closely and you will see that your mind goes through a complete cycle every twenty-eight days. As you become familiar with your cycle, you will be able to predict with great accuracy what moods you will have and when you will have them. You may be surprised to discover that you get angry not because of any outside influence, but because of what is going on inside you. The other person is just an excuse. Then, if you lose your temper, you will not blame the other person; on the contrary, you will ask for forgiveness.

You will ask for forgiveness. You will explain that your outburst has nothing to do with him, that you always get angry at this time of the month. It was just a coincidence that he was there to excuse your anger. Anyone else would have done just as well.

Through self-observation you will discover the circular motion of the mind. It is a mantra repeated over and over again. If you don't understand it, you will be going round and round for infinite births. That is why the Hindus have called the world samsara: the wheel that goes round and round. For endless lifetimes you do the same things over and over again, and you are not the only one who does it. Everyone else does it too. When you fall in love for the first time, you feel that nothing so wonderful has ever happened before. But it happens every moment somewhere in the world, even in the world of animals and plants. It's not just you that love happens to. It has been happening all the time. And anger also happens to everybody.

There is only one thing that is outside this circle, and that is meditation. It is the only event that does not happen by itself. The other events happen by themselves; you don't have to provoke them. All you have to do is to keep sitting on the wheel, which moves by itself, you will keep moving attached to it. Only by jumping off this wheel can you free yourself from it. There is only one thing that is outside this wheel, and that is meditation! But this does not happen by itself. It happens to one in a million, to an exceptional Buddha!

According to Arnold Toynbee, the great historian, only six people in the whole of human history have managed to jump out of this circle. If there are sixty and not six, it is still too small a number.

It is an unusual, almost impossible phenomenon. Anger, love, greed are common and ordinary occurrences; they happen not only to humans, but even to animals. This does not make you a human being. You will truly be a human being the day you step out of this circle of the mind, out of the whirling motion of the mind. When the circle of the mind is broken and you stand outside it, that is meditation!

Meditation is not circular. Meditation is a state of being, mind is a movement. Meditation is a condition of non-movement. The mind is another name for a wandering, and the places it wanders are not new. It is stuck in routine. It wanders in the same places over and over again, like an ox in the oil mill. If you observe this phenomenon consciously, you will know that it is not just a concept, but really a fact of life. It is not a doctrine of philosophy. The circular motion of your mind, that your mind is a mantra, is a fact of your life.

Those of you who have tried to understand life have discovered this fact. It is not a principle, not a theory, but a fact. A concept is just a circular motion in your mind. it is not a philosophical theory, but a fact of life, and you can get it from your experience. don't believe it just because i say so, or just because shiva says so. You have eyes to see. Look inside yourself; observe your mind. Observe your mind from within for a few days and you will be surprised at what you discover. You will find yourself chained and chained to this wheel; and not only you, the whole of creation is captive to the wheel. This is not the affirmation of your humanity, there is no dignity in this state.

The real dignity of your existence as a human being cannot be realised as long as you are a captive of this cycle of endless repetition; it is only born when you separate yourself from the wheel and stand aside. It is then that you attain buddhahood; it is then that you attain Shiva-ness.

Mind is mantra. Repetition is the very nature of mind; therefore, nothing new is ever born in the realm of mind. Nothing is original in the mind. Everything is old and stale, just leftovers and waste. And you keep chewing this cud! You are like a cow. With the mind you assimilate something, forget about it, and after a while you bring it up and chew it. You read a book and it keeps spinning in your mind. You hear me and my words go round and round in your mind.

Your mind will start a new circle, but nothing original ever happens in the mind, whereas the soul is an original entity. And God is the supreme originality. It is always new; there is nothing fresher than that. It cannot be reached through the mind; you will have to break the circuit of the mind.

Understand the sutra well:

***The mind is the mantra.***

***Effort is the seeker.***

Effort, the next sutra, means an attempt to get out of the circle of the mind. The one who comes out of this circle is a siddha, the one who has arrived; the one who keeps trying to get out of the circle is the sadhak, the seeker. Your effort must be great; in fact, the best that you are capable of. Only then will you be able to get out of it. You will have to make as much effort to get out of the mind as you did to chain yourself to it. There is a major obstacle in your way: you see everything through your mind and everything you see is coloured by your mind. This makes things very difficult.

I speak and you hear, but your mind gets in the way. Whatever I say, the mind will colour according to itself and give it its own shade of meaning. The whole meaning of my words changes.

Mulla Nasruddin had had too much to drink. He stank of alcohol, and the old woman sitting next to him felt sorry for him. She said, "Son, do you realise what you are doing? You've embarked on a road that leads straight to hell".

The Mulla stood up with a start. He shouted to the conductor: "Stop the bus! I've got the wrong bus.

The Mulla's alcohol-soaked mind gave its own meaning to the old woman's words. He was convinced that the bus was headed for hell. This is what the mind does all the time; therefore, the most difficult and complicated thing is to put the mind aside and listen. One who can do that is a Shravak, the right listener. This is right listening: Put the mind aside and listen directly.

***Effort is the seeker.*** You will have to make an effort, and a lot of it! You will have to make a Herculean effort. Laziness will not help you to get out of the circle. How can you get out of a circle by simply lying down in it? The circle will keep spinning and you will have to hold on even tighter for fear of falling out.

If you have watched the bird hunters in the forest, you will see that the method they use is very simple. The mind uses the same method to trap you. A rope is tied across two branches. The parrot comes and sits on it. Because of its weight, it turns upside down. Now it does not move, because it is afraid of falling down. It holds on tightly to the rope. Now it is in trouble. If he lets go of the rope, he will fall. You don't have to catch him, he gets caught himself. The bird catcher comes and catches him. The parrot is so scared that he forgets that he has wings; he forgets that he cannot fall to the ground. If you hang upside down on a rope, you'll have the same fear You're afraid too, if you get out of the circles you'll get lost, you'll go astray.

One of the characters in a novel written by Hemingway says: "I prefer to choose suffering over nothingness". You don't prefer emptiness. You'd rather choose hell, because then you have something to hold on to, even if it's hell. At least there is something to hold on to. You are used to it.

Besides, you don't have to do anything. Giving up old habits requires a lot of effort.

If you have been clenching your fist all your life, you will find it impossible to open it, because your fingers have become stiff and frozen. If you want to open it, you will have to make an effort to get the muscles stronger and the blood flowing through your veins again. One thing is certain: whoever makes a fist can also open it. The mere fact that the fist is clenched proves that it was open at one time, so it can be opened again. But if it is clenched for a long time, it will be difficult to open it.

This is the difficulty. That is why the effort is necessary.

Effort means: you will have to make an effort to leave the mind. And the mind will whisper in your ear again and again, "What nonsense this is! What madness!" The moment you abandon the mind, it does.

***Effort is the seeker.*** Unless you become a seeker, you will not strive. You strive, but half-heartedly. And half effort is meaningless. It is like grasping the wheel with one hand and letting go with the other. This does not solve the problem. Half-hearted effort is meaningless.

A businessman once told his wife that he was going to the Taj Mahal hotel to meet a very important client who was going to give him a very important order. So off he went. When he came home that evening, well stuffed with food and drink, his wife asked him, "Did you get the order?".

"Fifty-fifty," he replied.

The woman said: "At least you have something".

As they were about to go to bed, she suddenly asked: "What do you mean, fifty-fifty?

The husband replied: "I arrived at the hotel, but the client did not".

When you are also half and half, you are like that. Nothing is gained, because the other half is always missing. You are always fragmented; you are never whole. When you are whole, a revolution takes place, a transformation begins in your life. That's when you reach the boiling point; and only at the boiling point does water become steam. Then you cannot flow downwards like water; you can only rise upwards like steam. So your direction is not downwards, but upwards.

***Effort is the seeker.*** You have to abandon laziness.

People come to see me and tell me that morning meditation is a bit difficult. Six o'clock is too early. If getting up at six in the morning is difficult, it will be much more difficult and painful to get out of the mind. If getting up at six in the morning is so difficult, how are you going to jump off the wheel of life? If you are not even willing to give up the little habit of sleeping in? for a day or two you may feel lazy. But you allow laziness to win you over. That shows that you value your laziness more than meditation. If you didn't, you would never have brought it up.

Someone comes and complains that the four meditations you do during the camp are too exhausting.

"Why can't we just do two every day?" But then, why do two? Forget about four. If four meditations tire you, two will tire you half as much, but you'll get tired for sure. And I know that if I tell you that two will be all right, you will immediately come back with the request to do only one, because it is the same mind doing its own thing. Even two meditations will tire you to some extent.

If you approach things this way, you will become lazier and lazier over time. Effort is necessary for everything. Remember, life is effort; death is rest. If you want to be dead you don't need to do anything. If you want to live you will have to do something. If you want to live life to the full you will have to make a great effort. If you want to reach God these small efforts will not be enough. Your whole life must become one gigantic effort. You must gamble everything you have. If you hold back even a little of yourself, you will fail. You have to risk everything; only then will you be saved. That is why so few succeed. The reason is none other than laziness.

While doing the active meditations you are very careful not to hurt yourself, not to fall on someone or not to get tired. Why do you do it? Who asked you to do it? You have no inner clarity and that is the problem. You live in a fog where everything is hazy and foggy. It's not even clear to you how you came here and why. Someone was coming and you came with him, just to see what was going on.

You have been pushed and pulled like this for infinite lifetimes, but you will never arrive at your destination this way. You will never get there by blind chance. You will not arrive at the destination accidentally. It requires a well-directed effort. You will reach the destination when all the currents of your life flow in one direction. The destination is your concentrated willpower. As soon as you are fully resolved, your energy accumulates in one point and your mind flows in one stream. This energy within you is limitless. Therefore, if you think that you do not have enough energy, that you will get tired very soon, you are wrong.

There are three layers of energy in your body. The top layer is for everyday life; it's like the small change you carry in your pocket. It's not all the money you have. It's just the pocket money that you use for petty cash.

Mulla Nasruddin was passing through a village when four men pounced on him. The night was dark, but Mulla fought them so fiercely that he outwitted the four. With great difficulty they were able to overpower him, but when they searched his pockets, they found only seven paise! One of them said: "You are the limit Nasruddin! I don't know why you have fought so hard for only seven paise".

Nasruddin replied: "I didn't think you would fight for seven pence from my pocket. I have hidden five hundred rupees in my shoe".

But now the robbers would not dare to attack him. If he could fight so dangerously for only seven paise... They said: "Goodbye! Maybe next time ......".

The energy you use for your daily life is not worth more than seven paise. You use it for sitting, standing, walking, eating, sleeping and other light work. This is your superficial energy, the small change in your purse. When you start meditating, this energy is used up in a jiffy, because you are not used to using it for meditation; it is a new activity. Now, if you let this exhaustion rule you and stop meditating, you will never be able to enter deeply into meditation. Ignore your tiredness. If you continue, you will find that your persistence has harnessed the energy that lies in the second level.

You have often experienced this phenomenon. For example, you are about to go to bed at night.

You are so tired, so sleepy that you can hardly keep your eyes open, and suddenly an alarm goes off - your house is on fire! Suddenly an alarm goes off - your house is on fire! Can you sleep after that? You say "I'm sleepy"?

Your sleep is completely gone. Sleep is the last thing on your mind. Where has all this energy come from? A moment ago you were dozing. If someone had asked you to read the Gita, you would have found it impossible; but now that the house is on fire, you spring into action. You run here and there to put out the fire. And when all the fuss has died down, you will still find it impossible to sleep, no matter how hard you try. You have broken through your second layer of energy, which is not a layer of your daily routine. That layer is broken. Now this avalanche of newly released energy makes sleep impossible.

If you persist in your meditation without giving up, you will soon discover a second source of energy at your disposal. Once you have this energy, no matter how much you meditate, your body will never tire. You will have something inexhaustible. This is the second layer.

There is also a third layer of energy. This second source of energy is your treasure. It can be consumed, though not as easily as the first. If you continue to exert yourself, without ceasing, this source of energy will also be depleted, and the third layer will fall away. This third source does not belong to you. It belongs to God, and it never dries up. However, if you become lazy, you will not reach the second, let alone the third. ***God is the supreme energy hidden in you.***

The first layer is that of your mind; the second is that of your soul; the third is that of God. Exhaust the mind and you will reach the energy of the soul. Exhaust the soul and you reach the energy of God, which is eternal and inexhaustible. Then you are one with the whole.

That is why Shiva says: effort is the *seeker.* The continuous effort that becomes more and more intense is the seeker. You have to keep on striving until you reach the third level of energy and attain the supreme power. Then you are a siddha, someone who has arrived. Then you can relax. Before that, any relaxation is suicidal.

The third sutra:

### *The guru is the way.*

This search for life cannot be carried out individually, because by yourself you are trapped in your own circle. You cannot see outside it. You don't even know that there is anything beyond it. You live in a cocoon and for you that is the only life there is. Only someone who has known the Absolute can bring you the news of the outside world. You are a prisoner inside your house, alien to the stars and the moon and the open skies. Someone from outside who has seen the moon and the stars will have to come knocking at your door and tell you to come out from behind your closed doors.

But before you move an inch you will ask yourself the question: Is there an outside? That's what people ask themselves: Does God exist? Does the soul exist? And you want someone sitting inside the house to prove the existence of heaven. How can it be proved if you are sitting inside the four walls? How can you be convinced of the vast outer space unless you are willing to go out of your house?

You will have to step outside. You will have to take a few steps outside with the one who says that heaven exists, because heaven can only be shown, it cannot be proved. If someone wants to prove the existence of sitting under the roof, you will be able to defeat him. You will say, "What nonsense, there is only the roof and the walls, what is the proof that there is any vastness outside? Bring some sky inside and prove it to me The sky is not something that can be brought inside. Heaven can't be broken into fragments, nor can God break into pieces and show it to you.

Therefore, *the guru is the way.* Guru only means the one who has had the experience, the one who has known, the one who has escaped from the prison. He alone can make you aware of your imprisonment, he alone can tell you that you can escape from here, and he alone can suggest to you the means of escape. And only he can lead you out of the prison, because he knows the door through which you can escape. There are doors in this prison where the guards are asleep and there are doors in this prison where the guards are awake and alert, and if you try to escape through those doors you will find yourself in great trouble. Now, at least, you are free inside your prison, but if you try to escape through the main entrance, where the guards are alert, you will be caught and thrown into a dark dungeon. Then the prison will get even tighter. And remember that if you try to get out by the method of denial you will fall into this dungeon.

If you fight with evil you will be thrown into a greater evil: that is the main gate. No one can ever escape through it. No one has ever escaped through there because there is a strong guard at the main gate, and every measure is taken to maintain complete security. But there are other openings in this prison which are hidden, where there is no guard; because the prisoners are unaware of these openings. Their eyes are fixed on the main gate.

During the French Revolution, the prisoners in a prison revolted. There were two thousand prisoners and only twenty guards to finish them off. In fact, the prisoners could have been released at any time. What could the twenty guards do? The prisoners never rebelled, but of course, prisoners are never friends with each other. They do not unite. They don't have the simplicity that can unite them. They are hostile to each other. So twenty guards were enough. However, on this occasion they united and rebelled.

The head jailer was very disturbed, what to do? He told the guards not to worry about the main gate, but to defend the smaller doors and windows. The guards said, "This is not the right decision." The jailer said, "Don't worry, leave the main gate unguarded," but they did as they were told and not a single prisoner escaped. The main gate was unguarded. They could have broken it down and let everyone out, but they ignored the main gate. they imagined it was heavily guarded as it had always been.

When the guards asked him how he had come up with the idea, the chief warden explained: "They rebelled because someone from outside got in among the prisoners and incited them to escape: a free person who knows. This someone, coming from outside, knows that we have a strong guard around the main gate, so I would advise them to use the smaller gates. So until yesterday we were guarding the main gate because those inside were ignorant, but it seems that some master, he has sneaked in among them."

In life, the fight against evil seems to be the main door. Your mind tells you Destroy evil and you will attain holiness. Abandon the wrong way, then the right way will appear. Renounce the world to make room for God to be enthroned in you.

This is the main gate. The master will never tell you to try, because no one has ever been able to get through it. This door is heavily guarded and anyone who tries to escape is thrown into deeper dungeons.

According to me, all your saints and monks are locked up in prisons worse than yours. You have no eyes to see, so you cannot see this. The worldly man is in great distress, but the so-called saints are in a worse situation. You at least have a little courtyard in front of you where you can feel a little free, but they are deprived of such courtyards. They are inside the prison, but they do not have the limited freedom that a normal prisoner has. They are locked up in dark and dreary cells twenty-four hours a day.

Sadhus and sannyasins come to me. I find their minds sick and maddened. A Jain sadhu told me: "I am sixty years old. I have been a saint for forty years, but one thought always torments me:

Could it be that the common man enjoys the world while I suffer these unnecessary tortures?

Such doubts are natural in an intelligent person. This man is not stupid, he is wise and his doubts are natural. He sees that fighting desire for forty years has gotten him nowhere. He has achieved nothing, and his anger, lust and greed have not been destroyed. They have only become more submerged and hidden.

You can fool people in the outside world and hide your passions from them, but how can you hide them from your own self? You know you have them all inside you, repressed. You look like a good person, you don't commit any crime, but the criminal is hiding inside you and can appear at any moment.

If given the opportunity, he will commit a crime.

The prison walls have come closer for this man. He has lost even the little freedom to walk that an ordinary person has. It is a dungeon.

He who tries to leave by the main door will be bound with even heavier chains; but there are secret doors that only the master can show you. There are keys to open the secret doors, but only the one who has already escaped can lead you out.

The Scriptures can help you to some extent. You can stay in prison and read them, but you cannot find your way out through them; for who is going to find the meaning behind the words?

Who is it that will read the Scriptures to extract their meaning? It is you. Who will understand it? You! And you will understand it according to your own understanding. And if your understanding were right, you would not need the scriptures at all; but you are not wise, and that is a fact! The meanings that an ignorant person extracts from scripture only cause him more trouble and difficulty.

No! You need living scripture. ***The teacher is the living scripture.*** Seek a living guide to lead you on the right path.

Shiva says: ***the guru is the way.*** There is no other way. If you try to solve this problem by yourself, you will be drawn deeper into the problem, because the mind is a very subtle mechanism. Not to accept help from anyone, we try to solve our problems by ourselves. If you discover that your watch has stopped, your first impulse is to do something immediately to try to get it running again. The more stupid you are, the stronger your impulse is. A child doesn't hesitate at all; he thinks, what's the big problem? First it worked and now it doesn't. Let me figure it out myself. It's not a very complex machine.

If you try to repair your own watch you will find yourself in the same state as Mulla Nasruddin.

I heard: One day Mulla Nasruddin went to a watch repair shop. He put his watch on the counter. It was nothing but a pile of little wheels and parts. The watchmaker looked at the mess and then looked at Mulla.

Nasruddin said: "I dropped it. I don't understand how he could fall.

"I don't understand why you bothered to pick it up," said the watchmaker. "It's irreparable. Anyway, a watch doesn't fall into a thousand pieces just by dropping it."

"Well, the fact is," Mulla confessed, "I tried to fix it myself.

A clock is a simple mechanism compared to the mind. There is no mechanism on earth as complicated as the brain. In your brain there are seventy million cells, each capable of collecting ten million messages. Psychologists say that a brain can store all the written matter in the world.

All the knowledge in the world can be stored in a small brain. And it is such a tiny thing. It weighs barely a kilo and a half, yet it has seventy million tiny neurons, each one invisible to the naked eye.

Once you understand the immense complexity of the brain, you can understand why brain surgery is still in its infancy. If you try to cut something, thousands of other neurons are destroyed. It's all so delicate. A single touch of a surgeon's scalpel and a huge number of neurons are destroyed.

You don't even need the knife; try standing on your head for half an hour every day and your brain will be damaged. Standing on your head floods the brain with excess blood and damages the delicate tissue. People who practise this posture for a long time are never very intelligent.

Man's brain developed as it did because at some point in his evolution he stood upright on his hind legs, and the blood flow to his brain was reduced as a result. For this reason, animals' brains did not develop further, because their brains and their bodies are at the same level. Their nerve fibres are thicker, not thinner. The whole dignity and speciality of man lies in the fact that he stood upright. By standing on two legs, the gravitational force makes his blood flow downwards. His lungs and heart have to work harder to pump the blood upwards, only then does the blood flow to the brain. And so a limited amount reaches the brain. This has facilitated the evolution of finer, more delicate tissues and fibres. If there is a flood, the biggest trees will be swept away; what about the tiny bushes? Thus, the tissues are so delicate that the slightest increase in blood pressure destroys them, as if they were being swept away by a flood.

If you were to dismantle the delicate machinery of all these seventy million cells and try to work things out for yourself, you would never succeed. Failure and great damage are certain. Yet this is what people do: they try to open their own brains! They try to meditate on their own and practice their own yoga postures. They pick up clues from books and from people they know. They pick up ideas floating freely in the air and start working with them. The only result is disaster!

They brought me to a Buddhist monk. He had been unable to sleep for three years. He had undergone extensive treatment, but to no avail. His insomnia had defied all tranquillisers and no treatment seemed to work. You can imagine his condition: a man who hasn't slept for three years is almost insane!

However, no doctor had asked him the same questions I had. All the doctors did the usual tests; they took his blood pressure, did a cardiogram and started treating him. But this was not his problem. This man was practising a particular meditation technique used by Buddhists, Vipassana. He himself had chosen this meditation from the scriptures and started practising it. A guru will take care of each and every disciple. If he develops a group exercise, he will take care of the group. The scriptures cannot take care of you in this way. Who is going to read them The scriptures can live for thousands of years, and anyone can read them in his own way.

The vipassana technique is a very ancient technique. This man read about it and set out to practice it. Then he began to enjoy it. As a method it is a jewel. The Buddha himself used it a lot. Once you start enjoying it, you don't know when to stop. Enjoyment, once it becomes extreme, becomes poison. This man was so intoxicated by vipassana that he started practising it twenty-four hours a day.

If you practice something incessantly, day and night, sleep will be destroyed. You have created a great torrent of energy within you, and its continuous movement will not allow you to sleep. Moreover, I had been doing this practice for so many years that all the brain tissue that caused sleep had been destroyed. A doctor can only help if the brain tissue itself is still in order. Tranquillisers can make the cells in question relax, but if they are not, what can the doctor do?

I suggested that he forget meditation altogether and become a lazy person for a whole year. Forget meditation altogether. He should encourage idleness: eat, drink and sleep as much as he could for a year; become a completely worldly man for a whole year.

He was disappointed. He objected: "I never expected to hear you say such a thing, are you trying to ruin me?

I told him he could think that way if he wanted to, but that was my opinion. "Do what I say for a year and then come to me," I told him.

She came back after three months, radiant and happy. Then I had to give him a new technique. At that point I have to judge what is appropriate and how much a particular person can endure. Gradually the duration is increased according to the seeker's progress. I have to be aware of all aspects of the seeker's state of mind. I have to observe the whole picture.

That is why Shiva says: ***the guru is the path.*** Don't be a path for yourself or you will spoil everything. First of all, it is a difficult task to meet a living person, because surrendering to a living person is difficult; the ego gets hurt! That's why people are more interested in scriptures; scriptures don't hurt the ego so much. You can throw them in the dustbin or keep them in a place of worship: the scriptures will not object. You cannot do that with a living guru. Your ego will have to bow down to him.

You also bow to the scriptures, but you are still your own master. At any time you can throw them away; they can do nothing against your will. Bowing at the feet of a living person is a crushing blow to the ego. That's why people first look in books. Then, when they get tired, they look for a teacher; but by then the books have so corrupted them with words that they cannot recognise the teacher when he comes.

When you finally approach the teacher, you bring your bookish knowledge of the teacher and try to judge him or her accordingly. No book can tell you what a teacher should be like. A book can tell you about a guru.

If there is a book about Kabir it will tell you all about what Kabir was like, but Kabir is not going to be born again. Those are the characteristics of Kabir, but not the characteristics of a master. If you are a follower of Kabir and you are totally full of him, and therefore you look for the same qualities in someone else before accepting him as a master, you will never find a master for yourself. Kabir cannot be born again.

The digambara jainas do not accept a master unless he is totally naked. Mahavira liked to take off his clothes; I don't like to take off my clothes. If the seeker seeks a Mahavir, Mahavir no longer exists. It is an irony of fate that during Mahavira's lifetime it was this very nakedness that prevented people from accepting him, perhaps because nakedness was not mentioned as a necessary quality in the books circulating at that time. None of the Tirthankaras before Mahavir had renounced clothing, so the Jainas themselves were not prepared to accept him, because nudity seemed to them uncivilised. They rejected Mahavir, for nowhere in the scriptures is there any mention of naked gurus. Then Mahavir died and scriptures were created around him and the present day Jainas who carried Mahavira's burden. As a result, when Parshwanath appears clothed he cannot be accepted as a guru, he is not naked!

Remember, any particular scripture you read speaks to you of a particular master. It cannot go back. A master is incomparable, unique! That is why, if your eyes are full of scriptures, you will never be able to recognise a living master. The scriptures speak of those who have been and those who will not be again. Those who believed in Mahavir will never accept the Buddha. At best they may consider him a great soul, a Mahatma, but not Bhagwan.

I know a man, a Jain. He has written a book. He is really a good man, but that does not give him understanding. Bad people are often foolish, but so are good people; foolishness is so deeply ingrained that goodness makes no difference. He is a good man and respects all religions equally. The book he wrote is called ***bhagwan mahavir and mahatma buddha - god mahavir and great soul buddha.*** My friend is a writer. He is known to the people of Poona; in fact, it was he who brought me to Poona for the first time. He is an old devotee of Gandhiji, from whom he got this feeling that all human beings are one. So he wrote this book, but his Jain mind persisted. I was with him at that time. I asked him, "Why were you differentiating between Mahavir and Buddha, calling one 'Bhagwan' and the other only 'Mahatma'?"

He replied, "You see, Mahavir is indeed Bhagwan, but we can accept Buddha at best as a Mahatma, not as God, because God does not wear clothes. He is naked.

So this is the difficulty! It is not that only the Jainas have this difficulty. Everybody has it. That is why a Jain cannot accept Rama as God, because Sita is by his side. A Jain cannot understand a woman present with God. When he has renounced everything, how can a woman be there? That is why a priceless jewel like Sita is lost to the Jainas. They cannot understand its significance.

And Krishna? They put him in hell, for he has not one, but sixteen thousand women around him. No one is more fit for hell than Krishna. As the Jainas are merchants and caste merchants, they are afraid to start any dispute with the Hindus. Perhaps this is the reason why they have advocated non-violence.

It is always a coward who advocates non-violence. Violence requires guts, so cowards believe in not killing and not being killed. As a principle it is fine: Don't kill others - live and let live! But it implies that they want to survive and don't care at all about others, so they use the idea of non-violence; there is no other meaning behind it. Having thrown Krishna into hell, they feared the wrath of the Hindus, so out of fear they have played another trick: they declared that Krishna will be a Tirthankara in the age to come. It does not fit into any part of their doctrine, yet if they have to live among the Hindus, they have to accept it. They came to a compromise, as any businessman will calculate his mind! Now the Hindus will not be angry, that's fine. And their own concept remains intact. They have avoided conflict.

If you look for the master through the scriptures, you will never find him, for by the time the scriptures are compiled the person around whom they are written is gone. And every teacher belongs to his own class. He is different and unique. You cannot find another like him. You cannot find Mahavir or Buddha or Krishna again. But in all your search you just look for those same people and go round and round. When they were alive, you were looking for someone else, again, someone who was long gone. You are still always lost.

If you want to find a master, put aside all the scriptures. Try to get close to someone. If you want to meet a master, bathe in his presence. Don't take your concepts with you and don't try to judge him by your measure. Let your heart beat with his heartbeat; do not allow the intellect to interfere.

If you allow the mind to interfere, the hearts will not meet and you will not be able to recognise the master.

The master is recognised through the heart and not through the head. Whenever you put aside the intellect and see with the heart, something happens immediately. If it is possible for you to connect with this master, it will happen immediately, without delay. You will find yourself merging with him and he merging with you. From that day on you will be an integral part of him. From that day you become his shadow; you can flow into him. The master can be sought with the heart, and without the master there is no path.

### *The body is the offering.*

Remember that what you call your body and what you consider your whole being is but an offering. Just as you make offerings in the sacrificial fire as part of a ceremony, so you have to surrender your body, little by little, in the course of meditation. All other offerings are useless. You can offer ghee and wheat to the sacred fire, but it will do you no good. You will have to throw yourself into the flames to kindle the fire of life. You have to stake your whole body. If you try to save a part of it, your fire will not ignite and the sacrifice will not take place. Give it all! ***The body is the offering!***

***Knowledge is food.***

Now you live on food. Food comes into your body. It is necessary. Realisation, knowledge, meditation, awareness are food for the soul. So far you have only fed the body and left the soul hungry. Your body is well fed, but your soul is hungry.

Knowledge is the food of the soul, so the more awake, aware, the more you know, and by this I don't mean book knowledge. Knowledge means awareness. The more you establish yourself in the fourth state, turiya, the more your soul will be filled with vital energy. Your soul is almost dry; you have denied it all nourishment. You have practically forgotten that it needs to be fed.

Your body consumes food while your soul fasts. This is why many religions have used fasting. Reverse the process: Let the body fast for a few days and let the soul feed. This does not mean that the body has to starve. Give the body its normal needs, but don't let all your effort in life be exhausted in feeding it. Let an important part of your life's work be the awakening of knowledge, for that is the food of your soul. Knowledge is food.

***When knowledge is destroyed, the dream is seen.***

If the knowledge of the soul does not penetrate you, and if the inner flame does not get its fuel, then dreams arise in your life; then desires arise, and your life loses its way and flounders in darkness. Then you live in illusion, in desires; then you do nothing but think and weave webs of fantasy.

I asked Nasruddin: "Mulla, where are you planning to go on holiday this year?

"I only go on holiday every three years," he replied.

"What are you doing in the two years you have left?"

"One year is spent reflecting on the previous holiday and reliving it in our minds, and another year is spent planning the next holiday".

At least Nasruddin goes on a trip every three years, but you don't go at all! Half your life is spent thinking about the past and the other half thinking about the future. The journey never begins.

Either you wander in the ways of your memory, which is a dead dream, or you wander in your imagination, which is a dream of the future, which is yet to come. You are divided into these two. The present is in the middle, and that is where life is, but you miss it!

Knowledge, awareness, will awaken you, here and now, to this very moment. Knowledge will bring you to the present. The past will fade away. In fact, it has already faded. It is you who foolishly persists in carrying the ashes. The future is coming. You cannot make it happen. It will come when it comes, but the present is now. The present is reality, the truth. To dream is to wander into what is not present.

Remember the sutra: when **knowledge** is **destroyed, you see the dream.** When knowledge is absent, when the soul does not awaken, you lose yourself in dreams. The past and the future become everything to you, and the present is meaningless; but, in fact, it is the present that is everything. When you begin to awaken, the past and the future will become less and less and the present will begin to have more and more meaning for you. The day when you are fully awake there will be only the present. Then there will be no past and no future. When there is no past and no future, all the diseases of the mind, all its repetitions and circles are destroyed. Then you are here in the present, pure, immaculate, innocent, fresh as the morning dew. Then you are here in the present, like the lotus flower. If you are present in your wholeness in a given moment, in that moment you are God.

Because you are not present in this moment, you are the mind and the body, but not the soul.

Meditation is an effort to draw yourself from the past and the future into the present. You don't have to go backwards or forwards; you just have to be here. To be here and now totally peaceful and aware is meditation! Through it knowledge is born and through knowledge you reach the highest peak and attain the bliss of ultimate samadhi.

Whoever loses this, loses everything! Whoever achieves this, achieves everything!

Enough for today.

# Knowledge that is Self-Knowledge

*Atman chittam kaladinam tatvanamaviveko maya mohavarnat siddih mohajayadanattabhogatsahaja vidyajayah jagrad dvitiya karah.*

*The soul is the mind.*

*The lack of discrimination of essentials is an illusion.*

*The yogi trapped in attachments can attain powers, but not self-knowledge.*

*After the definitive overcoming of attachments, spontaneous wisdom is attained.*

*The awakened yogi realises that the whole universe is an emanation of his own energy.*

*The soul is mind,*

This sutra is very significant. The waves are seen in the ocean, but the wave is also the ocean. However shallow, however choppy the wave may be, it still contains within itself the infinite ocean. The most despicable, the most insignificant, also contains the absolute within itself. God is hidden in each and every particle No matter how mad you are, no matter how troubled your mind, no matter how many disturbances and illnesses surround you... you are still God. It does not matter that you are asleep, unconscious. In your unconsciousness it is God who lies unconscious within you. It does not matter that you have committed, or thought of committing, many sins. It is God who thinks within you. It is through God that sins are committed.

**Soul is mind** means that your mind is a form of your soul. It is important, very important, that you understand this; otherwise you will begin to fight with your mind, and he who fights with his mind loses. The way to victory lies in the acceptance of the mind: that it too is God. Caught in the state of struggle - futile struggle - and duality, know that the wave is also the ocean. Once this is seen and accepted, the distortions and diseases of the mind begin to fade away.

The day you begin to understand that the absolute is hidden even in the most insignificant, you will stop calling it insignificant. It is you who have drawn its limits. The tiniest grain has no limits; it is part of the limitless. The limits are created by your eyes. The day you begin to see the unlimited in the limited, all limits and boundaries will disappear.

The most profound experience in a person's life occurs when he begins to see God in his own mind, when he begins to see Him in his own wrongdoings, when he sees His footprints - and only His footprints - in all his wanderings. Then he stops wandering. Wandering shows that you consider yourself separate and apart from God. In this separateness lies your disease; this separateness is the root cause of all that disturbs your natural harmony. That you consider yourself aloof and separate, that is your ego!

Strange as it may seem, as far as the ego is concerned, there is no difference between a good man and a bad man. The sinner is as full of ego as the so-called man of virtue. Their actions may be different, but the feeling is the same: both consider themselves apart from the rest. One considers himself bad, the other good. You set yourself apart from the rest as long as you consider yourself one or the other. You are not different from the others. It is your own belief that has squeezed you into this narrow position. Your own concepts bind you; you are imprisoned within the cage of your own beliefs. Otherwise, there are no walls anywhere; all around you are open skies. No one stops you. No one obstructs your path.

How can your ego melt away? ***Soul is mind*** means: you are not you! You are God! You are part of the whole. You are not a small wave; you are the whole ocean. If you meet and experience this vastness - the whole - it will make your ego fall. And where there is no ego, there can be no evil. There is only one evil, there is only one sin: "I am separate!" This feeling of separateness is also found in those whom we consider our sadhus.

It is said that a yogi once died. He reached heaven and knocked on the door, which opened.

The guard said: "Welcome! Please come in. The hatha yogi stopped there, shocked. He said, "What kind of heaven is this that you let anyone in without asking any questions? You have never asked who I was or what my deeds on earth were, good or bad. I don't want to be in a place that is open to everyone. No reservations, no questions: this is how you are welcome! This is not my idea of heaven.

His ego is full of good deeds, not of evil. This man has performed so many austerities, so many spiritual practices; he may have attained siddhis, powers; but it is all in vain, for all the siddhis he has attained have only added to his ego. His sadhanas (austerities or spiritual practices) have been a total failure.

Bernard Shaw had received the Nobel Prize. He was invited to join an exclusive club in Europe that has only one hundred members in the world. Each member must be an outstanding world figure in his or her own field: Nobel laureates, celebrities, great sculptors, painters, writers. But only one hundred, no more. Only when a member dies is another one elected in his or her place. People wait all their lives to be invited. When Shaw got the Nobel Prize, he got the invitation from that club.

The invitation read: "We would be honoured to have you as a member of our club". Shaw responded: "Any organisation that is honoured by my membership is not an organisation to me. It is inferior to me. I only want to be a member of a club that is unwilling to admit me".

The ego always seeks the difficult, the unattainable; whereas life is very simple. That is why the ego always misses life. And there is nothing simpler than God. That is why the ego never seeks this door.

This door is always open. You are always welcome without asking questions. If you are questioned at the entrance, that is not the door of God; it is the door of the marketplace. The fact is that you stand at this gate. If your back is turned to it, it is your own fault.

The door hasn't turned you away - if you'd only look! The door is always open and the sign says "Welcome!

*Soul is mind* means: never consider yourself separate, no matter how bad you are.

This does not give you licence to be bad. On the contrary. Once you see that you are not separate, evil will be impossible.

Psychologists say that an individual becomes what he believes himself to be. Our belief becomes our very existence. They say that we should not call a bad man bad, because by constant repetition: "You are bad! You are bad!" - it becomes a mantra. If a man is constantly told by everyone around him, "You are bad", he realises within himself that he is bad. Not only that, but he tries to behave as others expect him to behave. Evil becomes his habit. People who explored the field of religion made this discovery a long time ago. That is why they have asked the ultimate reality to make their mantra. *The soul is the mind.*

You are God. Your own soul is your mantra. This is the greatest statement that can be made about you. If this becomes your mantra, if it mixes and mingles with every particle of your being, if its vibrations penetrate every pore of your body, you will gradually come to feel that you are becoming what you believe yourself to be. What you have chanted within you becomes a reality in your life.

The principle of religion is: You are not, God is! Start with this sutra. You are in a deep sleep.

Even if you are a great evildoer, even if you are guilty of countless sins, it does not affect your basic nature. Purity is your nature. No matter what sins you have committed, once this thought takes root in you - that you are God! - all evil is erased. You can destroy your vices one by one, but it will be an arduous task, which will go on for many, many lifetimes, because vices are infinite.

In your effort to destroy one evil you create ten more. When you eradicate one vice and replace it with virtue, there are still ninety-nine vices within you; they will quickly spoil your one virtue. Then all your good acts will also appear sinful. If you touch the nectar, it becomes poison, because the evil in you quickly contaminates it. Building a temple does not bring you humility. On the contrary, it inflates your ego even more. The ways by which the ego enters are very subtle; something useless can feed it.

Mulla Nasruddin had a dog. Its pedigree was unknown. It was a thin, ugly, weak creature that walked with its tail between its legs, always frightened, always trembling, but the Mulla never tired of praising it. He had named him after Adolf Hitler. When asked about the dog, the Mulla would say: "There may be doubts about Hitler's family background, but my dog is a very valuable thoroughbred.

No stranger can pass by my house without our knowing about it. Hitler warns me immediately.

"What does your Hitler do," I asked him, "does he bark or bite, what does he do?

He runs in and hides under my bed," said the Mulla. It has not happened to me once that a stranger has come and I have not noticed him". Even cowardice is praised!

Your ego is like Mulla Nasruddin's Hitler. You don't know his race. Do you know where your ego is born? How can that which does not exist be born? The ego is an illusion. Its race is unknown. You are born of God. Where does your ego come from? Have you observed your ego closely? You may call him Adolf Hitler, but his feet are made of clay. He is so torn and tattered!

The biggest ego is weak and miserable. Why? Because even the biggest ego is impotent; it has no power of its own. Power belongs to the soul. The source of power is different. That is why the ego has to be cared for twenty-four hours a day. It needs support. It has no legs to stand on. We have to prop it up with wealth or position - if nothing works we prop it up with sin!

You can visit the prison. Men locked up in prison tell stories about crimes they never committed.

A man who has killed one person boasts that he has killed a hundred. This is the only way to inflate the ego in prison. There, the bigger the crime, the bigger the criminal. The petty criminal has no prestige, so prisoners compete to establish who is the biggest criminal. Those who are tried for a single crime are not respected. Those who are tried for multiple offences, they appear in court every day, they are the bosses. They magnify their real crimes and attribute totally fictitious ones to themselves.

The ego can be sustained by good deeds, by bad deeds, by wealth, by position... and yet it is a cripple, death brings it down. Death destroys that which is not; that which is cannot be destroyed. You will remain, but remember, when I say you will remain, I am talking about that part of which you know nothing.

What you think you are will not remain, because it is nothing but your ego. Your name, your looks, your wealth, your honour, your abilities, whatever you have earned, none of it will remain. If you find the slightest trace of connection between this and what you really are, what you have not worked for, what you were born with and what is beyond all your capacity, you will find that what was with you before you were born will remain with you after death.

***The soul is mind.*** That soul is worth searching for. Your mind also carries a ray of the soul, otherwise it would not work. Even if you want to sin, who will? You need energy to sin. The energy comes from the same source; you are simply misusing the energy, but you cannot go from misuse to right use, because at the root is the ego.

There is only one sin: to consider oneself on the margins of existence. All other evils follow it like a shadow. There is only one virtue: to know oneself and to be one with existence. When the wave merges with the ocean, all virtues follow in its wake.

***The soul is mind.***

***Illusion is the lack of discrimination of what is essential.***

What is this illusion, this maya, why is the mind clouded with darkness if the soul itself is the mind?

Why this inability to discriminate what reality is? You are unconscious of the doer, the true artist in you. You are unconscious of the fundamental principle in you. What you assume to be the doer does not exist. You cling to what is not; hence the anguish and confusion. All your life you slave and strive, and your problems do not diminish; in fact, they have increased. In spite of working hard all your life, at the end you find that you have not gained a drop of joy; there are only mountains and mountains of sorrow and pain. Yet man runs in this senseless rat race until his last breath.

Why this infatuation for what is worthless and meaningless? Try to understand it. Everything that is meaningless and worthless has a common quality.

A man bought a new bungalow. He laid out a garden and planted some flower seeds. When they started to sprout, he found that they had grown weeds mixed with the flowers. He was worried, so he went to his neighbour, Mulla Nasruddin, for advice.

"How do I know which plants are flowers and which are weeds?"

"That's very simple," Nasruddin replied, "Pull them all out! The ones that come back out are the weeds".

This is the quality of all that is worthless: if you tear it out, it is not destroyed. That which has meaning, that which has purpose, is destroyed if you uproot it; that which is meaningless, that which has no purpose, is not. You sow the seeds of that which has meaning and you are not even sure if it will bear fruit, because there are thousands of obstacles ahead. This is the speciality of the pointless. Uproot it and it will grow on its own. The useless and the ineffective flourish on their own. Uproot them a thousand times, and they will still persist.

The meaningless grows effortlessly, but the meaningful requires great effort. That is why you have chosen the meaningless; it grows by itself. You don't have to do anything to become a thief. The habit of stealing grows like weeds. Do you have to make an effort to become or to become sexual? You don't have to do any prayer, any sadhana, any yoga. Do you have to go somewhere to learn how to get angry, to some university? No, it grows like weeds. But when it comes to meditation the difficulty begins. If you want to learn to be truly loving, there are many difficulties on the way, while attachments grow and flourish like weeds. You only learn to love with great difficulty. Every moment you have to uproot all the weeds before you can plant the seedling of love. If you want love to grow, you have to constantly control the weeds, or the young plant will suffocate, as if it were covered by a heap of rubbish.

The useless and the meaningless have one outstanding quality: they require no effort. You can loaf about, they will take root and blossom of their own accord, and cling to you until your last breath.

A seeker is one who has begun his search for significance. Reaching the meaningful is a journey, an uphill journey. Reaching the useless is like rolling down a mountain; you don't have to do anything, for the force of gravitation will do it all.

So far you have done nothing in your life, so you are good for nothing. You may not agree. You may state: "I have worked hard and succeeded in my life. I have wealth and prestige. I have obtained these degrees and these diplomas...". Yet, I will tell you that you have done nothing to achieve it. Your successes have sprung up like weeds, and if you take a good look at yourself you will find that you have done nothing to earn your wealth and your position. You allowed ambition to grow in you, and these are simply the fruits of ambition.

The ambition and the desires were already there. They have grown in your mind like weeds, and they cling to you until you die.

A seeker is one who has realised that what grows on its own is useless, and that he has to plant something.

One woman went to a psychiatrist and said: "I need help now. I've been putting it off, but now it's time. I'll have to talk. He asked her what her problem was. She replied: "It's not me, it's my husband. He is not as affectionate as he was when we were first married, nor is his desire for me as it used to be. He used to be like a flood, but now he is like a river that has dried up.

The psychiatrist was amused, but kept his composure. After all, business is business. So he asked him: "How old are you?

"Only seventy-two," she replied.

"And what is your husband's age?"

"He is only eighty-six years old".

Everybody thinks like this. The word "only" - "only eighty-six", "only seventy-two" - this "only" is used against death. They feel that they are still very young, that they have just started to live.

The psychiatrist then asked the lady: "And when did you start noticing that his sexual desire was diminishing?

She replied: "Last night and again this morning".

To the end, man clings to what is worthless. He has nothing to do about it; it grows by itself.

People come to me and say: "We try to meditate, but we fail again and again. We meditate for two days, but then it stops. Then, after a few days, we remember again, and again it stops.

It is not the same with your desires and passions. You have never forgotten to be angry and you have never forgotten to be greedy, but you have to remind yourself to meditate. Try to understand this fact, because meditation has to be actively practised. It slips away again and again. It is a seed that has to be sown and cared for. Rubbish grows by itself; weeds grow by themselves.

You must know that everything that happens for its own sake is worthless. As long as you live like this, you will achieve nothing. At the moment of death you will find yourself going out empty-handed, just as you went in empty-handed. And this blindness, this lack of discrimination, is maya, the illusion. It is the state of unconsciousness in which you cannot discriminate between the useful and the useless.

Shankara has defined knowledge as the discrimination between what makes sense and what does not. In life there are both: both flowering bushes and weeds. You will have to distinguish one from the other by your own experience. If your attention is not fixed on the meaningful but on the worthless, you will wander in illusion.

You don't know who you are, you don't know where you are going, you don't know where you come from.

You have become entangled with the rubbish by the roadside. You have made a home for yourself by the roadside, and you are so full of worries and anxieties, just because of this worthless rubbish, that it is there whether you deal with it or not. You have nothing to worry about.

Indiscrimination is Maya. Indiscrimination means inability to distinguish the diamond from the pebble. You have to become the jeweller of life, because only that leads to the birth of discrimination.

You possess life. Now search within it. The test of your search is to know that whatever happens for its own sake is worthless, and that which refuses to happen in spite of your efforts, is worth attaining. This is the test. The day you discover that what was so difficult to achieve has begun to happen, then you will know that the flowers are about to bloom. And the day when everything that was growing on its own stops growing, you will know that maya is over.

***The yogi trapped in attachments can attain occult powers, but not self-knowledge.***

Meaningless rubbish has become so meaningful to us that, when we set out to realise the meaningful, we end up achieving only the useless.

I am amazed at the motives of the people who come here to meditate. They only desire the useless even through meditation. They come to me and say, "I want to meditate to get rid of physical ailments. Can you assure me that they will disappear through meditation? It would be better if they went to a doctor. When they go to a spiritual doctor, it is only to cure their physical ailments. For them, meditation is only a medicine for the body.

People come to me and say My economic situation is very bad. Will meditation make things better? This cover of attachments is so dense and thick that even when you look for nectar it is only for poison.

Isn't it unbelievable? You come for the elixir, but you only want to kill yourself by drinking it! But you can't kill yourself with the elixir of life. Once you drink it you become immortal, but when you go for the elixir, the nectar, your goal is suicide. You want to satisfy some earthly desire or other, even through religion.

Go to the temples and listen to the prayers of the people. You will see that their requests are all mundane: someone's son needs a wife, someone else's son needs a job, someone wants peace in his home. Even in the temple they ask for mundane objects. Anyone would say that your temples are supermarkets where everything is sold. You have no idea what a temple should be. Your priests are nothing but shopkeepers. The people who go to temples are buyers of worldly things. You will always avoid the real temple.

I was once a guest at a dentist friend's house. One day, as I was sitting in his living room, a small boy came in, looking frightened. He looked around furtively. I could almost see him trembling inside. Then he asked me, "Could you tell me if the doctor is in?". I told him that I had just gone out. The boy's eyes lit up with joy.

"My mother has sent me to have my teeth checked," he said. "May I ask when you're going out again?"

Such is your condition. If you come across a real temple, you will run away as fast as you can.

You can bear the pain of a toothache, but you are not prepared to bear the pain of a dentist. We are all like little children.

You can bear all the pain that the world inflicts on you, but you are not willing to suffer any pain for religion. And religion is bound to cause you pain. Actually, it is not religion that causes you pain.

Your teeth have decayed so much that pain is inevitable.

Religion does not cause pain. Religion is the supreme bliss. But you have always lived in pain. You have accumulated so much pain around you that all your teeth are full of pain and suffering. You will really find it difficult to pull them out, so you prefer to live with this pain and suffering. The poison spreads throughout your body. Your life is upside down, but this pain is familiar to you. these pains are familiar to you.

Man is ready to endure familiar suffering. Ready to bear the unknown suffering. These teeth are yours and the pain is yours. You have known them for millions of lifetimes, but you are not aware that, once these teeth are extracted, this pain disappears, the gates of bliss will open for the first time in your life.

Even if you go to the temple you ask the priest when will God come out next time? - When can I go? You go and you don't want to go. It is difficult to evaluate the games you play with yourself.

Observing you and your problems over a period of time, I have come to the conclusion that your problem is only one. You don't know exactly what you want. You are not sure you want to meditate, but it bothers you that you can't meditate. Now, if your mind is not fully made up, whatever you do will be half-hearted. Nothing is ever half achieved. The useless needs no effort; it goes on by its own momentum. What is meaningful in life demands that you stake your life on it.

This sutra says: *the yogi caught in attachments can attain occult powers, but not self-knowledge.*

The curtain of attachments is so thick and dense that even if you go to religion you are looking for miracles. If you find Buddha before you, you will not recognise him. If Buddha and Satya Sai Baba are present, you will certainly go towards Satya Sai Baba, and not towards Buddha, because Buddha is not so stupid as to conjure things out of thin air! You are looking for magicians.

You are impressed by miracles, because your deepest desire is for the world and not for God.

When you see a miracle you are impressed. You think you have found a guru. Now you wait for your wishes to be fulfilled. A guru who can produce an amulet out of nothing must surely also produce the Kohinoor Diamond, so you wait patiently and serve the guru, for you never know when his compassion may fulfil your wish. What difference does it make to the guru to produce an amulet of the Kohinoor. You desire the Kohinoor, and even a great man will become a thief for the Kohinoor. Today he sheds ashes from his hands, tomorrow he may shed the elixir of life; nothing is impossible for such a guru. You have only to serve him!

No, you will never go to Buddha, because there are no miracles happening around him. When all your desires are over, there is no question of fulfilling them. The greatest miracle that takes place with Buddha is the light of desirelessness; but your desire-filled eyes cannot see this. You can only see the Buddha, you can only understand him, you can only bow to him when the meaninglessness of the world has really and truly enlightened you, and the curtain of attachments and cravings has really fallen.

Attachment is an intoxication.... Just as an intoxicated drug addict does not know where he is going or what he is doing, so too you move in this almost dazed condition. No matter how hard you try to watch your step, it makes no difference. All drunks try to control themselves; they try to prove to themselves that they are not intoxicated. They only fool themselves! The more they try to disguise it, the more obvious it becomes. Attachment is intoxication.

When I say that attachment is an intoxication I am speaking in chemical terms. In the state of attachment, your whole body is filled with intoxicating chemicals, even in the scientific sense. When you fall in love with a woman, your blood fills with certain chemicals. These chemicals are the same chemicals found in LSD, hashish and marijuana. That's why the woman who falls in love starts to look so wonderful; she never looks dull or ordinary. Likewise, the woman who falls in love sees her man as something otherworldly. When the intoxication wears off, he seems worthless.

That is why your love affairs cannot be permanent: they all develop in a state of drunkenness; it is a form of attachment. it has not happened consciously. You were unconscious when it happened.

That is why we say: "Love is blind". In reality, love is not blind, but attachment. We confuse attachment with love. Love is "the eye". No eye is sharper than the eye of love. It is the eye of love that sees God hidden in all His creation.

Attachment is blind. It sees things that do not exist. Attachment is a dream; and those whom we call yogis also fall prey to it. They acquire certain occult powers; that is not difficult at all.

You can read another person's thoughts with a little practice. You can influence another person's thoughts with a little practice. You can implant your thoughts in another, also with a little effort. This is science, and religion has nothing to do with it, any more than reading a book is science. When an illiterate sees you reading a book, for him it is nothing short of a miracle. He sees only a few spots on the piece of paper and you are deriving great pleasure from reading the poetry Vedas Upanishads. He is mesmerised by them. An illiterate man is amazed to see this.

Mulla Nasruddin was the only one in his village who could read and write. When there is only one literate person, it is difficult to judge whether he is really literate. Who can tell? One day an old woman came to him and asked him to write her a letter.

"I am sorry. I won't be able to write it," Nasruddin said. "My foot hurts."

"But how is it possible that your foot prevents you from writing?" the old woman asked.

"Don't worry about the detail. My foot hurts and I can't write your letter".

But the woman was stubborn. "I won't go unless I know the truth. I may be illiterate, but I've never heard of pain in the foot having anything to do with writing a letter".

"If you insist, I will tell you," Nasruddin said. "Who will go to the next village to read the letter? It will be me.

I can write, but I'm the only one who can read what I write. now my foot hurts. I'm not going to write it.

An uneducated person is astonished to see someone lost in the book. But anyone can be taught to read; there is a method to it. You see your thoughts moving within you, and another person can also learn to see them. There is a method, an art, but this art has nothing to do with religion. Just as reading a book has nothing to do with religion, reading another person's thoughts has nothing to do with religion. These are the tricks of a juggler, of a magician, and those who can perform them are not those who have achieved.

But I'm sure you're impressed. You go to a monk and he calls you by name. He says: "You come from such and such a village, and there is a neem tree in the right corner of your courtyard". You go crazy! But what has the real saint got to do with knowing your name, your village, your house and even a neem tree? He is a saint who has realised that nobody has a name, nobody belongs to a village. This name, this family, this village, all belong to the worldly world.

You are a worldly person, so the monk impresses you because he himself is more deeply involved in the world. He has learned a higher art. He speaks without being asked. He wants to impress you. Remember, as long as you want to impress someone, you are possessed by the ego. The soul never wants to impress anyone; what is the point? It is like drawing a line in the water.

What difference does it make to me whether I impress ten thousand people or twenty billion? What am I to gain from it? The desire to impress a crowd of ignorant people only shows your own ignorance. It only betrays my own ignorance. When a politician tries to impress people, it is understandable, but why should a religious person do it?

Be clear about one thing: whenever you try to impress others, it shows that you are not established in your soul; it shows that you are very ego-centred. The ego feeds itself by influencing others; it functions as food for the ego. The more I am known, the bigger my ego is. If everyone recognises me, my ego becomes invincible. If I pass through a village and nobody recognises me, nobody even looks at me, there is no flicker in anybody's eyes, as if I don't exist, then my ego takes a hit.

The ego desires the attention of others. This is very interesting. The ego does not want to pay any attention to others, but it certainly wants the attention of others. It wants to be the centre of the world.

A religious person does not care whether others look at him or not. He is more concerned about looking at himself, because it is that self that will ultimately remain with him. It is childish! It is natural for children to be anxious to impress their elders; they bring a school certificate home and show it to everyone. But if they keep looking for certificates in old age, then they have missed out on life altogether.

The desire for occult powers is part of the desire to impress others. It has nothing to do with religious quest. It is essentially worldly.

This sutra says that the yogi who is caught in his attachments attains occult powers, but lacks self-knowledge. No matter how great his achievement - he can raise the dead, he can cure diseases, he can turn water into wine - it has nothing to do with self-knowledge. In fact, the truth is that the more power he acquires, the further he moves away from self-realisation, because as the ego gets bigger and bigger, the emptier and emptier the soul becomes. And as the ego empties, the soul becomes richer and richer. You cannot empower the ego and the soul at the same time.

Abandon the desire to impress and influence others or your yoga will be corrupted. In that case, even if you practice yoga, it will be politically motivated, not religiously motivated. And politics is tricky. In politics you want to influence others by hook or by crook. You don't care whether you use right or wrong methods to do it. And the reason you want to influence others is that you want to exploit them.

I heard: Elections were being held and three people were taken to prison. It was quite dark inside when the three of them showed up.

One of them said: "I am Sardar Sant Singh. I work for Sardar Sirfod Singh".

The second one said: "How strange! I am Sardar Shaitan Singh and I am working against Sardar Sirfod Singh".

The third one said: "Unbelievable! I am Sardar Sirfod Singh".

The leaders and supporters of the ruling or opposition party, all of them, are fit only for prison. That is the right place for them. The roots of sin lie in the desire to influence others. The ego knows neither good nor evil; it only knows how to fulfil itself. How it fulfils itself is secondary. The ego's only aim is to feed and strengthen itself; but, because the ego is empty, it always remains empty regardless. As life goes on, man's ego becomes more and more insane. He realises that life is passing, that most of it has already passed, and yet the ego remains unsatisfied.

This is why the elderly are so irritable. This irritability is not because they have not succeeded in life. They are irritable because they have not been able to achieve what they wanted.

Their irritability is increasing because, as they get older, people stop noticing them. In fact, they simply wait for them to leave.

Mulla Nasruddin was a hundred years old. I asked him if he could tell me why God had granted him such a long life. Without batting an eyelid, Mulla replied: "It only tests the patience of the family.

All the elderly test the patience of their family They observe all the time that their relatives pay less and less attention to them. Death will destroy them. Death will destroy them much later, the lack of attention from relatives kills them much earlier. Hence the irritability.

You can't imagine how irritated Richard Nixon must be right now. All those people who wanted nothing more than a glance from him have now turned their backs on him. Those who were near and dear to him have become strangers. Friends have become enemies. Those who supported him have withdrawn their support. Nixon is disturbed, perplexed, unsettled. The first question he asks anyone is: "Wasn't what I did right? What do people say about me?".

Not long ago he was at the height of his power, and suddenly he was cast into oblivion. He is the same man as before. The only difference is: he was at the peak of his ego's glory, now he has been thrown into the pit, but the soul remains intact. If only he could remember that which has neither peak nor valley; for which there is neither victory nor defeat, which does not care whether people look at him or turn their backs on him, which is devoid of all change and is uniform.

You will only experience this uniformity when you stop seeking recognition from others. Abandon this beggar's attitude. What will you gain by attaining powers? People will call you a miracle man millions of people will flock to you. By attracting millions of idiots you will prove that you are the centre of attention of millions of idiots: you are a super-idiot!

What will you gain from the praise of the ignorant? How does the appreciation of the ignorant benefit you? What is the value of their praise? What is the advantage of being the leader of those who have already gone astray?

I heard: There was a Sufi saint, Farid. If people applauded when he spoke, he wept. One day his disciples asked him about the meaning of his tears. Farid said: "When they applaud, I know immediately that I have made some mistake; otherwise they would never applaud. Then, when they don't applaud, I know that they didn't understand me. Then I know that what I said was right".

What is the applause of the wrong people worth? Before whom do you want to prove yourself? If you want to be acclaimed as someone who has come through the world, you keep seeking recognition from fools. You yourself are a fool. If you want to demonstrate your powers before God and be recognised by Him, you are a greater fool, because ego has no place before God. You have to be extremely humble. You will only be accepted there if you have completely annihilated the ego. If you come there with your arrogance, it is in itself a great obstacle.

That is why the so-called siddhas, those who possess the powers, have never attained God. They acquire many powers, but they miss the real power. Self-realisation is the genuine power. Why do they miss out on it? Because the occult powers are also other-oriented. Would you crave for these powers if there were no one in existence, if you were all alone? Would you like to turn water into medicine? Would you like to touch a dead person and bring him back to life? If there were no one else in the world, would you still want to acquire such powers? You will say, "What are these powers for?

There are no spectators. The powers are for the spectators.

As long as your attention is directed towards others, you cannot direct it towards yourself. Only the one who turns his gaze away from others and directs it towards himself can attain self-knowledge.

***After the definitive overcoming of attachments, spontaneous wisdom is attained.***

Only when attachments are completely conquered is victory complete. What does attachment mean? It is the attitude: "I cannot live without others. The other is the centre of my life".

I'm sure you've read the children's stories in which there is a king whose life force is encased in a bird, perhaps a parrot or a mynah. It is impossible to kill the king. The bullet will go through his body, the king will live on. The arrow will pierce his heart, the king will not die. You can poison him, he will not die. You will have to find the bird in which his life force is hidden. Kill the bird and the king will die. These stories are very meaningful. Adults would do well to understand them.

Attachment means: you don't live in yourself; you live for something else. For example, someone's life revolves around his box. If you wring his neck he will not die, but if you steal his treasure he will drop dead. This man's life revolves around his wealth. His bank balance falls and it is a mortal blow to him. Kill him and he won't die. Try poisoning him and he will stay alive.

Attachment means that you have taken your life force out of yourself and placed it elsewhere.

Someone puts it in his child, someone else in his wife, someone else in his wealth or his position... but always somewhere else. The life force is not vibrating inside you. It is not where it should be, and then you will have problems.

This very attachment is a samsara, worldliness. Wherever you place your life force, you become a slave to it. The king whose life force is in the parrot is a slave to that parrot. His own life depends on the parrot. If the parrot dies, he dies, so he protects the parrot with his life.

I heard that once a king was very displeased with his astrologer. The astrologer had predicted the death of the prime minister the next day, and he died! The king was very worried. He suspected that his prime minister had died because of his prediction. He had died as a result of a spell cast on him by the astrologer's prediction. The king thought: "If he says the same thing about me, I will surely die. He will be influenced by his words.

He had the astrologer thrown into prison. When the astrologer asked the king why he was imprisoned, the king said, "You are a dangerous man. I don't think the prime minister will die a natural death. What you said had a profound influence on him. Your words hypnotised him. You are dangerous.

The astrologer said: "Before you throw me into the dungeon, listen to what I have to tell you about your future, I have calculated it too". The king refused to listen to him, but said: "You will die three days after my death". Now the king was really in a dilemma. He kept the astrologer in the palace and made himself look after him day and night. He himself looked after his body because his death meant the death of the king.

Wherever you place your own self, there you are enslaved. Watch the people approach their safe, with folded hands, as if they were going to the temple. On it they write all kinds of sacred inscriptions, as if it were the very place where God resides. They worship it.

At the festival of diwali you should see these crazy people worshipping their wealth, with so much feeling!

It is worth observing his attitude. Every year, on this day, the shopkeeper starts his new account book.

On the first page he draws a swastika, the symbol of Ganesh, and writes: "I bow to Ganesh".

This Ganesh is an old troublemaker. Ancient history tells us that Ganesh is the Lord of all obstacles, and he looks like a God of mischief-makers. First of all, he has no head of his own, and he who has no head of his own is really mad! He can do the impossible.

Everything about him is ambiguous and confused. He sits astride a mouse, which he rides. And the mouse is the symbol of reasoning and logic. And logic is as sharp as a mouse's teeth; it bites and chews things to pieces. You can never depend on logic, for wherever there is logic it creates a lot of obstacles. If a person's life is permeated with logic, he will be full of confusion and chaos; he will lose all peace and tranquillity.

An ancient story tells that Ganesh is a God who creates trouble. Whenever there is an auspicious occasion he appears. People used to fear him. They would come before him with folded hands and beg him not to create problems in their affairs. Gradually, people began to regard the problem-creating God as a problem solver, but they have forgotten the real story. They are right when they fold their hands and beg him to have mercy on them.

The curtain of attachments means that your soul is imprisoned elsewhere. Whether it is locked up in your child, in your wife or in your wealth is of no importance. What matters is the fact that your soul is not within you; that is what attachment means. The permanent conquest of attachment means that you have renounced all dependence on others. Now you are no longer dependent on anyone for your life. Your life is entirely dependent on you. You are centred in yourself. You have made your own existence your centre. Now, if your wife dies or your wealth disappears, it doesn't matter at all. For they are only superficial waves. So whether you succeed or fail, whether there is happiness or sorrow, it makes no difference, for the difference was caused by your dependence.

Victory over attachment means becoming completely independent. It means the feeling and the knowledge that "I depend on no one. I am enough for myself, alone". What satisfaction! What satisfaction! It is enough for me to exist. Such an attitude is the victory over attachments. As long as your being is dependent on another, attachment holds you captive. Until then you will cling to others so tightly for fear of losing them, because you cannot live without them.

Mulla Nasruddin's wife died. The Mulla wept obediently, but one of his friends could not contain his grief. He wept and howled, beat his chest and refused to be consoled. The Mulla could not bear it. He put his hand on his friend's shoulder and said, "Don't grieve, my friend, I will remarry. Now this man had been in love with the Mulla's wife; his life force was invested in her, so it was natural that he should be so distressed, but not the Mulla!

What is it that makes you cry? It's just your attachments. What do you miss when you lose it? It is the object of your attachment. Reflect on it. Find out what it is that clutches your own life, without which you feel miserable and destitute; that is the centre of your attachment. Before it is taken away from you, give up your attachment to it, for you are sure to lose it some day.

Nothing is stable in this life, neither love nor friendship. Constant change is the very nature of this world. The world is like a river... constantly flowing. Nothing is lasting, nothing is constant; and nothing can be made lasting, no matter how hard you try. You cannot hold that which is always moving, always flowing. You want to hold it, to freeze it. You will not succeed, because you go against the very nature of things. It is because of the effort you put into this futile effort that you are so disturbed.

Change is the other name for the world; yet you try to find in it some permanent support on which your life may depend. This cannot be! Every moment of your life is filled with sadness, for each moment further erodes the support on which you lean.

This is what you should do: try hard to find out what things would hurt to lose. Then, before you lose them, slowly open your hands, relax your grip on them. This is the method of overcoming attachment. There will be pain, but you must bear it; this is your penance. It is not necessary to give up anything. It is not that you should abandon your wife and flee to the Himalayas. Stay there, where you are, but gradually stop depending on her. There is no need to cause any pain; your wife need not even know. There is no need to tell her.

Jesus said, "Only when your right hand does not know what your left hand is doing, are you a true seeker". The desire to let others know what you are doing is, again, a desire of the ego. You want the world to know: "Look at that man! He has left his wife and is going to the Himalayas. Isn't that wonderful? It is not wonderful at all. Ask any husband. He is delighted to go to the Himalayas.

I may not be able to go, but that is another matter.

Mulla Nasruddin ran to the local asylum and knocked on the door. When the superintendent asked him what was wrong, he said: "Has some lunatic escaped from your asylum?

The superintendent wondered, "Why do you ask, have you seen anyone running?"

"Someone has run away with my wife," said the Mulla. "It must be a madman who has escaped from here.

Ask any husband. He who lives in the world has no end to his tales of woe. He cannot escape because he sees no joy anywhere. Where can he go? Wherever he goes, the world follows him like a shadow. Besides, with great expectations he has made a place for himself in the world and now it is difficult to destroy it, because then life is meaningless.

Look for attachments. Try gradually to live without the things without which you now think you cannot live. Create within yourself such a state that, when those things are lost, there will not be the slightest tremor in you. Then you will have attained victory over those attachments. This can be possible. It has been possible. And if it has happened to one, it can happen to all.

This Shiva sutra says: *after overcoming attachments, spontaneous wisdom is attained.* The day you finally overcome your attachments, you will begin to experience that knowledge, the knowledge that is not learned from others, but is innate and natural. That very knowledge is self-knowledge. There is no way to learn the knowledge of self from others. It comes naturally from within you.

As flowers grow on trees, as streams flow down mountains, so gurgles this knowledge within you; and it is your own innate knowledge. You don't have to get it from anyone else. No guru can give it to you; all gurus only point to it. When you get it, you will find that it was already within you. It is your own wealth, and that is why it is called innate, natural knowledge.

There are two kinds of knowledge. Knowledge of the world must be learned from each other.

It is not innate, nor spontaneous. However intelligent a person may be, he only acquires worldly knowledge through others. However clumsy and stupid a person may be, even he cannot gain knowledge of himself through others. It is within you. The only obstacle is attachment. When attachments are removed, when the clouds disperse, the sun shines.

*The awakened yogi realises that the whole universe is an emanation of his own energy.*

The day the natural knowledge unfolds in a person, he wakes up and can see that everything in this world emanates from his pulsations. He becomes the centre. You wanted with all your might to be the centre of the whole world, but because of the ego you could not achieve it. Every attempt ended in defeat. How as soon as the ego falls, you become the centre.

What you want to achieve, you will achieve. Only now you are looking in the wrong direction. You are following the wrong path; you have fallen into error. What you desire you will attain, only you have chosen the wrong support, the wrong charioteer, the wrong vehicle. You can never be the centre of the universe along with your ego. The egoless person immediately becomes the centre of the universe.

Buddhahood is only attained under the bodhi tree. Then the whole world becomes the circumference and buddhahood becomes the focal point. Then the whole world is only my expansion. Then all the rays are mine. All life is mine, but this only happens when the self, the ego, no longer exists. This is the complication, as long as the self exists, no matter how much you expand, no matter how big your empire is, you are only deluding yourself.

You have travelled a lot. Lives and lives you have wandered and yet you have not realised it.

Mulla Nasruddin once boarded a plane. Before settling into his seat, he called out to the stewardess and said: "Look! Have you checked the oil, gas and water properly?

The stewardess assured him: "Relax, sir. That's our concern, not yours.

"Then don't ask me half-heartedly to go out and push!" said the Mulla.

I happened to hear about this incident, so I asked the Mulla, "Did you have any problems? Did you have to push the plane?"

He responded with the proverb: "He who has scalded himself with hot milk never forgets to blow, even on his buttermilk. If you had ever been made to push a bus, you would have been on the plane too".

You've been scalded many times, and you haven't even learned how to cool milk, let alone buttermilk. The biggest problem in life is that we don't learn from experience. People say they learn from experience, but there is no proof of that, because over and over again you repeat the same mistakes. If you made some new mistakes, it would show some ability, some skill, and it would bring some momentum and maturity to your life.

The mind is a circle. You keep turning and turning on the wheel of ind, and this wheel receives energy from your attachments. Break your attachments and the wheel will stop, and as soon as the wheel stops you will realise that you are the centre. You don't need to become the centre, there is no need to become God; you already are! Therefore, this knowledge is innate.

Such an awakened yogi realises that this world is the result of rays emanating from his own being. Such is the experience, and it provides the supreme bliss. There is supreme nectar in sensation. All darkness flees from your life as soon as this knowledge comes to you; all suffering, pain and anxiety vanish into thin air. You are overcome with a joy, an ecstasy. You are drunk, intoxicated with it, and the song within you awakens. You throb with every breath; you are filled with a fragrance that comes from an unknown source.

This is a natural knowledge that no scripture can teach, no guru can teach, but the guru can help you to remove the obstacles. Keep this in mind. There is no way to "learn" this supreme knowledge. You have to learn to remove the obstacles that stand in its way. Meditation will not give you this supreme treasure; it will only give you the key to the door. With this key you can open the door. The treasure is within you.

You are that! Tat-tvam-si! You are the brahma!

All methods serve to remove obstacles from the path. You have to remove all your stones. You carry your destiny with you. There is no difficulty in attaining Brahma. The difficulty is that you cling to your attachments. You cling too much to the world, and as long as you cling to the world, you only postpone the meeting with God. It is up to you. Give up this very moment and you will reach this very moment. If you wish to delay, if you wish to delay, you can delay for many more births. You have seen delay since time immemorial. You have delayed long enough and you can delay for many more lifetimes, but I think there is no point in waiting any longer.

The time has come for you to fall from the world tree. Do not be afraid to disappear.

You will be lost, but only the useless you will be lost. What makes sense will multiply endlessly.

# The Mad Projectionist

*Nartakah atma rangoantaratma dhivashat satvasiddhih siddhah swatantra bhavah visargaswabhavyadabahih sthitestatsthiti.*

*The soul is a dancer.*

*The inner soul is the stage.*

*Through the control of the mind, reality is attained, and from that attainment comes a freedom.*

*And because of this sense of freedom, it moves freely in and out.*

Before going into the sutras let us understand a few things, Friedrich Nietzsche has said somewhere, "I only believe in a God who knows how to dance. To believe in a sad God is a sign of a sick man".

There is truth in this statement. You mould your God in your own image. If you are sad, your God will be sad. If you are happy, your God will be happy. If you can dance, your God will dance. Existence appears to you as you are yourself. ***Creation is an extension of your own vision.*** As long as you cannot believe in a dancing God, you are not healthy. The concept of a sad, weeping, sick God speaks of your own sick state.

Today's first sutra is

***The soul is a dancer There are*** a few things to understand about a dancer. Dance is the only activity in which the act and the actor become one. When someone draws a picture, the picture and the person who draws it separate; when a poet writes a poem, the poem and the poet separate; when a sculptor makes a statue, the sculptor and the statue separate. Dance is the only activity in which the dancer and the dance are one; the two cannot be separated. If the dancer disappears, the dance ceases to exist. If the dance is lost, then that man cannot be called a dancer.

The dancer and the dance are one.

That is why it is very meaningful to call God a dancer. This world is not apart from him. It is his dance; it is not his work. It is not a sculpture that God has created and finished. He is present within His creation at every moment. The moment He steps aside, the dance will stop. And remember, the moment the dance stops, God will also disappear. He cannot exist without the dance. He manifests Himself in every flower, in every leaf, in every grain and particle. It is not that the work of creation took place in some ancient past and stopped. The act of creation is happening every moment; therefore, everything is new. God is dancing, within and without as well.

*The soul is a dancer.* This means that whatever you have done, whatever you are doing, whatever you are going to do, it is not separate and apart from you. It is your own game. If you suffer, it is your choice. If you are blissful, it is your choice. No one else is responsible.

I was a newly appointed professor at a university. As the faculty was quite a distance from the city, the professors used to bring their lunch and sit together at a table at lunchtime. It was by chance that when the person sitting next to me opened his box and looked inside, he said: "It's potatoes and chapatis again! I thought maybe he didn't like potatoes and chapatis.

But as I was new there, I didn't say anything. The next day the same thing happened. She opened her lunch box, looked inside and sighed: "Same potatoes, same chapatis! Then I said to him: "If you don't like potatoes, why don't you tell your wife to make something else? He replied: "Wife! What wife?

Shall I make my own food?

This is your life. There is no one else. If you laugh, you laugh; if you cry, you cry. No one else is responsible. However, it may happen that you have cried for so long that it has become a habit and you have forgotten how to laugh. It may also be that you have cried so much that you don't know how to do anything else. You have had a lot of practice. It is also possible that you have cried for so many lifetimes that you have now forgotten that it was you yourself who chose to cry, but your lack of memory does not make a lie out of the truth. You have chosen it; you are the master, and therefore, the moment you make up your mind, that weeping will cease.

To be filled with the knowledge that I am the master. I am the creator and the one responsible for all my actions, brings about a transformation in your life. As long as you hold others responsible, transformation will not be possible because until then you will be dependent. You believe that others make you unhappy, so how can you be happy? It is impossible, it is not in your hands to change others. It is only in your hands the power to change your own self.

If you believe that it is your destiny to be unhappy, then the matter is no longer in your hands. How can you change your destiny? Destiny is above you. And if you believe that everything that happens is destined for you by God, then you will be nothing more than a machine, dependent on external factors and without a soul of your own.

The very meaning of the soul is that you are independent. However great your suffering may be, it is your own doing. The day you decide otherwise, your life will change. It all depends on your outlook on life.

I was a guest in Mulla Nasruddin's house. In the morning, while walking in the garden, I happened to see Mulla's wife throw a cup at his head. It missed his head and crashed against the wall. Nasruddin also realised that I had seen it. Then he came out and said: "Forgive me!

But don't think otherwise. We are very happy. Sometimes women throw some things away, but that doesn't influence our happiness.

I was a bit surprised. I asked him: "Mulla, would you mind explaining it to me in more detail?

He said: "You see, if she hits the target, she's happy, and if she misses, I'm happy. But that doesn't affect our happiness. Sometimes you hit and sometimes you miss. Then we are both happy.

It all depends on how you see life. You are the one who makes it, you are the one who experiences it and you are the one who interprets it. You are absolutely alone. Nobody ever enters your life. No one can ever do it.

If someone does it, it is because you give them permission. Now, this understanding poses a problem, and because of this problem you have chosen to forget your understanding.

The problem is: if you realise that you alone are responsible, then you cannot suffer. And yet, if you choose to suffer, you cannot complain. You enjoy both suffering and complaining.

You enjoy pain and suffering because then you feel like a martyr. There is great pleasure in martyrdom. When you are unhappy, you ask for sympathy, and sympathy is very pleasant, and that is why people exaggerate their suffering tenfold, while telling others. That's why people exaggerate their suffering tenfold, while telling it to others. What could be the reason that people keep telling their stories of suffering when nobody wants to listen to them?

Who cares about your suffering? Your tales of woe only make others sad; they cannot make flowers bloom in their lives, and yet you insist on telling them. And the other only listens until he hopes that you will listen to his sorrows too. If he thinks that won't happen, he slips away.

You only call people boring if they don't let you talk. So there is a kind of contract: you bore us and we bore you. You bore me with your stories of suffering, I'll bore you with mine and then we'll be even.

Why is there so much talk about suffering? The reason is that man seeks sympathy. If you pass on your sorrows, someone will caress and soothe you. Someone will say, "Oh, you are suffering so much. You are asking for love from each other in this way. That is why you have invested so much in your suffering. You have invested a lot in your suffering.

When you are unhappy, only then do you see a little hope around you. People seem to offer you help and support. They are sympathetic. You have never received love in your life and sympathy is rubbish, but it is the closest thing to love. He who has never had real gold begins to settle for unreal gold.

Sympathy is false love. What you really wanted was love, but love has to be earned, because only a person capable of giving love can get it. Love is a reflection of what you give. You are incapable of giving; you only beg. You are a beggar, not a king! It is much easier to beg when you are suffering.

Look at the beggar on the road. He has made artificial wounds on his body. Those wounds are not real. But he looks so painful that it is very difficult for you to say "no"; you feel guilty, your ego hurts, because how can you say "no" to a person who is suffering so much? If he looks healthy, you will also say, "You are healthy; do something, earn something; you can earn something! But when you see a man suffering you can't say anything. You have to show compassion even if it is false.

You cling to suffering because you have not received love. Whoever has received love in life will be full of joy and bliss; he will cling to joy and bliss and not to suffering. Suffering is not worth clinging to. But then you have the advantage of complaining; because when you say that others make you suffer, the burden of responsibility is no longer on you. And when I tell you, all the scriptures tell you and all the sages have said one thing only, that you alone are responsible and no one else, it becomes all a burden on you. The most burdensome thought is that you can no longer put the blame on someone else. Even more burdensome is the fact that if you are solely responsible, from whom will you ask for sympathy? And in the background another difficulty arises: that if you are responsible, then change is possible. And change is a revolution, it is a transformation.

You have to break all your old habits. You have an old shell, which is all wrong. The house you've built so far is complete hell. But you have created it; no matter how big it is, it has to come down. Your whole life's work seems to go down the drain. So you try to avoid the truth, but the more you avoid it, the more lost you are.

Realise first and foremost that you are the centre of your existence; no one else is responsible. No matter how burdensome it may seem to you, but you alone are responsible. If you accept this truth, all sorrows will soon disappear. Because once it is clear that I am creating this game, how long will it take you to destroy it? Then there is no one else involved. And yet, if you want to enjoy suffering, it is your choice, but then there is no reason to complain. If you want to wander aimlessly in the world, that is your sweet will. If you want to descend into hell, it is your own choice. But then, don't complain! Then be happy in your suffering!

These sutras are very valuable in this context.

The first sutra is: ***the soul is a dancer.*** Your actions and your being are not two different things. Your actions come out of your own being, just as the dance comes out of the dancer. And if the dancer starts complaining, "I'm tired of this dance. I don't want to do it", what would you say to him? You would say: "Stop! Then don't dance. Who is asking you to dance? It is you who dances. Stop! if everything is useless and you don't find pleasure in it. If it is painful, stop! The dance will disappear.

***The soul is the dancer.*** This means that whatever you do, it is you who does it. It has come out of your own being. Just as the leaves come out of the tree, your actions come out of your being.

Stop! And that's the end of the action!

Another thing to understand from this sutra - the soul is the dancer - is: if you stop your dance of suffering, if you put an end to your life of misery and pain, the dance will not stop, but will change form. The dance cannot stop; it is part of your existence. It is your very nature. You will continue to dance, but then there will be no tears, only laughter. Then your dance will have a rhythm, a melody.

It will be a pulsation of joy, of intense pleasure, an intoxication. Right now your dance is the dance of hell, then it will be a divine dance.

There was a Mohammedan fakir: Ibrahim. He was a king who later became a fakir. He came to India during his travels. He saw a sadhu who was sad and depressed. Sadhus are usually sad and depressed because their life was full of pleasure when they were in family life. They know no other pleasure than that. They give up the world and family life and all pleasure is lost.

They may not suffer, but they are sad and joyless.

There is a little difference between sadness and grief. Sadness means that there is a sharpness, a taste, in sadness. Sadness also has a sting, a passion. There are two kinds of ardour: the ardour of sadness and the ardour of happiness. One, when you are so full of sadness that tears begin to flow, and the other, when you are so full of happiness that tears begin to flow: both are a kind of burning.

When a man flees the world because it is full of sorrows, he also leaves the joys behind.

Then it is filled with sadness; there is no torrent, neither of joy nor of sadness.

Look at your sadhus and sannyasins. They are dead; as if they are ghosts, as if the dance has stopped. They ran away from sorrow, but they also lost their joy. They thought that if they left sorrow behind, only joy would be left. That was their mistake.

In this world, where there is joy, there is also sorrow. You want to keep the joys and get rid of the sorrows. So you run away from sorrows; but in the process you also lose the joys.

The sadhu was sad. He must have been an ordinary sadhu. A true sadhu gives up both happiness and unhappiness. He does not want to keep happiness, he simply gives up both. And the moment he gives them up, all sadness disappears, for sadness is the middle point between the two.

When you give up both, the middle ground is also lost. Then a whole new dimensional journey begins, you can call it bliss, tranquillity, nirvana... whatever you like.

There is no ardour in bliss; it is a cold ray, a cold light; there is no passion. In a way, bliss is like sadness. Sadness is in the midst of joy and sorrow. Bliss is beyond joy and sorrow. Sadness is a state of darkness in which everything has become motionless, a state of death in which everything languishes in inertia. Bliss is a radiant state of consciousness, where there is neither joy nor sadness. In this sense, bliss is also like sadness, where there is neither joy nor sorrow. There is light there, but the light is not that of joy, because the light of joy also has an edge, an intensity that makes you sweat.

Therefore, people get tired of happiness. You can't be happy for long. Happiness tires because it has a fever, an intensity. If you won the lottery every day, you would die, you wouldn't live. It's all right if you win once in a while. If you hit the lottery every day, the tension would be so great that you wouldn't be able to sleep. Your heart would pound so hard that you wouldn't be able to rest. The excitement would be so great that it would kill you. So happiness can only be taken in homeopathic doses. You will not be able to take an allopathic dose. A lot of unhappiness along with a little joy is all you can bear, because it is also a tension. It also has heat and intensity.

Grief is tension, as is joy.... There is excitement in both. Bliss is the state of an unexcited, unstimulated mind; there is light but no heat. There is dance, but no excitement. There is a silent and serene dance in which there is no sound. It is a dance in emptiness, which produces no fatigue.

It is not of the body. Joy and sorrow are of the body, and joy is of the soul. It is a totally different dance.

This sadhu was an ordinary sadhu, the kind you find everywhere. Ibrahim was surprised to see him sad, for his idea of a sadhu was that he should be happy. So he asked the sadhu, "What are the characteristics of a sadhu?

That sadhu said: "If he gets food, he accepts; if not, he is content". Ibrahim said, "Those are the qualities of a dog. What is holy about it? That is exactly what a dog does. If he gets something, he is happy, if not, he is content".

The sadhu was dumbfounded. He asked: "Then how do you define a sadhu? Ibrahim replied: "If he gets something, he shares it, and if he doesn't get it, he dances and thanks God for giving me the opportunity to practice austerity". The definition of sadhu is: one who shares with others when he gets something. One who shares what he gets is a true sadhu. If he retains it, he is a householder. If he treasures it, he is a householder; if he shares it, he is a sadhu; whatever it is - blessing, knowledge or even meditation - he shares it all.

It is an interesting fact that worldly things, if you share them, become less and less; that is why we hold on to them. If you start sharing from your vault, then your vault will not remain a vault for long.

Because everything in the world is limited: the moment you start sharing it, it disappears. That's why you have to hold on to what is limited in the world. But we don't need to apply this to the soul, because that treasure is unlimited; the more you give, the more it becomes. The more you take out, the more new comes out. It is a limitless ocean.

Ibrahim is right; if he gets it, he shares it; he does not eat alone. If he does not succeed, he dances and thanks God. To be content is not enough, for there is still sadness in contentment.

People often say: "A contented man is a happy man". This is not true. A contented man is not a happy man.

He just thinks he is happy. Deep down he is unhappy, but he can't do anything about it. He is powerless, so he disguises it as contentment. No, contentment is not enough. Contentment is part of sadness. When you endure it without protest, when you don't complain, these are signs of a dead conscience.

Ibrahim said: "If you receive nothing, then dance and be grateful that you have given me the opportunity to practice austerity; today there will be fasting. If you receive, then gratitude because then you could share it, spread it! If you don't receive, then also gratitude!

You cannot destroy the bliss of a sadhu. On the other hand, if you destroy his sorrows, the result will be nothing but sadness. Even when you somehow manage to abandon your sorrows, you become sad. Sadness keeps you busy, busy. You may not have realised it, but if all your sorrows are taken away, you will commit suicide; for what will you do then? There will be nothing left for you to do.

The father is busy working because he has to educate his children, so that they will get married. If they all get married and settle down right now, what will the father do? Life will seem pointless to him. You are busy with meaningless things. It makes you feel that you are doing something, that you are important, necessary. The world cannot go on without you; what will become of your child, your wife! It gives strength and support to your ego, that you are indispensable; everything happens because of you. Whereas the simple fact is that things can go on just as well without you. When you were gone, things went on; and after you are gone, things will go on. But only for a while in between do you dream, the dream of your indispensability.

So, even if you drop the sadness, the best thing you can do is to feel content. But there is a sorrow hidden beneath the contentment. Contentment is only on the surface; deep down there is a wound of sorrow.

Contentment is like a bandage, it is not a remedy.

No! A true sadhu is not content, he is blissful! Whatever the circumstances, if he gets something, he will share it and be blissful; even if he gets nothing, then he will also dance and be happy.

The nature of the soul is to dance, and it can dance in two ways. It can dance in such a way that there is sadness and suffering everywhere, that there is darkness and gloom everywhere; or it can dance in such a way that everything begins to dance with it and flowers bloom everywhere.

Sannyas is the dance of bliss; worldly life is the dance of pain. There is no hell anywhere else! Do not sit in the hope that there is hell elsewhere. Hell is your wrong way of dancing, which creates sorrow and suffering. Heaven is also nowhere else. It is your right way of dancing, which creates heaven wherever you are. Heaven and hell are qualities of your dance.

You don't know how to dance, but you still think it's the dance floor's fault. There is nothing wrong with the dance floor. For those who know how to dance, the dance floor is of no importance.

And for the one who doesn't know how to dance, a floor made exactly at a 90 degree angle doesn't help him. He will not be able to dance because of that.

I heard that a man went for an operation on his eyesight. Before the operation he asked the doctor: "I can't see anything, will I be able to see after the operation? The doctor examined him and said, "Of course you will see". The man said, "And will I be able to read? The doctor replied, "Of course. The operation was successful and the man could see. But he was very angry with the doctor.

He went home and said, "You lied to me. I still can't read. "How is that possible?" the doctor asked. "You can see everything, why can't you read? I never learned to read.

the man replied.

Even if you regain your sight, that doesn't make you able to read if you have never learned to read. It doesn't matter how smooth the floor is, if you don't know how to dance.....; dancing doesn't depend on the smoothness of the floor, you have to learn it. And remember that there is no one else who can teach you! You are all alone! The enlightened ones can give you hints, but it's you who has to learn. No one can take you by the hand and teach you. The dance of life is so deep within, so profound, that outside hands cannot reach it. No one but you can enter it. You are all alone there. Everyone else is outside.

The soul is a dancer. Sadness and joy are the two ways in which it can dance. If you are unhappy, you have chosen the wrong way to dance. Change your way. Don't blame anyone. Don't complain. As long as you complain, you will go on dancing the wrong way; because you will never realise that the mistake is mine....; it is always the other person you try to blame.

Stop complaining. Look at yourself and wherever you find sorrow arising, look carefully, you will find the cause within you. Abandon those causes! What is the purpose of doing things that bring only sorrow and pain? Why do you keep sowing seeds that bear only poisonous fruits? Why do you keep reaping their harvest every year? The best thing would be not to sow the harvest. Even if it remains empty, it is not bad. In fact, it is better for the field to remain unsown for a while, so that all the old seeds have time to die and you can sow new ones.

Why are you so afraid of being empty? Meditation is this empty state. It is like a farmer who leaves the land empty for a year or two, he doesn't sow anything; meditation is that in-between state; it is the empty space between heaven and hell. Leave it alone for a few days. Don't sow anything.

Remember one thing: rather than doing something wrong, it is better to do nothing. Stop for a moment and do nothing. Until you know how to do it right, it is better not to do it at all; for every action, every wrong action results in a chain of actions. One wrong action triggers a chain of wrong actions. This is what we call karma, a web of our actions.

You are always doing something. You can't sit and do nothing, you will go on doing something. Sitting and doing nothing is meditation. Sit and do nothing, so that the old habit disappears and gradually you begin to see things clearly. But you are so busy that you have no time or comfort to see.

The only point of meditation is for you to sit quietly and do nothing for one, two, three hours, whatever time you have. Just look, observe, so that, little by little, your vision becomes sharp and penetrating, and you begin to realise that, whatever has happened in my life so far, I have been the cause. As soon as you realise this, you will stop sowing useless seeds. A meaningful dance will be born in you.

Religion is the supreme bliss; it is not the sadness of renunciation, but the enjoyment of existence. It is to merge with the supreme joy. It is to become one with the dance of existence. Never think of religion in terms of sadness and renunciation. Religion that thinks in terms of sadness and renunciation is wrong. True religion is always a dance. It is always bliss. True religion is always a flute playing.

*The soul is a dancer.*
*The inner soul is the stage.*

And this dance, which is happening, is not happening anywhere outside; it is happening inside you.

This world is not a stage; it is the inner soul that is the stage. No matter how much you think you have come out, you cannot; how can you come out? You will always remain inside yourself.

Everything happens only in there. The play unfolds in there, and then the results become visible outside. It's like when you go to a movie theatre and you see the drama on the screen, but in reality it's all happening in the projector behind you, what we see on the screen is just the reflection.

The screen is not the real stage, but your eyes are so glued to it that you forget that the real image is behind you, on the projector. The real image is behind you, what you see on the screen is just a reflection.

The inner soul is the stage; the projector is inside. All the seeds of drama come from within; outside you only get news; you only hear the echoes. And if outside there is sadness, you must know that inside you have the wrong film. And if everything you do outside seems to go wrong, it means that what you bring out of you is wrong.

A screen change won't make any difference. Whatever you do to improve the screen will make no difference. If your film comes out badly from inside you, the screen will keep repeating the same story. And then you are not only a film, but also a broken record repeating the same line.

Have you ever tried to find out what's inside your skull? You'll find that things keep repeating over and over again, like a broken record. You keep repeating the same thing over and over again.

Nothing new ever happens there, and whatever you repeat there, its echoes are heard all around you, reflected on the world's screens.

Mulla Nasruddin went to see a film with his wife and son, and you can imagine Nasruddin's child, he can't be a tidy child because when everything is messy inside what comes out is also messy. The child was crying, howling and making a lot of noise. The manager had to come and ask Mulla at least seven times to either return the money and leave, or shut the child up. But why would he shut the child up? The manager had to come again and again. Mulla would nod his head and continue to watch the film in silence. And then, as the film was about to end, Mulla asked his wife, "What did you think? Did you like the film?" She replied, "It's absolutely hopeless." Then he said, "Well, don't waste any more time. "Give the boy a good pinch; then we'll get our money back and go home".

You have been observing for a long time. You have observed for many lifetimes that everything is wrong.

When will you pinch? You will have to do it yourself; there is no one else here. When will you wake up and come back? What is the purpose of watching this wrong show that is filling you with so much pain and anguish; that gives birth to nothing but sorrows and nightmares? You are in this house only because of yourself; why do you delay? Have you not had enough? If you have not had enough, why do you listen to the ravings of people like Buddha, Mahavir, Krishna, Shiva and Jesus? Don't listen to them. Stay away from them, for their words only make sense to those who are fed up with the film, who feel they have seen enough; to those who are bored and restless and uneasy in this hell; to those in whom the desire for the celestial dance has arisen; to those whose desires have turned towards God.

Your state of mind is such that you want to travel in two boats. This adds to your problems. No matter how much pain it causes you, you still want to continue to pursue the pleasures of the world. There is always a faint glimmer of hope that you will find happiness. Happiness always seems so close!

And you are sustained by this hope, that the goal is almost within your reach; but your experience tells you that nothing is going to happen. Experience is on the side of the Buddhas; hope is opposed to them. And you support both. You have one foot in each boat.

One foot is on the boat of hope. You always say that everything will be alright soon. One woman doesn't bring you happiness, you change to another. One son disappoints you, maybe the other one won't. One business is not profitable, maybe another one will be. You are always changing things around you. If one house hasn't brought you happiness, maybe another one will. Your safe is small; a bigger one would suit you better. You keep doing this with everything around you: you just change the screen! The story inside you is the same, so the same story is projected on the screen outside again and again.

Everywhere you meet sorrow. Your experience is sorrow; your hope is happiness. These are the two boats. If you hear Buddha or Mahavir or Krishna, they talk about experience. They urge you to get off the boat of hope and get into the boat of experience. And you listen to them. You cannot deny them completely. In their presence you feel they have achieved something you have not. It looks like the rat race is over for them, but you are not one hundred percent sure; they could be a fraud. Who knows if they've really made it. They might just be faking it. And who knows? - Maybe we'll get it too. Maybe the wise men are just saying that the grapes are sour and not worth eating; maybe they couldn't reach them. Maybe we can reach them in our own way.

So you are in a dilemma. Certainly, you cannot deny your experience, but still hope persists. This dilemma is your folly.

These two boats go in different directions, so get on the boat of your choice. It doesn't matter if you decide to get on the boat of hope, but at least get on one boat and leave the other. Get totally into the boat of the word and you will soon get bored. This half-hearted affair gets you nowhere. Keeping one foot in the boat of the Buddhas prevents you from having a full experience of the world. You remain half-hearted; you go to the temple as well as to the tent. In this way, neither the temple is well taken care of, nor the stand; you can't manage both at the same time. Take care of your shop wholeheartedly. Forget that there was ever anyone like Mahavir, Buddha, Krishna or Shiva. Forget that there are scriptures. Let the ledgers of your shop be everything to you. Throw yourself into it with all your heart and very soon you will come out of it. Your own experience will show you the futility of it all.

But you realise that you can't do it; one foot is still stuck in the other boat. Again the problem: you are not quite in the second boat. The reason you haven't left the first one is that your mind keeps whispering to you: 'There's no hurry. You are still young. These are things for old people to worry about. When you have one foot in the grave, put the other foot in the Buddha's boat'.

People think that religion is for old people; they will only need the water of the Ganges when they are about to die. Only then will they need someone to recite the prayers for them. When you are about to die, when there is no energy or power left in you, then you start preparing for the journey. You are destined to fall back into samsara, back into the world; you will get back into the same boat, just as you have done for countless lifetimes.

*The soul is the dancer.*
*The inner soul is the stage.*

Remember that what you see outside is what you project from within. In life, all you see is what you project, and life presents you with many situations that prove that this is so.

I have heard: Once three travellers were together in a waiting room. One was an old man of sixty, another a middle-aged fellow of about forty-five, and the third a young man of thirty. The young man was telling the others: "Last night I spent the night with the most beautiful woman in the world; the pleasure of having her is indescribable".

The forty-five year old man replied: "Nonsense! I have known many women in my life. They seemed incomparable to me then, but now I see that the pleasure they gave me was not as great as I imagined then; in fact, it was no pleasure at all. Now I know the true meaning of joy. Last night I was invited to the king's house, and oh, what a glorious feast! I have never tasted such wonderful food.

"That's nonsense," said the old man. "Ask me what real pleasure is. This morning my bowels were completely emptied. The pleasure of an empty stomach is indescribable. I have never known such bliss.

That's earthly joy: it changes over the years. The problem is you, who forget it. In your thirties, the sex drive seems to give the most pleasure. At forty-five, food seems to give the most pleasure, so people tend to put on weight around that age. At sixty the interest in food disappears; the interest that remains is to keep the bowels empty. The pleasure of samadhi comes from a totally different dimension.

The inner soul is the stage. Whatever you have put inside. Sexual desires spring from the eyes of the young man. His whole body is filled with aspects of sexual desire; wherever he looks, he sees the woman.

Sexual desire grips him from all sides.

Mulla Nasruddin was a young man. He went to see an art exhibition with his wife. They were newly married, so they went to many places together. There were many masterpieces in the exhibition. Mulla stopped at one painting in particular. He froze. It didn't move. It was a nude covered only by leaves. The caption read: Spring. He was paralysed. The Mulla's wife shook his arm and said: "Are you waiting for autumn?

Such is the mind of man. His wife got it right. Wives usually get it right. They know it.

Whatever force has surfaced in you becomes the whole world around you. You colour the world with your own brush. We have an earlier word in our language, raga. No other language has a word like it. It means both fascination and colour. All your fascination is the result of the colour projected by your own eyes. You colour everything, and the fascination of what you have coloured is what catches you.

Raga means: you have coloured. A woman is not beautiful. The colour of your sexual desire makes her beautiful. A boy is not bothered by the appearance of a woman, for the colour of his sexual desire has not yet developed. The old man has long since passed this stage. He laughs at your nonsense, though he himself did the same when he was young. You will laugh too when it is your turn, but the one who wises up realises the moment it happens that it is nonsense; and wakes up. There is not much point in laughing later on; anyone can do it; But when the foolishness has taken hold of you and the colour is in full swing, then you must become aware that all this is a play from within, and the outside is a mere screen.

*The inner soul is the stage.* It is the projector through which the outer world becomes an extension of the inner drama.

*Reality is achieved through control of the mind.*

This game continues, and you will continue to wander in it as long as the mind is not under your control. It is through the control of the mind that reality is achieved. As soon as you realise that all the drama is projected from within, you forget about conquering the world, for it is only a screen.

Put your mind under your control and the whole world will be yours to control. When you come to know that you are the producer, the actor, the writer and also the stage of the play, everything will cease to interest you for any external change. Then you will become concerned with integral possession, that is, with taking possession of your mind, with being its master.

You are not the master of your mind. Your thoughts are not your slaves; rather, you are the slave of your mind. You meekly follow where your thoughts lead you; they never go where you want them to go.

Try to give a slight twist to even a very insignificant thought and it resists you. Tell an insignificant thought to shut up, and it immediately rebels.

You never consider this situation, because it is too painful. The very thought "I am not my master" is killing you, because you have set out to be the master of the whole world! How can you be the master of anything if you are not even the master of yourself?

Take a good look at your mind. Examine it closely. The first thing you will discover is that the mind has become the master, not you or your soul! The mind says: "Do this"! And you do it! If you don't do it, the mind creates problems. It becomes sad, and the sadness of the mind becomes your sadness. If you do what it says you get nowhere, because the mind is blind. Where can you get to by obeying the mind! The mind is unconscious. If you listen to it you will get nowhere.

It must be clear to you that if a bound man follows a bound man, they will both end up in a ditch, but that is what every one of us does. Your mind is absolutely bound; it knows nothing, and yet you follow it as blindly as your shadow follows you. You have forgotten that you are the master.

The association with slaves brings this about. Gradually, the slaves become the master, for as you become more and more dependent on them, their ownership begins to be established.

All sadhanas, all spiritual practices, have only one aim: to break and destroy the domination of the mind. What will you do to destroy this domination? First: if you want to overthrow the domination of the mind, destroy all identifications with it. A thought arises within you: do not identify with it!

If you become one with it, you give it strength; stay away. Stand as if you were on the roadside watching people go by. Look at it as you would look at a cloud in the distant sky while you are on the earth below. Don't identify yourself. Don't join your thoughts.

Don't say, "This is my thought". As soon as you say "my", you identify yourself; as soon as you identify yourself with it, all your energy flows into that thought. It is this energy that makes you a slave, and it is your own energy!

Don't identify yourself. When you start to turn away from your thoughts, they start to lose strength and become lifeless, because they don't receive energy. Your problem is: you want to extinguish the lamp, but you yourself also keep adding oil to it. On the one hand you blow on the lamp to turn it off, and on the other hand you pour more oil into it. Stop replenishing the oil. The old one won't last long.

What is oil? Whenever a thought takes hold of you - for example, whenever anger takes hold of you - you immediately become one with it. You say, "I am angry. Now the truth is: you have become so identified with anger that all your energy flows into it. You have become the shadow and your anger is the master. When anger arises, step away from it and watch. Let anger arise; let it permeate your body. It will envelop you everywhere. Let it go! You have only to remember one small fact: that you are not your anger! Don't be in too much of a hurry to immerse yourself in it, because then you will find it difficult to come out of it.

Watch your anger, but be firm on one point: if you really must respond to the man who has insulted you, do so when your anger has passed. Under no circumstances should you respond before then. At first this will be difficult, very difficult. You will have to be very alert and on your guard, but little by little it will become easy. Keep your mouth shut as long as the anger lasts; respond only when the anger has gone! This is the right thing to do. The right response can only come in serene moments. Responding in anger is as good as responding under the influence of alcohol.

When sexual desire takes hold of you, stand back and watch. The greater the distance you create between you and your thoughts, the more you establish your control: but you are so close, so close to your desires, that you have even forgotten that there is any distance between them and you, that there is any gap between the two.

Start today. The results will not come immediately, for your closeness, your association, has existed for countless births. These old associations cannot be broken in a day; it will take time, but a little effort on your part will bring results, for it is a false identification. If it were genuine, you could never break it. But this identification with your thoughts is only your conception, and yet it creates all your problems.

When you are hungry, don't say, "I am hungry". Rather say, "I see that the body is hungry". This is the fact.

You are the observer. It is the body that is hungry. Consciousness is never hungry. Food only enters the body. It is the body, the flesh and blood, that has needs. It is the body that gets tired; never consciousness. Consciousness is a lamp that burns without wick or oil. It needs no nourishment or fuel. It never needs anything.

The body needs fuel and water. The body is a machine; the soul is not. Feed the body when it is hungry, but know one thing: the body is hungry and I am watching it. If it is thirsty, give it water. It is necessary, for the body is an instrument dependent upon food and water. It is a foolish man who says, "I am not the body, so I will not give it food and water. If you don't put gas in your car, how will you make it go? You can sit in it, but it will not move. You have to give the car fuel. Only then it will run. Just don't become one with the car. Be the master and satisfy its needs.

The needs of the body have to be me; it is a machine that you have to use. It is a very useful instrument, because it is the ladder that leads to bliss; but the rungs can also lead to sorrow. The body is a ladder. The characteristics of a ladder are that one end of the ladder always rests on the ground, and the other end always touches the sky. With the same ladder you can ascend and descend.

It is through the body that you have descended to hell; it is through the body that you can ascend to heaven. And it is through the body that you will attain liberation. It is your medium. You have to take care of it. You have to satisfy all its needs, but you need not become one with the medium! Let the instrument remain an instrument. You write with the pen, but you are not the pen. You walk with the feet, but you are not the feet.

The body is a machine, a valuable machine. Take care of it and don't spoil it. It can be spoiled in two ways: there are people who spoil it by overindulgence; there are others who spoil it by renunciation.

Both are enemies of the body and both are foolish, ignorant. One resorts to prostitution or overeating to spoil it; the other does the damage by fasting. Either you flood it with petrol or you don't put a drop in it. These are the two extremes. You have to give the body enough to satisfy its needs. You have to maintain your servant, but that doesn't make him master.

*Through the control of the mind, reality is attained.* As your mind begins to come under your control, as you gradually begin to become the witness, you will find that reality; your soul, your real existence, begins to awaken.

It is the misuse and failure of the mind that leads to samsara, the world. Control of the mind leads to the soul. Where the mind is the master, there is the world; where the mind is the slave, there is God.

The mind is a ladder. You don't need to use it to go down; you have to go up and up. But only the one who is master can go up; the one who is a slave goes lower and lower. The slavery of the mind is very dangerous, because the mind is not one. It is a multitude. One moment it commands you to be angry, and the next to repent. One thought tells you: Enjoy the world! Another says: You must accumulate wealth, even if you have to steal! Another thought says:

That is sin! There are countless other thoughts and their sum total is the mind.

If your mind were just one thought, that would be enough to allow you a peaceful life, but it is not just one. Your mind is a crowd, a marketplace. The mind is like this: in a classroom, as long as the teacher is present, the children sit quietly and study. As soon as the teacher leaves, the classroom turns into chaos. The children start shouting, throwing books, knocking over desks and fighting among themselves. There is no one to control them. As soon as the teacher returns, all is quiet; the books are in place and so are the children.

As soon as you gain mastery over yourself, the mind begins to function in a more orderly way. As soon as you lose mastery over the mind, chaos and confusion ensue. It is very difficult to obey this chaos, for it leads you nowhere. It is not just one note, but a discord of many different notes.

Mahavir has said that man has many minds. Man has not one mind, but many. Modern psychology supports Mahavira's view. They say that man is "polypsychic". It is as if there is one servant and thousands of masters, and each master gives orders to the poor servant. Whom should he obey? He will go mad. This is exactly the state of your mind.

Seek the one, so that the master may return to the classroom. Seek the one so that the slaves can go to work in their proper places. If the master is one, he will give a direction to your life, and reality will assert itself. Then you will be able to know yourself. Then this affirmation of existence will bring with it a natural freedom. As long as your mind is your master, you will remain a slave.

The moment you realise the reality, natural freedom comes.

It is necessary to understand what is meant by "natural freedom". Why is it not simply called "freedom"?

Why "natural"? The answer is very subtle. There are two kinds of freedom. A freedom is directed against someone. In that case it is obstinate and stubborn. It is not a real freedom, because in it you are forced to take the opposite direction.

For example, the mind says, 'Be angry'. Now, if you want to do just the opposite of what the mind tells you, you will say, 'No, I will not be angry; on the contrary, I will be indulgent'. The mind says, 'Kill!' and you will say, 'No! On the contrary, I will offer him my head to cut it off'.

We do exactly the opposite of what the mind tells us, as our sadhus usually do. The mind says, 'Go and find a woman'. The sadhu flees into the jungle. The mind says: 'Pursue wealth'.

The sadhu refuses to touch the money. The mind says: "Rest". The sadhu stands in the scorching sun or sleeps on a bed of nails. This is not true freedom, for you go on listening to the master, even if you go against his directions. You do the opposite of what he says, which still makes him the master.

Understand. It is a bit complicated. The struggle continues; it is not over. Once you are the true master, all struggle is over, for the slave is a slave and is no longer worth fighting against.

Imagine that a slave in your house becomes the master, and you sit or stand as he orders you to sit or stand. If you decide not to obey him and do just the opposite of what he says, he is still the master, because he is the one who motivates you. And if he is clever, he can tell you to sit down when he wants you to stand up. You can't escape him.

Mulla Nasruddin had guests in his house and his young son was making a lot of noise. The Mulla told him to be quiet, but the more he told him, the louder he became. Normally, children tend to become noisy in the presence of strangers to make their presence felt. It's a battle of egos: father versus son.

Finally the Mulla said: "Look! Do what you want. Now we will see if you are capable of disobeying me".

The boy must have been perplexed.

If you go against the mind, natural freedom will not work. It is not freedom. The result is rebellion.

We are always linked to those against whom we rebel. We have a relationship with the person we are fighting against. We are not yet masters, for the initiative still comes from the opposite camp. When the signal comes we do the opposite.

If you then practise celibacy, it will make no difference, because your celibacy will be a revolt; it will not be natural. The mind is full of sexual desire and you set out to fight against it. This is war! And who goes to war with his own slaves? He who fights against his slave considers him his equal, and not his servant.

So your sadhus may be the opposite of you, but they are not different from you. They do the opposite of what you do, but as far as the property of the mind is concerned, the sadhu is not one iota different from you.

Natural freedom is something quite different. Natural freedom means: I am the master. Now there is no question of obeying or disobeying the mind. It is no longer a question of being for or against. Now I give orders to the mind. There are two ways of obeying the mind: to accept its orders or to go against them. In both cases you are a slave to the mind.

When the mind becomes the master, its ownership can be of two kinds: positive or negative. If you want you can be a householder, a worldly man; if you want you can become a sadhu. There is no difference. Sadhus are the opposite of you. You stand on your feet; they stand on their heads. They have more difficulty, because it is easier to stand on your legs than on your head. Sadhus do exactly the opposite of the home: you love wealth, he renounces it; you take care of your body, he neglects it; you live on a soft bed, he lies on rocks; you enjoy good food, he fasts; you wear fine clothes, he goes naked. This is not natural freedom. It is a state of tension.

That is why the sutra says: ***through control of the mind, reality is attained.*** This leads to natural freedom. Then you are free. Then you don't seek the guidance of the mind. Then your actions become natural. Then it is you who decides, and the mind merely follows you. But this happens only when you become the master, and you can only become the master if you have become the witness.

Do not fight against the mind. If you fight, you will not get natural freedom. If you fight, you give the mind an equal status. You fight against a person only when you consider him your equal. Before he was a friend, now he is an enemy. The master is not an equal; the master is always above - in the heavens, and the servant is always below - on the ground. When you are a master you acquire the freedom that is natural, and this freedom is unique.

I have heard: There was a Muslim fakir, Bayazid, who undertook the holy pilgrimage to Mecca with a hundred of his disciples. They fasted along the way. He was a well-known and respected scholar. On his way he stopped in a village. All the people came running to meet him. They informed him that a devotee of his who lived in the village had invited the whole village to a feast in honour of his arrival. This man was very poor. He had sold his hut, his cattle and his land to celebrate Bayazid's visit to the village.

Bayazid and his disciples had decided to fast for forty days, of which only five days had elapsed. They decided not to break the fast until the journey was completed. Bayazid seemed unperturbed, but all the disciples became very tense. Bayazid went and sat down to fast, so the disciples had to sit down too. Had Bayazid forgotten that they were fasting, or had he succumbed to the savoury smells of the food?

They had to sit down and eat, for they had to follow their master, but they were very unhappy.

And there Bayazid was, eating copiously without a trace of guilt or tension. When everyone else went to sleep, the disciples cornered him and demanded an explanation. They expressed their displeasure that he had broken his fast.

Bayazid said to them: "Why are you so upset, have you not seen with what love the poor man prepared the feast? For that love it was good to break your fast. Besides, fasts can be broken and resumed again, but a heart in love should not be broken so easily. If he had broken his heart there would be no way to mend it. And what did it matter that we had broken the fast? We had decided to fast for forty days. We will start again and fast for forty-five days!

This is the difference. The freedom of the disciple was not natural. They were concerned that Bayazid had surrendered to the mind and that they had been taught to obey the mind. This was slavery to the mind!

Bayazid was his own master. It was his own decision to break the fast or to keep it; the mind had nothing to do with it. Moreover, there was no hostility or opposition to his mind, nor vice versa.

his attitude was: 'I am the master. If I wish to keep the fast, I will; if not, I will not. The decision is entirely mine.

Both the master and the disciples were fasting, but there was a world of difference in their attitudes.

Bayazid's freedom is natural. He can stay in one place and be completely relaxed, or he can stay in a hut and be completely at ease. But his disciples would be uneasy if they had to stay in a palace, for that would be gratification of the senses.

This is very interesting. Sometimes you are caught in a palace, and sometimes in a hut; but you are always in the clutches of one or the other; but nothing can stand in the way of Bayazid, for his decision comes from his own soul. His freedom is natural. The soul is the criterion.

Natural freedom only arises when reality is the inner result. All other freedoms prior to this are false freedoms.

***And spontaneous freedom springs from this.***

*Thanks to this freedom, it moves freely indoors and outdoors.*

This is a priceless sutra: *thanks to this freedom, it moves freely in and out.*

Kabir never gave up his trade as a weaver. It doesn't suit you now. You are no longer the head of the family. It's no longer good for you to weave cloth and go to the market to sell it.

Kabir laughed and said: "Everything is His game. Inside and outside are one.

We cannot understand it, because we are so trapped by the outside world that the inside and the outside can never be one for us.

Zen masters have said: "Samsara and moksha are one: the world and liberation are one and the same thing". We are shocked by this. How can this be? We are caught in the clutches of the world, we are tormented by the world. Liberation is exactly the opposite: it is where we will be free, calm, blissful, where there is no pain. In our mind, liberation is opposed to the world, but when a person is liberated he finds nothing opposing or conflicting in this world. All conflicts and oppositions cease, all distances between inside and outside vanish, because all distances are created by the ego.

What is inside and what is outside, all is one! But the ego gets in the way like a wall and creates the differences. If we were to get into the river with a vessel and fill the vessel with the water of the river, we could say that there is water inside the vessel and water outside the vessel; but what is the difference? Simply a wall of clay! What happens when this wall is broken? So what is outside and what is inside? What is inside is outside; what is outside is inside.

That is why Kabir says: "When I sit and when I stand that is my worship. When I walk that is my prayer.

Now Kabir no longer goes to the temple, for there is no distance between the tent and the temple; they are one and the same. Now Kabir does not flee to the Himalayas, for there is no difference between the market and the mountains. Kabir does not even give up the house, for he sees no difference between "mine" and "yours". So what should he flee from?

All distances fall when the ego falls. Then there is nothing inside and nothing outside. Then there is neither matter nor God; then both are one. That is non-duality, the indivisible, where all is one and all boundaries fall, but this can only happen when natural freedom enters one's life. Then that person, because of his independent nature, can go out into the world and, remaining in the world, can also live within himself. For him there are no obstacles. Inside a palace he is as much a sannyasin as outside in the street. If he has a million rupees, he is still not possessive, he is not an owner; and if he has nothing, he is still the greatest of possessors, for all the world is at his command.

However, it is very difficult for us to recognise it, because we only know one side of existence. You affirm the difference between the water outside and the water inside the vessel. What is hidden inside you is what is outside you. The space inside is the space outside. Your body is the clay vessel that creates this slight difference.

Samsara, the world, and sannyas are not two things. They seem to be two, because you know only one of them: the world; you don't know sannyas. That is why you think of sannyas in terms of the world.

Your concept of sannyas arises from your concept of the world; that is why you call him a sannyasin who is the complete opposite of a worldly man. You say: Look! What a great sannyasin. He goes barefoot! He remains naked, standing in the sun and rain, and sleeps on the grass.

You can never think of a sannyasin in any other terms. King Janak can never be a sannyasin for you.

How can it be? He lives in a place. Krishna cannot be a sannyasin for you. How can he be? He wears his peacock crown and plays the flute. No! For you they cannot be sannyasins.

When your bondage to the mind ends and the essence within you is released, you will come to know that liberation is everywhere. Then the tent will no longer be a hindrance nor the palace an obstacle.

For liberation is the state of your experience. When you attain salvation, the world no longer exists; then there is no inside and outside. All is one! Then worship and work are the same. Then a person accepts life as it comes, as it is. There is no need to make the slightest change. Thus, even the butchers have attained supreme knowledge. It has also happened that the sannyasin who runs away from the world swims.

This sutra has an intrinsic meaning: *because of this freedom, he moves freely in and out.* It is now free. He is beyond definition. If you try to define him, you will never know him. Now he is beyond all explanations, he has no goals. It is difficult to know where you will find him; he can be anywhere.

It happened once that one of Buddha's monks was passing through a village. The village courtesan saw him by chance and immediately fell in love with him. The monk was young and handsome; moreover, he had the unique beauty that only a monk can have, which cannot belong to the ordinary man. He who renounces everything is filled with a certain inner light. He who has abandoned all that is meaningless finds flowers of meaning blooming within him. His life is filled with a grandeur, a dignity, which is not seen in ordinary life.

It was only natural that the courtesan should fall in love with such a blissful dancing monk. The woman was very beautiful and many had tried to win her favours; even kings were knocking at her door. She was not within everyone's reach. She came running to the monk and said: "Please, sir, I beg you to be my guest during this rainy season.

The monk said, "I will ask my guru and do what he orders me to do". Notice that he did not say yes or no, but promised to ask his guru. The next morning, the monk went to the Buddha and said, "I have received an invitation to stay with a prostitute. What should I do?"

Buddha replied, "If the prostitute was not afraid of you, why should you be afraid of her? Is my sannyasin so weak that a prostitute can frighten him? Go on! Accept the invitation. Stay with her during the rainy season".

There was great commotion among the rest of the monks. Many of them had taken notice of the beautiful courtesan. Many of them were filled with desire for her, how they wished she had invited them instead!

A monk stood up and said, "This is not right. A sannyasin staying with a harlot? That is not right. There is every chance that he will fall.

Buddha replied, "If you had received the invitation, you would not have obtained my permission, for there is a possibility that you may become defiled; even differences between the inner and the outer. The one I send, I know well. Whether he stays inside or outside makes no difference to him".

The monks were not convinced. They said to the Buddha, "You are making a mistake. You are setting a wrong precedent. All the rules of propriety are at stake".

Every day the monks brought alarming news of their activities.

Some said they saw him watching her dance. Others said he was sitting on velvet cushions. Others said he was dressed in beautiful clothes. Others swore they saw him embracing the prostitute.

To all this Buddha would say: "What until the rains are over. What is the hurry? Why are you bringing this rum of ours? What do you have to do with them? It is not you who is getting polluted. The one who is will come back after the rains".

After the rains, the monk returned with the courtesan walking behind him. She bowed to the Buddha and said, "Please do sannyasin for me. The monk has won. I have lost. I did everything I could. He did not object to anything. He did not move when I hugged him. When I made him sit on a velvet cushion, he did not object, saying it was forbidden for a monk. I gave him the best of meals, and he never complained that it was against his principles, that it might arouse desires in him.

I offered him all kinds of invitations and he never said no; he remained quiet and unperturbed in all situations, as if nothing had happened. I am immensely touched by his behaviour. I want to acquire the same bliss he enjoys. I want to be in the same state he is in, where the inside and the outside don't matter: a bliss that nothing can destroy."

Buddha thus addressed the other monks "Look! He whose inside and outside no longer exist, makes a sannyasin of a prostitute. If you had stayed with her, you would have become her shadow".

The good that fears evil is worthless. The sadhu fears the sinner; the true saint does not.

The saint is beyond both. The saint is one whom no circumstance can change. Remaining in the outer world, he is firmly established in himself. The world cannot penetrate him, even if he chooses to remain in the world.

Buddha said: "The highest state of sannyas is when you cross a river but the water does not touch your feet. If you are afraid of the river for fear of getting your feet wet, that is not the highest state; it is a state of fear.

You must keep these sutras in mind. You have to break the dominance of the mind. This happens with the witnessing state, which creates the difference between the mind and you.

You have to assert your own mastery, not through hostility, but by rising above the mind. Independence will come. If it comes through opposition it is a false freedom; there will be tension and anguish. It will not be sarian or spontaneous. In religion there is no place for a warrior. In religion you have only to rise. Do not fight, for you will stagnate at that level. Don't be at enmity with your mind; you have to go beyond it, transcend it.

The key to going beyond the mind is the ability to witness. As you rise, spontaneous freedom arises. This freedom is not against anyone or anything. In such freedom you reach a state where, whether you live inside or outside yourself, there is no difference, for distances have fallen; there is no inside or outside. Samsara and moksha, the world and liberation, are one. All dualities have ended. All dichotomy is gone. You have attained the non-dual, non-dichotomous state.

# Meditation is the seed

*Bijavdhanam asnasthah sukham hridae nimajjati svamatra nirmanapadayati vidya-avinashe janmavinashah.*

*Meditation is the seed.*

*Simply sitting, relaxed in himself, he spontaneously enters the lake of the supreme being.*

*It achieves self-creation or becomes "twice-born".*

*Eternal knowledge leads to the cessation of birth and death.*

Jesus' disciples said to him, "Tell us about the Kingdom of God". Jesus answered: "The Kingdom of God is like a seed". In our discussion today we will talk about this very seed that Jesus is talking about.

Meditation is that seed. The seed itself has no meaning. The seed is only a means; it is a potential tree. The seed is not a state of being; it is a stage on the path. When the seed grows into a tree, it reaches the goal. It blossoms and bears fruit. This is its success. In the same way, when the seed of meditation becomes a tree, it also blossoms and bears fruit, and that blossoming is God.

It is necessary to understand the state of the seed. You constantly ask about God, but this is a futile enquiry. Why do you ask about the tree if you have not cared for the seed? Without planting the seed, how do you expect to see the tree? And God is not an external event that you can see with your eyes. God is your own purified state; God is your own development. You will not be able to see God in others until the hidden seed within you sprouts and becomes the tree.

Try as they may, no Mahavir, Buddha, Shiva or Krishna can reveal God to you, for your God is hidden within yourself. At present it is in the form of a seed; it is not yet a tree. You cannot see anything in a seed. When the seed bursts and the tree sprouts, when it develops, it will manifest. The flame within you will be lit, and then you will know that God is.

It is difficult to beat an atheist for this very reason. He always asks: "Where is your God? Show me. His very question is wrong, so any answer given to him will also be wrong. God hides with you. He hides inside the questioner. And you cannot see the God of the other, for it is an inner happening. When your own seed sprouts you will know.

Right now you are like the seed, but you don't understand this seed, so you look outside. As long as you look outside, your seed will remain dormant; it will not sprout, because it needs water and soil.

It needs light and love, just like a small child. When you turn your eyes inward, when your attention flows inward and your life energy is directed inward, the seed will receive that energy; it will come alive, it will sprout. ***Meditation is the seed.***

People come to me and say, "We are restless, how can we calm down?

Mulla Nasruddin came to see me early one morning. I was about to say something when he blurted out a question. "You have to help me," said the Mulla.

"What's the problem?" I asked.

"It is a very complex problem," said Mulla. "I have a strong desire to bathe ten to twenty times a day. This obsession is driving me crazy. I can't think of anything else. Please help me.

"When did you last bathe? I asked.

"As far as I can remember, I have never given in to this annoying practice," Mulla said.

If you refuse to bathe and if the desire to bathe overtakes you, then the desire is not the problem; the problem is you. You are restless. You don't know. You have never meditated. You have never indulged in this annoying practice, and you want to eradicate your restlessness? It can never be eradicated without bathing in meditation.

Meditation is an inner bath. Just as the body is freed from dust and dirt, and becomes clean and fresh after a bath, so meditation is a bath of the inner soul; and when everything becomes fresh within, where is the agitation? Where is the sorrow and the worry? Then you are thrilled. You are joyful and blooming. You have bells on your ankles and your life becomes a dance. Before you are sad, tired and distressed. And if you think the cause of your distress is outside, you are wrong.

There is only one cause for your restlessness: you have not let your seed of meditation grow into a tree. No matter how hard you try, you will remain restless. You may imagine that peace will come if you accumulate the right things: wealth, status, honour, honour, health, sons and daughters... but there is no end to your restlessness. The more of these things you accumulate, the more your life will be filled with restlessness, and the more intense it will become.

A poor man is restless, a rich man more so! Why is it so, why does restlessness increase with wealth? It is not so. The poor man is restless too, but he has not time enough to realise it. The rich man has time to notice; it pricks him like a thorn, and he sees it all around him.

When you have satisfied all your needs, you will suddenly realise that the real need is meditation. All other needs were for the body, not for your self.

This sutra says: *meditation is the seed.*

In your great journey, in your quest for life, in your pilgrimage to the temple of truth, meditation is the seed. What is meditation? Why is it so precious? So precious that if it blossoms you will become God, and if it rots you will rot in hell? What is meditation? Meditation is the state of thoughtless awareness, in which you are fully conscious but thoughts are absent. You are, but the mind is not.

The death of the mind is meditation.

At present, you are not. There is the mind and only the mind. It should be just the opposite: there should be only you, without any mind. Right now the mind consumes all your energy. All your life energy is being absorbed by the mind.

Have you ever seen the air plant, the amar-bel? It is a parasite that attaches itself to a tree and lives off it, sucking its energy. In the end, the tree withers and dies. It is called amar-bel, the immortal vine. It is just like the mind. It has no roots. It doesn't need roots, because it lives off the mother plant. It sucks the tree dry while it nourishes itself. The Hindus have given it an appropriate name, the immortal creeper.

Your mind is also an immortal vine. It does not die. It lives indefinitely. It follows you for countless lifetimes. The interesting thing is that it has no roots, no seeds. Its existence is rootless. It should be dead, but it lives in you.

Your mind envelops you. You are completely suffocated by it. All your vital energy is absorbed by the mind. You are almost dry. Your mind allows you to have just enough to keep you alive. The parasite does not completely kill its host, but allows it to retain just enough for its most basic needs. A master treats his slave in a similar way: the slave is given just enough to keep him alive.

Your mind gives you just enough to allow you to survive. It gobbles up ninety-nine percent of your energy and allows you only one percent so that you can maintain the body. In a non-meditative state, the mind is ninety-nine percent and you are one percent; in a meditative individual, the individual is ninety-nine percent and the mind is only one percent. If you become one hundred percent and the mind is zero, that is the state of samadhi.

Then you will be completely liberated; the seed will have developed into a full-grown tree. There is nothing left to achieve. All that was to be achieved has been achieved. All potentiality has become reality; all that was hidden has become manifest. Then existence is filled with your fragrance; then the music of your dance is heard in every corner of the earth, and even far away, in the moon and the stars. It is not that you alone are thrilled: the vital current of all existence throbs in you. Then existence is filled with celebration. Every time a Buddha is born, all existence celebrates.

All existence longs to see your seed grow into a spreading tree.

Meditation means: where the mind is as if disappeared. Samadhi means: where the mind is completely empty and only you remain.

This Shiva sutra says: ***meditation is the seed.***

That is why we have to start with meditation. Right now, in sleep and in wakefulness, in consciousness and in unconsciousness, the mind has you in its clutches. Thoughts invade you by day and dreams by night. Twenty-four hours a day the mind argues and debates, and the most surprising thing is that it all leads to nothing. What have you achieved with all your reasoning and thinking?

Where has it taken you? What goals have you achieved?

The great philosopher Immanuel Kant was returning home one evening when a little boy stopped him on the road and said: "Good evening, uncle. I have just been to your house. Tomorrow we are going on a picnic with some of the boys and I came to borrow your camera. As you weren't there, I asked your servant for it.

Is it all right, uncle, for a servant to say 'no' like that? The boy was boiling with rage.

Kant said: "Certainly, the servant was not right; who is he to refuse when I am here? Come with me.

The boy was happy. They arrived at Kant's house. They called the servant and reprimanded him in front of the child. Then Kant turned to the boy and said: "Now I will tell you. The fact is that I have no camera. All the joy, the excitement, the hope that the boy nurtured of getting the camera, vanished into thin air when he learned that his uncle did not even own one.

This is the state of your mind. All your life you strive, you slave, you groan with the burden you carry because you still have hope. In the end, the mind will admit that it does not possess what you seek.

It has always been like that. It does not possess what you really seek, but it holds out hope:

"Maybe today, or tomorrow... tomorrow.

No one can offer you such seductive wooing as the mind. And you are a fool. If the mind had something to give, it would have given it by now. The fact is that it keeps on giving you the runaround and you keep on believing it. How many times have you believed the mind? Every day it says, "Tomorrow", and when tomorrow comes the mind again says, "Tomorrow". Now it has become your unconscious habit, and the habit has become so ingrained that you hardly think about it. Even while you sleep, the mind seduces you with new assurances about the future.

Mulla Nasruddin was in bed with a very high fever. I went to see him. I asked his wife how long he had been in this state. The wife said: "He has had a fever of 40 degrees for an hour".

The Mulla was unconscious. I put a thermometer in his mouth to see what his temperature was. Instantly he said: "A match, please! He was a heavy smoker and the habit was so ingrained that even in that unconscious state the thermometer reminded him of a cigarette.

And when you die your state will be exactly like that of the Mulla. "Your mind continues to weave its webs even in your unconsciousness. At the time of death you will be full of the mind. Whether you worship or pray or go to the temple or the holy places... the mind is with you and as long as the mind is with you, you will not be able to establish contact with religion.

There lived a Muslim fakir named Haji Mohammed. He was a sadhu. One night he dreamt that he had died and was at the crossroads between heaven and hell. One path led to the world and the other to moksha. At the crossroads there was an angel who guided and directed people according to their actions.

Haji Mohammed had nothing to fear. All his life he had been a good and pious man. He prayed five times a day and had performed the holy pilgrimage, the Haj, sixty times. In fact, that is why he was known as "Haji" Mohammed. When his turn came, he stood bare-chested before the angel.

"Hayy Mohammed," called the angel.

"Yes," Haji said.

"This is the road to hell," said the angel pointing to a road.

"I'm sure there's some mistake," Haji said. "Maybe your account books are mixed up. I have been to the Haj sixty times during my life on earth."

"All that has gone to waste," said the angel, "for you made it a matter of prestige and started calling yourself 'haji'. You have already reaped the benefits of your haj. What else have you done?"

Now the Haji was not so sure of himself. When sixty pilgrimages counted for nothing, what more did he have to prove? Nevertheless, he persisted: "I have religiously recited my prayers five times a day".

That too was fruitless," said the angel, "for you; you prayed louder and longer when there were people, and little when there were none. Your attention was on people, not on God. You wanted to be known as a religious man, a pious man. Do you have anything else to prove?"

The Haji was now so terrified that he woke up! This dream changed his life. He became the simple Mohammed of Haji Mohammed; he also began to pray in secret so that no one would know.

Word spread through the village that the Haji was no longer religious. He had even stopped praying. Thus he reached old age. The Haji never refuted what people said. His prayers began to make sense and to be sincere. It is said that it was not difficult for him to reach heaven.

If your mind prays, it will not allow prayer to take place. It will make prayer another way to fill its ego. Do not talk about your meditation. Hide your meditation as you would hide your precious jewels.

You always protect your valuables from the gaze of others: do the same with meditation. Don't talk about it, don't fill your ego with it, or the creeper of the mind will also get there and suck it in.

Where the mind reaches, there is no religion. Where the mind is not, there is religion. The mind is always outgoing, extraverted; its attention is on the other, and not on itself. Meditation is introverted. It is introverted.

Meditation means: attention is focused on oneself and not on the other. Mindfulness means that attention is focused on the other. Observe yourself: when you give a two paise coin to a beggar you look around to see whether people are looking at you or not. When you build a temple, you take care to inscribe your name in bold letters on a marble slab right at the entrance. You give to charity, but you see to it that it is mentioned in the newspapers. Everything you do is in vain. You can't get there by becoming a "Haji".

Muhammad. Do not keep track of your fasts and austerities. The kingdom of God is not a place of business. God is not impressed by your balance sheet.

Now look at the Jain munis. Every year they announce in writing how many vows they have taken, how many fasts they have observed in the rainy season. They keep a record of it all. They are shopkeepers who happen to occupy our temples; they have not yet got out of the habit of keeping accounts. All their fasts and meditations are spoiled; they are becoming "Haji" Mohammeds.

Don't worry about the outside world; don't worry about whether people know that you are religious or not. What others say is unimportant and not worth thinking about, for it is your mind that relates to others, not you. The day the mind disappears, you will disassociate yourself from everyone. It is the mind that binds you. As long as the mind binds you to the world, you will remain detached from God. The day you divorce yourself from the mind, the mind annihilated, you will be united with God. You disengage on the one hand, while you begin to associate on the other. You break relationships here, you establish relationships there. Once your eyes are closed here, they are opened there.

*Meditation is the seed*, and meditation means: thoughtless awareness.

Now for the second sutra:

*Simply sitting, relaxed in himself, he spontaneously enters the lake of the supreme being.*

This sutra is very revolutionary. It is easy and also difficult. The individual, once truly established in himself, drowns in the lake of the supreme being.

If you were to ask the Zen Buddhists in Japan what you should do to meditate, they would say, "Do nothing! Now, remember that when they say do nothing, they mean that you don't have to do anything at all - just sit - because if you do something, the mind is immediately activated. At first glance it looks very easy, but in reality it is very difficult to sit. That's the problem:

You sit with your eyes closed and your mind starts to race. Your body seems quite still sitting motionless, but in your mind there is a great commotion.

If you sit and do nothing, that is meditation. If you just sit and do nothing, there is no Ram-Ram, no Krishna-Krishna, no thought-wave, because that is also an activity. If you simply do nothing, if you do not even try to stop the thoughts - for you can do it only with another thought - if you do not repeat the name of God or remember the world, if you do not say "I am the soul" or "I am Brahma", for such repetitions are also of no use, they are mere thoughts, if you sit, like a rock, with nothing happening inside or outside, then you are *"simply sitting"*. This state is called "zazen" in Japan: just sitting. Zen masters use this method. It takes twenty or thirty years for the disciple to reach this state of just sitting.

This seemingly easy sutra is very difficult. The easiest things are the most difficult things in the world. If you are told to climb the Himalayas, it will not seem so difficult. You may get tired, you may face difficulties, but still you will climb; but as soon as you try to do nothing, it will seem to you that a great calamity has befallen you.

What happens when you sit quietly? You notice that, as soon as you sit down, all kinds of movements occur in different parts of your body. You feel needles pricking your feet, you feel itching somewhere else; suddenly you feel a pain in your neck or back. A moment before you didn't feel any of this, you were absolutely fine. Suddenly, your body rebels and tells you to do something; even if you have been able to ignore everything else, you feel compelled to change your position.

Life is sustained by action in this mundane world. When you begin to empty yourself of action, the world is lost. As soon as you try to be still, the body pushes you into one activity or another.

People come to me and complain: "We don't suffer from aches and pains, but as soon as we start meditating, all sorts of discomforts start. You feel like coughing when there is no reason to. You are the teacher, and if you don't listen to the body, it will calm down, for how long can it remain agitated?

It is the attention you pay to it that acts as its nourishment. You must firmly tell the body Whatever happens, I am not going to do anything during this hour. Are you itching? So what? What harm is it going to do to you?

Have you noticed that if you don't scratch for a minute or two, the itching stops on its own? The itching sensation never goes away when you scratch, but increases. If you have firmly resolved that you are the master and not the body, you will find that your throat has calmed down: there is no coughing. However, you will have to assert your mastery for a few days. For too long you have allowed the slave to lord it over you, so when you begin to rob it of its power it is sure to rebel and defy you.

You've decided to sit still for an hour - what's the worst that can happen? Your feet go numb...

All right, let them! They feel itchy... So what! It's not a matter of life and death. You'll find that if you stick to your resolution, your feet will stop being numb. This was nothing but a ploy of the body to frustrate your purpose. If you had heeded the feet, your hands would have clamoured for attention, then your neck and so on; but if you ignore the feet, the itch will subside once and for all. A beggar does not beg for long in front of an empty house, but if you make the mistake of saying, "There is no one here. Go somewhere else", he won't budge from your door. Once you have answered, he is sure to say something.

A beggar asked for alms in front of the house of a miserly marwari. What a wrong place! He knocked and asked for a loaf of bread.

"There is no bread here," replied the marwari.

"Then give me a paisa or two," the beggar shouted.

"There is no money here.

"Well, old clothes!"

"Didn't I say there is nothing here?" the Marwari shouted.

"Then why do you stay here," the beggar replied. "Why don't you join me and we can go begging together.

One answer and you are trapped. Your answer means yes, and you are willing. At least you're responding. That's enough. You feel itchy! Just observe it and do nothing, don't react. In a short time you will be surprised to find that the sensation has disappeared. When you feel pain, watch it and it will go away. It takes about six months to get the body to "just feel" like this. Choose any posture in which you feel comfortable. Don't choose an inappropriate posture that might give you problems. That's why I say choose a comfortable and easy posture. Don't adopt an uncomfortable posture that tortures the body unnecessarily. You don't have to sit on pebbles or thorns. As it is, the body will give you enough trouble: don't increase your pains.

Sit in an easy posture and make up your mind to sit like that for an hour. Then do not listen to the body at all. If you zealously keep your resolution and do not yield to the body, in three weeks you will find that the body ceases to agitate. Then, when the body stops disturbing you, turn to the mind.

Don't worry about the mind at all in the beginning. You have to make the body stand still before you fight with the mind. The day you find that the body has become passive and no longer gives you trouble, that it is now ready to be still, know that half the journey is over. In fact, more than half the journey is over, because the mind is also part of the body, and if the body has been subdued, the mind cannot hold out for long. If the whole body has been trained to accept a certain posture, this part of the body cannot wander for long; it will also have to settle down.

To stabilise the body, to bring it into a certain posture, means to stop all the turbulences and disturbances in the body. Now you sit as if you have no body, as if you have no body. Now you are aware of the body: you are just sitting.

Next, concentrate on the mind. The method is the same: don't do anything the mind says.

Don't react to them. Observe the thoughts with an indifferent attitude, as if you had nothing to do with them, as if you were witnessing someone else's thoughts while standing on the sidelines, as if you were watching a rioting mob on the road, as if you were watching the clouds pass in the sky.

Observe with indifference. Be absolutely neutral.

First let the body calm down. This state comes gradually over the course of three weeks. The mind takes about three months. It may be a little more or a little less. It all depends on your seriousness and sincerity of purpose, but in a period of six months this state of "just sitting" can be reached. Now neither the body indulges in activities nor the mind.

Don't fight the mind. Do not repress it. Do not command it not to think, for remember that this too is thinking. Even this thinking can keep the mind moving. The mind will cause great chaos, but don't fight it. Your reactions will show that you are still willing to yield to it, that you have not succeeded in ignoring it.

Indifference is the key. Just observe. Don't say anything. It's going to be difficult, because the habits are old and deep-rooted. You have always been in the habit of talking to the mind, of talking back. Gradually, if you persist, you will come to a stage where, by constant observation, there is only you and nothing happens, neither in the body nor in the mind. When all the activities of mind and body are stilled, that state is called the state of "just sitting".

Here the word "posture" does not mean some intricate yoga posture. If you do yoga asanas it will be useful, for it will give you the strength to sit for a longer time, but this is not necessary. If you learn simply to sit, that is the supreme asana. You don't need to sit on the floor either; you can even sit on a chair. There is only one thing to remember: you have to keep the same posture for the whole given period.

Sit comfortably so that the body has no reason to complain. Take all necessary measures to keep the body comfortable: if it is cold, bring a blanket; if it is hot, turn on the fan. Be prepared for the body's comfort. Do not indulge in torturing the body, for that is nothing but cruelty Whether you torture another body or your own, both are acts of violence, and no one has ever attained God by violence. This body is also His, there is no need to torture it. When you have sat down, do not listen to the demands of the body. Remain seated. Ignore the mind, be indifferent towards it. It will create chaos, indulge in all kinds of rampages, perhaps more than ever.

People come to me and say, "When I wasn't meditating, my mind was never so restless. Now it is a hundred times more restless than before. Now there is so much noise and turmoil". It has always been like that, only you were not aware of it, because your mind was always outside you. You were so caught up in the outside world that you were not aware of the turmoil within. The fact that you sit in silence does not create it. In fact, when you are quiet, this chaos can only subside. It is impossible for it to increase. But you were so involved in the outside world, in your home, your family, your business, your wealth, that you couldn't hear what was going on inside. Now that you have closed your eyes to the outside world, all your attention has gone within, all the focus, all the light is now concentrated within. Then, in this first experience, when the light falls inside, you discover the chaos that reigns there.

But remember: be indifferent! You have to remember one thing: don't put anything out of your mind. If you cling to the slightest hope you will not be able to disengage yourself from the mind. Abandon all desires; nourish no hopes and sit in total indifference; be neutral and impartial. Difficult as it may be at first, it will become easier if you persist. Don't worry about time - today, tomorrow or the day after tomorrow - don't worry about when you will arrive, for the greater the hurry the more you will be delayed. To hurry is the nature of the mind. If you hurry, the mind will beat you. If you are patient and not in a hurry, if you are willing to wait for the event when it comes, you will find that in six months the mind becomes calm.

The state of "just sitting" means that there is no activity in the body, no thought in the mind. This Shiva sutra is revolutionary. It says that the moment you attain the state of "just sitting" you find yourself bathed in the lake of the supreme being. That lake is within you.

When all movements of the body are stopped, energy cannot come out. When all activities of the mind are stopped, all energy outlets are sealed. For the first time the bucket of your mind has no holes in it. Now there is nothing flowing out. All the vital energy flows inside, and inside is the great lake. This energy flowing within you then meets the supreme lake. You - your drop - beings to drown in the ocean. Then there is a natural bathing in the supreme lake. And that is God Himself.

When you go outwards, you wander. When you go inwards, the goal is reached. You seek outside what is hidden inside you. In reality, what you seek is you, yourself, and that is why the search never succeeds. What you seek remains forever hidden within you. That is the difficulty.

That is the complexity of the whole thing, for you never look there. Wherever you look, He is not there, and so you wander and wander endlessly.

One night, Mulla Nasruddin was in the street with a lamp looking for something. He was frantic.

Darkness was approaching and his friends offered to help him.

"What are you looking for?" they asked.

"I have lost my needle," said Mulla.

After a while, one of them said: "Mulla, where exactly did you drop the needle? The road is so wide and the needle is so small.

Nasruddin said: "Don't ask that question. It's a sore point.

The friends were perplexed. "What do you mean?" they asked.

Nasruddin said: "The needle is lost in the house, but inside there is no light. It is so dark, so terribly dark that I am afraid to go inside even in the daytime. That's why I look outside.

"Have you gone mad, Mulla?" they exclaimed. "How can you find outside what was lost inside?".

Nasruddin burst out laughing. "Everyone does the same thing!" he exclaimed. "What is lost inside we look for outside, and no one else is considered crazy, only me!".

What are you looking for? Surely you seek something, but what is it? If we were to find the sum total of all our quests, we would discover that what we seek is bliss. Some people seek wealth, but in reality they seek bliss; some seek love, but in reality they seek bliss; some seek honour, but in reality they seek bliss; some seek fame, but in reality they seek bliss. In essence, all seek bliss. Your quests may have different names, but the deeper meaning is one and only one: bliss! You seek bliss whether your feet point towards the tavern or the temple. Whether a man acts out of sin or virtue, whether he commits a good deed or an evil one, he is seeking bliss.

Have you ever wondered where the joy was lost? Look in the place where you lost it. Look in places other than where you left it. You certainly didn't lose it somewhere outside. It was an inner taste, a taste you know well.

Psychologists have made a significant claim. They say that the child is in a most blissful state in the womb. And so it should be. It has no worries, no responsibilities, no anxiety about food or the weather. The temperature in the womb is constant. It makes no difference to the child whether it is scorching hot or bitterly cold outside. It is not affected if the mother is hungry or under emotional or physical stress. The child is totally protected. It simply floats in the womb.

You have surely seen the image of Lord Vishnu floating in a sea of milk. So it is with a child in the womb. This image of Vishnu symbolises the blissful state of rest enjoyed by a child in the womb. From Vishnu's navel sprouts a flower. This represents the umbilical cord that binds the child to the mother. That is the source of its life. Just as there is water in the ocean, there is water in the mother's womb; even the proportion of salt is the same. That is why the mother feels the urge to eat salty things, because the salt in her body is absorbed by the womb.

The child floats in this water inside the mother's womb. It is in complete bliss. It knows no worries:

Before he is hungry, he feeds himself. It does not need to cry. He doesn't even need to breathe; the mother breathes for him. The child is attached to the mother. It is not yet separate. It has no ego: it is not aware that "I am". The fact is: the child is, but it is completely bathed in existence, and the bliss of this condition is the bliss it seeks throughout its life.

Psychologists say that your lifelong search is an attempt to regain your mother's womb. We devise a thousand and one ways to regain this bliss. If you look closely, you will observe this fact. You try to find a comfortable bed to sleep in; a comfortable bed is one in which the temperature is about the same as that of a child snuggled up to its mother. People who sleep well do so in this position; they are babies again.

All your efforts are directed towards freeing yourself from your responsibilities and worries. You are trying to become rich, for if you are rich you can use your wealth as a means of dissolving your worries about the future.

You seek friendship, you seek love and protection. Alone, you are afraid, because all around you are enemies, unknown and unfamiliar. You make a house for yourself and feel safe within its four walls; look closely and you will see that it is an attempt to create a womb within which you can feel safe.

The child experiences bliss in the mother's womb. All children experience it. Then he spends his whole life searching for the same bliss. That is why, whenever he catches a glimpse of this bliss, he feels happy.

All your moments of happiness are glimpses of bliss. Psychologists say that the search for liberation is a search for the womb. The day when this whole existence becomes a womb for you, when you are completely drowned in it, when your ego is completely annihilated and you have no worries, no anxiety, you will attain this bliss again. This bliss is within you, but you have lost it; and as you seek it outside you, you do not find it.

In the state of "just sitting", in the state of meditation, your own body becomes a womb for you. In this state, when all activities are stilled, when all thoughts are lost, your mind and body become the circumference and you re-enter the womb. That is why we call a meditative person "DVIJ", which means twice-born. There is one birth where you pass through your mother's womb; this is the birth you get through your parents. And there is a second birth in which you have to give birth to yourself. This birth is the one that makes you a dvij.

In the state of "just sitting", a person naturally bathes in the lake of the supreme being. And bathing in the ocean of awareness.... When the ocean of the body has given you so much pleasure, imagine how much more the ocean of consciousness can give you! It is more than your imagination can encompass, infinitely more. It has no limits. The bliss you tasted in your mother's womb was the bliss that comes from drowning in the body, but the bliss you will know when you sink into the soul, that is the real bliss. The Hindus have called it brahma. No taste can equal the taste of Brahma. It is sat-chit-ananda, truth-consciousness-bliss.

As soon as you drown in the ocean of consciousness you become dvij, for now the soul is born in you. In the present your soul is hidden within the seed. It is the present and it is not present; it is present as a seed, but not as a tree. You are still only a potential, a promise of becoming. You have not yet become the tree, and this is your problem; this is your anguish. This is what distresses and troubles you.

If you analyse all this anguish correctly, it is the pain of being born. As long as you are not born twice, dvij, this discomfort will persist. The one who undergoes the second birth finds that the first birth ceases for him, for now it is of no use to him; otherwise, you will be born, you will die, and you will be born again.

You will be reincarnated again and again, but when you are born twice it will not be necessary for you to return to the body again.

Those of the Brahmin caste are called "dvij", twice-born. It would be more appropriate to call a dvij a brahmin, for not all brahmins are dvij, but all dvijs are brahmins. No one truly becomes a brahmin merely by being born into a family of brahmins. He only becomes a brahmin when he dissolves in Brahma, when he is born of Brahma.

Hindus have a unique concept. Each of us is born in the lowest caste, the sudras, and only a few attain Brahma status. So, whatever caste the child is born into, by birth we are all sudras. The son of a Brahmin family is initiated with the sacred thread. This is only to make him aware that he is now a Brahmin and not a member of a lower caste. It is only a custom. To become a brahmin is not so easy as to do it by simply putting a thread around your neck. Becoming a brahmin is the most difficult process in the world; it only happens when a person is completely drowned in his soul.

The one who gives a new birth to his self, is born twice, dvij. He is now his own mother, his own father.

It has not been born through an external agency. His relations with the world have been broken. He is now united with Brahma.

This sutra says: ***meditation is the seed***. The one who attains the state of meditation, the one who simply sits, immerses himself in his self. Thus his soul is born. Now he is "twice born".

Put aside all second-rate methods, shun them. Don't be satisfied with the sacred thread around your body. Would that it were so cheap and easy to attain Brahma-ness, to become one with Brahma. But that's the way we are; we're always searching until we come up with some easy method of deluding ourselves. How long can we maintain this self-deception? All your sacred threads, all the devices you use to deceive yourself, destroy them! They give false hope. What you need is a real birth, and that will only happen when you become your own womb. You will need a body in a state of "just sitting" and a mind in a state of meditation. Together they form the womb within you.

Nicodemus asked Jesus, "When will I attain your kingdom of God? Jesus answered, "When you die and are born again". You have to end your life as it is, be dead to it, and be born again as you should be. Only then can you enter the Kingdom of God. Then the answer is clear: destroy the seed form and become the tree.

As you are, you are but a dream, a promise, a promise that one day God will emerge from within you, but He has not yet done so. Bury this possibility in the ground like a seed. What is the danger?

What is the fear? I can understand the seed's apprehension. It is afraid of extinction. Besides, it does not know the tree inside it. It has never come face to face with the tree. For the tree to sprout, the seed must die. Moreover, the seed is not sure whether, at its death, the immense tree will come into existence. All the seed can think is Whatever I am will be lost. And where is the certainty of reaching that immensity? Exactly that is your anxiety. You ask all the Buddhas and Mahavirs and Shivas this same question: "What if we lose what we have without gaining anything?

Fear is natural. That is why you are afraid to approach the master. If you don't experience this fear, the master is worthless; run away from him. The master frightens you because he is like death itself. It will destroy you. And while it is destroying you, the mind says, "Run away from here". When the mind gives you that signal of danger, don't run away! When the mind tells you to wait a little longer and enjoy the company of the master, then it is time to run away! When the mind is fearful, know that something is going to happen, for the seed is only afraid of extinction.

You do not fear the priests. You do not fear the temples. And the holy places - Kashi and Bodh Gaya, Gunar, Kaaba, Jerusalem -

you can wander in them without worrying, for there is no one there to threaten your existence. All places of pilgrimage, all holy places, are dead places, for life is not in the place, in the teertha, but in the tirthankara, the master. When the tirthankara is gone, a place of pilgrimage is built around him, for now the master is not feared. A dead master cannot destroy you, so the mind worships the dead master with much love. You worship Mahavir and Buddha, because you know with certainty that a stone statue cannot harm you. After all, it is you who bought it and you can throw it away whenever you want.

The Hindus are clever, they make their idols out of mud, because after worshipping them for two or three weeks they throw them into the river. One thing is certain: we make them and we break them. You worship if you feel like it; if you don't feel like it, you don't worship. Who is going to ask you to explain? All this is just a more sophisticated version of the games children play. They play with dolls: we play with statues of God.

When Mahavir, Rama and Krishna are no more, then they are worshipped. When such a person is alive, people flee in terror. People who are mortally afraid of a teacher think lovingly of visiting the holy places of pilgrimage. Crowds of thousands flock to the annual Kumbha Mela, the gathering of all holy men. Have people ever gathered in such numbers around Mahavir or Krishna? Never.

The Kumbha does not come to your door, you have to make the journey to the sacred bathing place where it takes place, but Mahavir and Buddha knock at your door. Unfortunately, they find the door closed, for they frighten us. They are dangerous. They say, "Die as a seed and become a tree!".

That is why trust and faith are necessary, they are priceless. If you listen to reason, it will say: "First make sure, what is the guarantee? Logic is always right. It says: "A bird in the hand is better than two in the bush".

This is correct in reason, for how can you part with what little you have for a promise of greater gains yet to come?

Mulla Nasruddin was eager to learn to swim. He met a teacher who told him: "Come, I am going to the river". It so happened that Mulla slipped as soon as he entered the water. He fell in and almost drowned. Somehow he managed to reach the shore, got out of the water and fled.

The teacher shouted at him: "Where are you going, don't you want to learn to swim?

"First teach me to swim," said the Mulla, "and then I'll go back to the river".

"That's almost impossible," said the teacher. "If you don't get in the water, you can't learn."

But the Mulla said: "I will never set foot in the river again, at least not in this life".

You too reason like Nasruddin, and your reasoning is correct. The Mulla will only go into the river if he can swim, for wasn't he nearly drowned? It was pure luck that he was found alive!

One day I saw Nasruddin teaching his wife to drive. He was standing on the side of the road, far away from his wife, who was sitting behind the wheel of the car. He shouted instructions: "Push in the clutch!

Shift gears!"

I watched him in intrigue. I approached him and asked: "Mulla, I have seen many people teach driving, but yours is a unique method! How can you teach someone from outside the car?

The Mulla replied: "The car is insured; I am not".

Logic always demands insurance; it wants a guarantee. The seed also demands a guarantee that it will become a tree, but how is the seed insured? Faith is invaluable. There is no way to insure it. Faith is a leap in the dark, that's why the faithful come and the logical ones don't. The mind deceives, it leads you astray. The mind deceives, it leads you astray; the heart leads you to the destination.

When you are in love you never listen to the mind. Even when you pray you cannot pray if you listen to the mind. If you listen to the mind, its logic always seems one hundred percent correct, but the end result is zero. The seed remains a seed; not only does it remain a seed, but it begins to rot.

Ask yourself this question: "Is what I have real?" What does a seed possess? Do not ask whether the tree will or will not be; instead, ask the seed what it has that it is so afraid of losing. This is what faith always asks. Faith says: "What do I have that I fear to lose?". There is nothing apart from anxiety, anguish and affliction. Why fear to lose them? Is there in you any bliss, any joy, so that you are afraid to lose it and be so much the poorer for it? You have nothing. You are like the naked man who would not bathe because he had nowhere to dry his clothes. He had no clothes, so there was no question of washing and drying them, but such anxieties take over the mind.

You have nothing to lose, absolutely nothing, and everything to gain. This is false. Truth always looks inward: "What have I got?" Logic always looks into the future: "What will happen?" Truth looks to the present.

People come to me and I tell them to switch to sannyas. They say, "Not now, in a year", as if I am taking something away from them. As if they need a whole year to gather the courage. They want to postpone it as if I want them to give up something. They have nothing; they possess nothing except misery, wretchedness and poverty. I want to give them the glory of sannyas. I do not want to take anything from them; rather, I want to give them something. For me, sannyas is not renunciation, but a door to supreme enjoyment. You become... you feel... like a king for the first time in your life when you take sannyas, but, alas, you consider your beggarly attitude as a treasure.

Whenever I tell someone to jump into sannyas they look at me as if I am taking something away from them. I am surprised. If I had something to lose, then I could understand. You have nothing! Not even rubbish! All that you have, all that you possess, is a Pandora's box full of scorpions and snakes of anxiety, suffering, anguish and all kinds of evils. Why you cling to all this is beyond my comprehension. What is the reason? The reason is simple: you do not look in this direction at all. You are always worried about what you will get.

People ask me: "What will we achieve by meditating? And that is the mistake they make. I want them to ask themselves what they have achieved without meditating. We cannot answer what will be achieved, because the future is unknown. Besides, the seed and the tree never meet. The seed will remain a seed. How can we make the seed meet its future? When the seed perishes, only then is the tree formed. The moment the tree is formed, the seed no longer exists, so how can you show the tree to the seed? As long as you are a seed, you are a seed; when you become a tree, you are no longer a seed. The seed and the tree never meet.

You want a guarantee for the future. To whom is this guarantee to be given? The seed that you no longer exist: you will not remain. The man who trusts asks, "What do I have?" Then he discovers, "I have nothing. I am naked." Once he realises that he is naked, why bother to dry his clothes?

Once you have acquired this knowledge, you are ready to embark on the journey into the unknown, because then you are ready for anything. You are not afraid of losing anything. If you gain something, good! If you don't, you can't be any worse off than you already are. Or do you think you can be? People worry about falling into a worse state than they are in now.

Mulla Nasruddin would often say: "It could have been worse". When someone told him something, the Mulla would invariably reply: "It could have been worse". His friends were sick of hearing it.

Finally an incident occurred in the neighbourhood and the friends were confident that the Mulla could never use his favourite phrase in this context.

Mulla's neighbour had been out of town. He returned two days ahead of schedule.

When he opened the door and entered, he found his wife in the arms of a stranger. The husband took his pistol and shot them both. "And now, Mulla, what have you got to say about it," chuckled Mulla's friends, fully confident that they had him beaten for once.

"It could have been worse," Mulla said calmly.

"What could have been worse than this?" they all shouted together.

"Silence, my friends," said the Mulla. "If I had returned a day earlier it would have been me!".

But I tell you it can't get any worse. Drop this sentence. The state you are in now is the worst state you can be in. What could be worse?

Trust always thinks: "What have I got? What has the seed got? It's just a covering, a shell. It has nothing. It can become something, but only when the shell is broken". You are a shell, a covering.

Let the shell break... and then everything will be possible.

That is why Shiva says: ***meditation is the seed,*** and when the seed is destroyed you reach the state of "twice-born".

***Eternal knowledge leads to the cessation of birth and death.***

The day when the state of dual birth blossoms in you, your knowledge can never be destroyed. It will flow constantly. You will become a stream of knowledge. Everything will become knowledge, consciousness. When the seed of meditation is broken, there is nothing but awareness, and only awareness within you. You are transformed into a state of awareness and witnessing, where knowledge is indestructible, where it cannot be destroyed. Right now your consciousness is almost non-existent. You live as if you were asleep. Whatever you do, you don't do it in full awareness.

A man sitting in front of Buddha was wringing his big toe. Buddha said to him, "Brother, why is your big toe twisted like that?

The man stopped immediately. He was surprised. "I don't know myself," he replied. "Now that you've asked, I'm worried about it too, because he wasn't consciously moving.

"So is your whole life," said the Buddha.

What have you ever consciously done throughout your life? Have you ever been consciously angry? Have you ever consciously loved? Have you ever been consciously greedy or obsessed? What have you consciously done? Your life is like this: just twiddling your thumbs unconsciously. You set up a house, you started a family; you gave birth to your children. Have you done anything consciously? Everything has happened to you; you just participated in it mechanically.

What did you do consciously in your life? Was there an action you did consciously? No! You can't find a single act you did consciously. Did you fall in love? Love happened, you did not fall in love.

If you fought, the fights happened mechanically; you didn't fight. You see a person and you immediately decide whether they are good or bad, but in your full consciousness, who is good, who is bad?

What you have become is accidental. You have not done it with full awareness. Things happen around you and you flow unconsciously with them. You float like a blade of straw in a river; you go where the current takes you. The straw thinks it is travelling, and you also think you are doing something. How can you be the doer when you are totally unconscious?

This sutra says that knowledge only becomes indestructible when the seed of meditation breaks and gives way to the eternal spring of consciousness. Then, even when you sleep, you are not asleep.

You are never asleep; you are fully conscious within. So when you make love, you make love with full awareness. When you eat, drink, walk or talk, you are fully conscious. Then your whole life becomes an expanding awareness. This is what we call Buddhahood, and it means: the state in which a man lives who is in full consciousness.

Now knowledge cannot be destroyed, now wisdom never fades. The inner flame never goes out. It burns constantly and without flickering. When this happens - when the seed of meditation is broken and the eternal knowledge and the steady stream of consciousness arises from within you - then there will be no birth; then you will not be reincarnated again.

You return to the body only in a state of unconsciousness. You are asleep and so you descend back into the body. The day when your consciousness becomes constant, the journey of the body will end. You will no longer descend into this narrow prison. No one in his full consciousness would choose to live in a body, for it is a bondage; it is a chain that you have forged around you. It is a prison, a bondage; and why would you knowingly want to be a slave?

You descend into the body without knowing it. You are lost in the darkness. The day your eyes are filled with light you will cease to descend into the body. Where will you be then? You will be a part of the great void, a bodiless part. This we call Brahma. Others call it God; others call it nirvana or moksha. Call it whatever you like, it doesn't matter. Between religions there is only a difference of words, and all the words are correct, for each word indicates a quality of that supreme state.

Nirvana means: the extinction of the lamp. Buddha likes this word. He used to say: "When the lamp goes out, where does the light go? What would you say? Where has it gone? You will not be able to point to a particular place. The light is bound to be somewhere, for nothing in this existence is ever destroyed. What is, is! What is not,

is not! There is no way for something that is not, to be; and there is
no way for something that is, not to be. The flame, the light, must
be somewhere, somewhere in the vast expanse, attached to existence.
Hitherto it had a form, now it is formless. Now it is freed from the
lamp, but that does not mean it is lost.

The lamp was made of clay, the flame was totally separate. What
has the flame got to do with the clay? There is no relationship
between the two. The flame did not owe its existence to the lamp;
the lamp did not have to become the flame. The lamp was merely the
body that contained the flame.

You extinguished the flame and the connection between the
fuel and the flame was broken. The flame was lost in the vastness
and became part of the great light. This is why the Buddha referred
to this supreme state as nirvana, total extinction, as the flame is
extinguished and becomes one with the supreme sun.

Mahavir calls it kaivalya, total solitude. He says: "As your
attachments are broken, darkness disappears and ignorance vanishes.
All false knowledge is destroyed. Then there is you and you alone, no
one else. There remains only the consciousness that has no beginning
and no end".

Mahavir does not speak of God. He says: "The soul becomes
God, the Supreme Soul". It is the same thing. Either you say the drop
is lost in the ocean or the ocean has become one with the drop. The
Hindus say the drop falls into the sea. Mahavir says the ocean is
lost in the drop. The event is the same, only the expressions differ.
Mahavir liked the word kaivalya. You, and you alone, remain: pure
consciousness.

The Hindus call it moksha, liberation, because the body is a
prison, and you have gained your freedom from it. Jesus has called it
the Kingdom of God, because you are no longer poor and miserable.
You have become a king. Only the words differ, the basic event is
one: when the seed is broken you become the tree.

Take courage. It takes a lot of courage. It takes more courage than anything else in the world. There is no greater challenge to your courage than religion. That is why I say to you: Do not believe that the weak take the path of religion. The weak can never become religious, only the very strong can tread the path of religion. Where you see the weak becoming religious, kneeling in temples and mosques, there is no religion there; it is only a worldly institution. The greatest act of courage is to immerse oneself in religion.

What is this act of courage? The leap of the seed. It is the willingness of the seed to destroy itself without any hope or guarantee of becoming a tree, the destruction of the known in favour of the unknown, the unfamiliar. It is the abandonment of the beaten path to wander in the vast wilderness. It is the willingness to choose an unknown path, to leave the world and set out in search of Brahma, to leave the well-mapped world behind and enter the uncharted sea.

There are no maps or guides. There are no written books to help. All books are left behind when the world ceases to exist, for they are part of this world. Even the guru cannot accompany you. He can only give you a push while he remains on the shore. What does a swimming teacher do? He merely pushes the student into the water. You know that the guru is standing, so you throw yourself in with confidence; but the knowledge of swimming is within you. At first, you throw your arms and feet; that is also swimming, but in a rough and inexperienced way. In a few days you learn by yourself to move your limbs in the water. You could have done it without the trainer, but you were afraid. Someone is waiting for you on the shore to help you if necessary. That gives you courage, just like the guru is on the shore to give you moral support. He does nothing, because there is nothing to do. Everything is hidden within you. It just has to manifest itself. The presence of the guru only assures you that there is no danger. You feel assured that someone is looking after you, that someone will hear you if you should and do ask for help. The guru assures the disciple" "I am here. Don't be afraid to jump.

As soon as you dive in, you start flailing your arms and legs. At first it's out of fear, but little by little you learn to swim. What's the difference between swimming and waving your arms and legs? It's just a matter of a little experience. For the first few days, your limbs will only move ineffectively, without helping you to move forward. Over time, all your movements will become more coordinated and, as you learn to move more effectively, your confidence will increase.

After a while, the guru will tell you that you no longer need his presence. Besides, you can now guide others, if you want to.

This is what the guru does in meditation: he pushes you; and if you are confident enough, your seed will break and the tree will be born. If you choose to argue and debate, you will wander uselessly. Confidence is the door.

# The Fourth Estate

*Trishu chaturtham tailavadasechyam.*

*Magnah svachitte pravishet.*

*Pranasamachare samadarshanam.*

*Shivatulyo jayate.*

*The fourth state should serve as oil to impregnate the first three states.*

*Thus bathed, it enters the state of self-consciousness.*

*One who experiences the all-pervading divine energy, sees all things as equal, and attains Shivahood.*

Through the three states - wakefulness, sleep and deep sleep - turiya, the fourth state, runs like a thread through the beads of a mala. Even while you sleep there is someone awake within you. When you dream, there is someone who witnesses the dream. When you are awake during the day, there is a witness within you as you go about your daily routine. This is inevitable, for that which is your nature you cannot lose no matter how soundly you sleep. That which you are is bound to be present. It can be suppressed, hidden, forgotten, but never destroyed.

Whether you are asleep, dreaming or awake, turiya is always present. In the depths of your being you are always Buddha. No matter how much you wander, all wandering is only superficial and belongs to the surface waves. In the depths of your being you have never wandered, because in the depths there is no way to wander.

Therefore, the fourth state is not to be attained, but revealed. It is not to be reached, but to be discovered.

It hides inside you like buried treasure. Dig through a few layers of earth and become rich as a king. You don't need to look anywhere, the treasure is inside. You keep glimpsing it, but you don't pay attention to it.

In the morning you wake up and say that you have slept long and deeply, that the sleep has been very restful.

When you say this, have you ever wondered who it is that knows that the sleep was pleasant? If your whole being was asleep, who was there to remember it? Who is it that says the sleep was deep and restful? Surely someone saw into the depths of sleep. Some dim light shone throughout your sleep. The darkness was never total; you could see.

You dream at night. In the morning you remember some fragments of your dream. You say you had a nightmare. Then the observer was separate from your dream, not lost in the dream. A part of you stood aside and did not become one with the dream. You were the observer, the spectator, when the dream played out on the stage of the inner soul. But you were outside the play, otherwise you would not have remembered it.

When anger comes over you during the day, it is not that you are totally asleep; there are glimpses inside you. You are aware of the anger when it comes, you feel it coming. As the sky fills with clouds before the rain falls, you feel the smoke rising before the fire of anger breaks out.

When you are full of attachments, when you are quiet, when you are restless, there is someone within you who is constantly watching; but you do not notice that watcher. Your attention flows to what is seen in the world, and you are one with what you see; it does not occur to you to turn and look at the watcher within. This is all you have to do: turn inward and see the observer. Your unconsciousness will be broken and you will reach the fourth state. Whoever reaches the fourth state, reaches everything. The one who does not reach the fourth state, finds at the moment of death that all that he has gained, all that he has gathered, is not worth a penny. It is all worthless.

I have heard:

Once Nasruddin ran to the river to catch a boat. He was on a journey and was in a great hurry for fear of missing the boat. When he reached the river, he saw the boat a short distance from the shore. He jumped and landed on the deck, but in doing so he slipped and fell. His elbows were bruised and his clothes were torn, but he was happy: he had reached the boat. He looked at his fellow passengers and smiled: "Well, I made it.

One of them replied: "I don't understand, Mulla, why are you in such a hurry? This boat is not going anywhere, it is just approaching the shore.

In the hour of death you will also realise that all your rushing and scurrying is futile in the end. The boat you thought would take you away is actually approaching the shore. But then it will be too late and nothing can be done about it. Now you still have time. Something can be done.

For him who awakens before death claims him, there is no death; but for him who sleeps until the moment of death, there is no life. His life is a long sleep broken finally by death. He who awakens during his life sees and experiences his inner nature and knows that he is immortal.

Life goes on while you remain unconscious. You walk around like you're drunk, you don't know where you're going. It's not clear why you're going either.

Two beggars were talking on the side of the road. I was passing by and overheard them. One said: "I wonder what the purpose of life is.

"Life is just living, what else can you do," the other replied.

You are of the second beggar's opinion: what else is there to do in life but live?

And even that is out of your control; it depends on an infinite number of factors. It's all in your unconscious mind. Why sexual desire arose in you, why you started a family, how greed and anger entered you, why you were dishonest, why you accumulated wealth, why you made enemies... you have no idea! you have no idea! You are like a puppet, whose strings someone else pulls. You imagine you are dancing, but in reality it is someone else who makes you dance.

Look closely at your life and you will discover that you are nothing but a puppet. How can anything real happen in the life of a man who is not his own master, but merely a puppet?

One night, Mulla Nasruddin rushed to the station with two of his friends to catch a train. All three were very drunk. The Mulla stumbled and fell and missed the train, but the other two managed to get on board. The station master helped the Mulla to his feet and took pity on him for missing the train. The Mulla said, "Don't pity me. I can always catch the next train. I am worried about what will happen to the other two. They have only come to see me off.

In the world getting on the train is a success, missing it is a failure; but in reality the successful and the unsuccessful, the victor and the vanquished, are all the same, for they are all equally unconscious. Rich and poor, victor and vanquished, each one wipes the slate clean with death.

Only one kind of person escapes this treatment: the one who has realised the fourth state which is hidden with the first three. For him there is no death. He alone wins. All others, be they Alexander or Napoleon, are total failures. Occasionally, a Buddha is victorious.

Here the meaning of success is only one: that you have come to know Him for whom there is no death. That which perishes with death you must regard as defeat. Make this a definition of failure.

Do you have anything that death cannot take away from you? Constantly reflect on this: "Do I have one thing that death cannot take away from me? If you find that you don't, hurry up. You can't afford to waste any more time - it's time to wake up!

Your days and nights, the time you spend awake, the time you spend asleep and the time you spend dreaming, death will take them all away from you. You have no relationship with these three states; they are clouds that hide the sun from you. If your life is spent entirely within these three states, you will find yourself a miserable beggar when the hour of death comes, but if you have been able to discern through the mists even a glimmer of light, then you will know that the sun itself is not far away. Then you will be facing the sun and the clouds will be behind you.

The first sutra is:

***The fourth state should serve as oil and permeate the other three states.***

In all three states - whether you are awake, dreaming or in deep sleep - keep the memory of the fourth state alive. Whatever happens on the outside, let it be. It is, after all, only the periphery. Keep your attention in the centre. Be aware in every moment, whether you are sitting or standing, eating or sleeping, going home or going to your place of work. Always remember that you are the observer and not the doer. Don't take life as more than a performance. Don't identify too much with the action.

Whether you are a wife or husband, businessman or client, don't get too involved. Don't lose yourself in it, for you are only playing a part in the play. Stay out of it and inside yourself.

These are all necessary parts of life. You must go to work, it is necessary. Play is delightful if you see it as play, but it is fatal if you take it for life. There is no reason for you to disturb your life. You have to play the role that life has given you. You have to fulfil your obligations and not be an escapist.

There is no need to flee.

Escapists are always weak. What you consider sadhus and sannyasins are escapists.

They are weak; they could not face life as it is; they could not deal with the observer inside them.

You cannot become a sannyasin by running away. It just shows that the world was too overwhelming and too strong, and you were too weak. You couldn't cultivate your consciousness when you were at work. You could not deal with the observer in you while you were at home, so you had to run away.

If you couldn't become aware in your working world, how are you going to become aware in the mountains?

There is only one process of awakening and it has nothing to do with where you are or what you are doing. Geography is irrelevant. The process of cultivating consciousness is one and has nothing to do with place. It doesn't matter if you are sitting in a temple or sitting in your shop doing business. It doesn't matter whether you sit on a velvet cushion or on the bare floor; the method is the same. The method is to be conscious in every moment of the fact that you are separate from the action in which you are engaged, whether it is attending the shop or praying in the temple, business or worship, it is all the same. "My actions are separate from me. They are part of the world. I am only the observer. This must be the attitude. Don't be so absorbed that only the act remains and the witness is lost. Right now this is what is happening to you.

This sutra says Over the other three states continuously pour the fourth state. By continuous watering, the tree of the fourth state will begin to grow. Begin with the waking state, for it is closest to the fourth, it contains a slight ray of awakening, take advantage of it. How could you awaken immediately in your deep sleep or in your dreams? Well, start with the waking state, which is one percent consciousness and ninety-nine percent unconsciousness. Take advantage of this one percent and sprinkle it with turiya. Whenever the opportunity arises, shake yourself awake. Again and again your memory will slip. Give yourself a push, a jolt into wakefulness again and again. Just as a person ties knots in their handkerchief to help them remember something, tie knots in your consciousness that remind you again and again. Whatever you do, at whatever time, shake yourself into the awareness of the truth: that "I am not the doer, I am only the observer".

When this thought takes root in you, you will notice that all your tensions disappear. All tensions belong to the doer, to the ego. As soon as you begin to contact the observer in you, all tensions disappear.

If this happens even for a moment, you will glimpse a brief flash. The waves of the ocean will begin to dance within you. Again and again you will lose it. This is natural, because you have cultivated unconsciousness during many births. It will take you time to overcome this unconsciousness. You have to be persistent and courageous. You have to keep pouring the oil of the fourth estate into your waking state, say about twenty times throughout the day.

As you walk along the road, stop! Become the observer: realise that it is the body that is walking and you are a mere observer. As you eat, stop! Become the observer. The body eats. You just observe. While serving customers in your shop, stop! Become the observer. Don't become so absorbed that you forget the observer. Hold on to yourself again and again. It will take continuous effort. You will find, little by little, that the effort becomes easier day by day; from time to time you will have flashes of turiya.

When turiya appears easily during the day, you can gradually use it in your dreams. Then, when you are about to fall asleep, let the last thought in your mind be: "I am the observer". When sleep overcomes you, let this thought echo in your mind: "I am the witness, I am the witness...". And so you fall asleep. You will not be able to catch the moment when sleep comes and the repetition ceases.

If you cultivate the sensation until you fall asleep, the sensation will continue in sleep, for it is only the body that sleeps. As you cultivate this sensation more and more, one night you will suddenly become aware of the observer in your sleep. And as soon as you become aware of the observer, something unusual will happen: the dreams will disappear. The dreams only occur because of your unconsciousness.

When this takes place even in your dreams, the third event will be possible. Continue the repetition: "I am the witness.... I am the witness...": in your dream. The day this stream of consciousness enters your dream, the key to the supreme treasure will fall into your hands. Now nothing and no one can make you unconscious, unconscious. Whoever awakens even for an instant in his dream, his unconsciousness disappears forever.

The day you wake up in your sleep you become a yogi. You cannot become a yogi by doing asanas. These are nothing but exercises. They are good and useful for keeping the body healthy, but if you take them for real yoga, you are deluded. Yoga means: the art of awakening in sleep.

Thus, the awakener is a yogi.

This sutra tells you to bring the fourth state into the first three states, and then this event will take place one day. When you wake up, even in sleep, you will be fixed in the fourth state.

When a person is established in the fourth state, he becomes like a flame that burns without flickering, as if there were no breeze. Such will be your wisdom, such will be your knowledge; such will be your soul, flickerless, full of light. Then everything in you will be transformed.

The first thing is: for the one who wakes in his sleep, dreams end forever. He who attains Buddhahood never dreams. At first, when you wake up in your dream, that dream will be broken, but other dreams will continue; but if you wake up in a deep sleep in which there are no dreams, then you will never dream again. This happens because all dreams occur in a mind dominated by desire.

What is a dream? If you have a desire that remains unfulfilled during the day, you satisfy it during the night. Not everyone can be king: there is a lot of struggle and competition, so the beggar satisfies his desires by dreaming of becoming king. The balance is maintained: the one who is king during the day is not aware of his kingdom while he sleeps; the beggar begs all day and dreams that he is a king when he sleeps.

It happened once: Aurangzeb was very angry with a fakir. He sent for him one morning with the idea of punishing him. People had told Aurangzeb that it was impossible to displease this man. He said, "We shall see. It was a cold night, a cold Delhi night. He made the fakir lie naked all night in the Jamuna river, while the palace was warm and merry.

The fakir spent the night standing in the cold river. In the morning, Aurangzeb sent for him and asked, "How did it go last night?

The fakir replied: "For me it was the same as for you, and sometimes it was better".

"I don't follow you," said Aurangzeb.

I kept dreaming," said the fakir, "that I was king. I sat in a brightly lit palace and there was merriment everywhere. I took as much pleasure in my palace and my revelry as you did in yours, so that my night was sometimes like yours. And when I was filled with conscience, my sleep was broken. You still don't know what conscience is like.

You complete at night what you have left unfinished during the day. You cannot fulfil all your desires during the day; there are difficulties. Moreover, it is not easy to fulfil desires because they are really unrealisable.

There is no way to satisfy desires; in fact, the very nature of desire is that it can never be satisfied.

Even if you get all the wealth in the world, your desires will not be satisfied.

It is said: Diogenes said to Alexander the Great: "The day you conquer the whole world you will find yourself in real trouble. Forget about all this business. As it is, you are in big trouble. When you have conquered the world you will find yourself in even greater difficulties".

Alexander is said to have been saddened and replied: "Please don't talk like that, for the very thought of having conquered the whole world makes me sad. Once I have conquered the world, what shall I do?

There is no other world to conquer. My mind will torment me without end, for it is never satisfied.

Kings dream and so do beggars; each one completes what was left undone during the day. Dreams are kind to you; that is one of their qualities. If some sadhu or sannyasin tricks you into observing austerities and fasts, and if during the day you almost starve to death, at night, when you dream, you will find yourself as a guest at a feast. You will eat food of indescribable flavour. Dreams are infinitely kinder than your sadhus and sannyasins. And there is no difference between the taste of real food and dream food; possibly the dream food is tastier! If you have not been successful in your career after women, then in your dreams you will find yourself attracting women as beautiful as your mind can imagine.

Dreams open the door to the fulfilment of all your desires. If a man lives for sixty years, he spends twenty years sleeping, twenty years working and twenty years awake in other occupations. Now, if one man is king for twenty years in his real life and another is king for twenty years in his dreams, what is the difference? The sum total is the same. Besides, the one who is emperor during the day has a thousand and one worries on his mind, but the king of dreams has all the time free to enjoy his status.

Dreams are only lost when man wakes up in sleep. Then dreams are meaningless, for the one who wakes up in sleep has no desire left. All desires are part of unconsciousness.

Once Mulla Nasruddin got off a train looking very ill and unable to walk straight. "Are you ill?" a friend asked him.

Nasruddin replied: "Whenever I travel and sit looking back, I feel sick and dizzy.

The friend said: "You should have asked the man sitting in front of you to change seats with you, Mulla.

"I wanted to do it," said Mulla, "only there was no one in the seat in front of me".

You go through life exactly the same, as if you were completely drunk or on drugs. You will have to break this addiction. Where will you start? You will start in the waking state. When you wake up in the morning make a resolution: Today I will practice the attitude of witnessing. In the early morning, when you wake up, your mind is very light and fresh, no dreams, no thoughts.

After a full night's rest, there is an inner dawn, just as there is an outer dawn. There are no tensions and no clouds. You are light and free. Soon the world will claim you and then the difficulties will begin.

As soon as your sleep is interrupted, don't be in a hurry to open your eyes. At that time the mind is very sensitive. As soon as you wake up remember your resolution: "I am the witness". Be still for five minutes Be still for five minutes and meditate on this. Do not open your eyes, for once your eyes are open you have the world in front of you and you lose yourself in it. Keep your eyes closed and cultivate the feeling "I am not the doer, I am the witness". May this practice of witnessing accompany me throughout the day. May I remember to practise it all day long".

Now stand up, completely immersed in this feeling and try to hold it for a while. It will be easy at first. Get up and sit on the bed, then put your feet down. Be fully aware.

Take a bath; bathe with awareness. Eat your breakfast; be fully conscious as you eat it.

To be fully conscious means to be fully aware of the fact that all actions happen outside. They are the needs of the body, not your needs. You have no needs, and in fact there are no needs, for you yourself are God. What could you possibly need? You are complete, perfect. You are Brahma. Everything is yours. The soul has no needs, no fuel. The flame burns without wick and without oil. That is why you say: "I have no needs. All needs are of the body: to bathe, to eat, to work, to move".

Try to maintain this attitude. Keep this thread of witness as long as you can. It will soon get lost in the hustle and bustle of the day. Your habits are very old and deeply rooted. Keep at it and water it every day, and the shoot will sprout and grow. At first it will not be apparent, for the growth will be slow, very slow; but soon you will find a thin ribbon of light shining perpetually within you. This ray of light will bring about an alchemical change in your life. Your anger will diminish, for how can a witness be angry? Attachments will become less and less, for how can a witness have attachments?

There will be events. There will be successes and defeats, there will be sorrows, there will be joys, but they will affect you less, for how can the witness be affected? Joy will come and you will witness it, sorrow will come and you will witness it, while within you a continuous stream flows:

"I am the witness, not the one who enjoys all this".

No one can tell you how long it will take. It all depends on the sincerity of your purpose, on the intensity of your desire, on your speed of progress, on whether you crawl like an ant or run like a deer. People walk in the realm of religion as slowly as if they were in a wedding procession. That way you will get nowhere. The wedding procession has nowhere to go; it just circles around the city and comes back to the same place.

There was a man called Aesop. His moral fables are still the best the world has ever known. He was a man of great wisdom. One day Aesop was sitting by the roadside when a man came up to him and said: "Could you tell me, sir, how far it is to the village and how long it will take me to get there? Aesop said nothing. He got up and walked beside the man. The man was embarrassed and also a little frightened by this strange behaviour. He asked Aesop not to worry, that all he wanted to know was the distance, and then he would be on his way.

Aesop said nothing, but walked on with the man. After about fifteen minutes he stopped and said, "It will take you two hours to reach the village.

"You could have told me at the beginning!" the man exclaimed. "There was no need to walk a kilometre with me."

Aesop replied: "How could I calculate the time before I knew your walking speed? The distance is not decided by the length, but by the speed of the walker. Now I can tell you with certainty that it will take you two hours to reach the village".

It all depends on your speed. You can run and you'll get there first. You can wander, and then we can't say when you'll get there. Your speed can be such that in a moment you can make the leap. You can also move half-heartedly, half-heartedly; then you will take infinite births to arrive. If you bring your whole being into play without holding back any part of yourself, if you put in all your effort with the maximum intensity of your way of life, you can arrive here and now. Because it is not an outer journey, but an inner journey. You just have to turn inwards from wherever you are. If you put it off until tomorrow, or the day after tomorrow, or the day after tomorrow.... then that's what you've been doing for infinite lifetimes!

Remember that nature is not interested in your religious achievements. Nature leads only as far as man has already gone. If you wish to go further, only your own effort will take you. Nature can, at best, turn you into an animal, and no further. Humanity must be acquired. That is why man is in danger, lives in great danger.

All animals are calm, except man. They accept what nature gives them; they have no goals. You cannot agitate a dog by telling him that he is less of a dog than another. Whatever the breed, whatever the form, the essential feeling of being a dog is the same in all dogs. It is not the same with man; there is a lot of difference between one man and another. A skinny, scrawny man may become a great man, a strong, stout person may be very ordinary.

A new quality begins with man. What is this quality? The more conscious a person is, the more human he is. The day a person is filled with full consciousness, he becomes divine. But this carries with it a great risk, for he who can rise to the heights can also fall to the depths. He who does not rise cannot fall; that is why we do not find Buddhas and Krishnas among the animals, but neither will you find a Hitler, a Genghis Khan or a Stalin. The valleys are always at the foot of the peaks.

There is a zoo in Tokyo where there are animals from all over the world. There are lions and tigers, leopards and hippos, snakes and birds, deer and elephants and so on. After touring the zoo, when you reach the last cage you see a sign that reads: "The most dangerous animal in the world". You really want to see what it's all about. You go over to get a good look at it.

Inside there is only a mirror... and you reflect yourself in it!

Man is, in fact, the most dangerous of all animals. He has the potential to become divine, so it is also possible for him to fall. If he cannot rise, he cannot stay where he is: he will fall. In this world there is no place to stop; therefore, if you do not move towards consciousness, you will gradually slip into unconsciousness.

It is a source of astonishment and also of shame that young children are more aware than adults. Why are they so? After a lifetime of experience, an old man should become more aware, more alert; but, unfortunately, he only becomes more cunning. With all his experience he becomes more dishonest, he becomes an expert thief.

An old crow advised his young son: "Look, son, I tell you from experience, beware of man! You can never trust him. If you see a man crouching down, fly away, because he is sure to be picking up a stone.

The son asked: "What if he already has a stone hidden in his armpit?

The old crow flew away as fast as he could. This son of his seemed even more dangerous than the man!

It is not wise to stay close to him.

With experience, the elderly become more cunning and clever without becoming more aware, but what will they gain by their cunning? There is nothing in the world to be lost by innocence and nothing to be gained by cunning and cunning. Whatever we build here is but a sand castle. If you build it, it will break; if you don't, you lose nothing.

Children are more aware. Look into the eyes of a child. They are full of awareness, they are more alert. We have to find ways to temper their awareness. We don't allow them to laugh out loud or cry out loud; we don't allow them to run and jump as they please. We restrict their vital energy in all directions. We teach them to be dishonest as soon as possible.

I asked Mulla Nasruddin's son: "How old are you?

"Seven years at home, five years on the bus," the boy replied. The father has given him a good start on the road to dishonesty.

I was once a guest in a house. One night, the hostess was putting her son to bed in the room next to mine. As she put him to bed,

I heard her say, "Go to sleep now. If you need anything during the night, call me; your father will come running".

All mothers do it, but what is the child being initiated into? Lying, deceit, deceitfulness, deceitfulness. We feed poison along with the milk. Our effort is never directed towards making the child more alert and more aware. If ever the right culture is born on this earth, the first thing the child will be taught is to become more aware, more conscious. The fourth state is the only thing worth teaching; everything else is useless. Everything else simply helps you to go about your daily life.

The child is fresh, just as you are a little fresh in the morning. He is still in the morning of his life. If he is taught the art of the fourth estate from this very moment and learns the art of awakening while he is still fresh, he will reach the peak when he is an old man. He will attain buddhahood.

There is only one thing to practice, and that is: to water the first three states with the fourth state, with consciousness, with discernment, with vigilance, with wakefulness.

***Thus bathed, it enters the state of self-consciousness.***

In this state the person slips invariably into self-consciousness, and once he knows the light of the fourth state he discovers that there is no joy equal to it. The intoxication of wine is so ephemeral, whereas the intoxication of the fourth state never fades. It is an eternal stream. And he who is filled with the delight of the fourth estate, who dances and rejoices in it; he who is filled to the last pore with the fourth estate, whose way of being has become consciousness; he in whom it is the fourth estate that sits and stands and moves; he whose every atom is bathed in the fourth estate, enters into self-consciousness. Otherwise, you will still not know yourself. You may know the whole world, but you will be a stranger to your self.

You can say many things about others - their names, their addresses, their vocations, their lives - but about yourself you know nothing. Until you know yourself, all your knowledge is worthless, for it is based on ignorance.

If you continually feed the oil of the fourth state to the other three states, then you will see the fourth state manifest in your life.

The way the Buddha sits, stands or walks is unique. There is a wakefulness when he stands and when he walks. Everything that comes out of him does not arise from unconsciousness. He is fully conscious; everything that happens through him is full of consciousness.

Everything you have done so far you have done in a state of unconsciousness. You say you have done a thing knowingly, but it is not true. Your son comes home from school with a torn shirt and a broken blackboard. You scold him and hit him. You say you did it knowingly, and it's all for the good of the child. A bit of real introspection - did you really act consciously, or did something happen to you when you saw the torn shirt and the broken blackboard? You got angry with the child and took your anger out on him. You got angry because he disobeyed you. If you were in a state of anger, all your actions followed in unconsciousness, for anger is a state of non-consciousness. Everything you say only serves to justify your actions.

Mulla Nasruddin beat his son. "This is all for your own good," he told him. "A child like you has to be beaten at least twice a day to keep him straight. Look at me. My father never hit me when I was a child."

"Your father must have been a good man," said the Mulla's son.

You hit the child and think you are doing him a favour. The child thinks otherwise, because his attention is focused on your anger and not on your beating. No rationalisation can prove that you are right.

Just yesterday a man came to see me with his wife. The woman doesn't allow him to meditate; she doesn't think this is the right way to meditate. It is very traditional, but this is only superficial.

Deep down in the unconscious, the reason is very, very different. No wife wants her husband to meditate, no husband likes his wife to meditate; as soon as a person starts meditating, all the old relationships are in danger. As soon as a person begins to meditate, his sexual desire begins to decrease more and more. This is the unconscious reason; all other reasons are excuses. A wife would rather have her husband go to a brothel than meditate, because when he goes to a brothel he is not yet totally against women; he is still interested in women. But meditation means that he will soon lose his interest in women.

So, if a woman has to choose between him going to a brothel or taking sannyas, she will choose a brothel for her husband. She is also worried that if her husband loses himself in meditation something will happen to the family. The fact is that meditation disturbs neither family nor business. In fact, a man who meditates does his work more effectively than before, because meditation breaks your connection with the world within, not with the world outside. The outer work remains the same. A new light is kindled. Now you know that it is a work. A new light is born inside you, while the outer life goes on as usual.

There is no doubt that there are problems between husband and wife, he thinks; however much they may claim and even believe that the reason is different, the basic cause is the sexual relationship. Sexual relations begin to cool down when one enters meditation, and as meditation progresses, sex gradually fades away.

Every day I have husbands who complain: "My wife was never interested in sex, but since the day I started meditating she has become sexually aggressive! Normally wives are not sex-hungry, because they trust their husbands. In fact, they intend to do their husbands a favour.

They boast of their virtue and piety, but as soon as the husband takes an interest in meditation, they become enraged. Now it is necessary to bring the husband back into their body. It is the same with husbands when their wives become interested in meditation.

One of these ladies started to meditate. She is really interested, and could have had profound results if she had gone deeper into it, but her husband burns my books and throws them out of the house.

He says she doesn't need advice from any outside person as long as he is there! He says he can give her all the answers she needs, and the wife knows very well what his answers will be! The husband's ego is bruised. The husband can't bear to think that another man holds first place in his wife's heart. It is a blow he cannot bear, but he does not speak openly about it.

Whatever you do, whatever you say, it is not entirely authentic; the reason is different, deep down.

The meditator has to look deep within himself for the reasons. He has to get hold of the root cause, because the root cause can be changed. If you consider the reason to be something other than the root cause, no change can be made. As you become aware of life, you will begin to see the root cause of all your actions and reactions. Then you will realise that you are not angry with the child because he made a mistake, but because it gives you pleasure to be angry. The mistake was just an excuse.

The boss fires you from your job. You would have loved to retaliate, but it wasn't possible. You get home and want to take your anger out on someone, anyone. The wife is there and you could take it out on her, but it's not a good deal, because she'll make a big deal out of it for days, so the child becomes the target. He is a child. He's bound to tear his shirts. He's obliged to tear up his books. After all, he's not an old man. He's bound to play with the wrong kids, because except for your son, all the kids are the "wrong kind".

I once asked a little boy: "Tell me, son, are you a good boy? Everyone says you are.

The boy replied: "If I had to tell the truth, I'm the kind of kid they won't let me play with.

All children, except yours, are "bad", so this child must have played with one of those bad children and broken his clothes and books. He may even have hurt himself. You will catch him.

He is not very strong. You will vent your anger at him, but insist that you are correcting and guiding him.

Only when you start to become aware, you will begin to recognise the real reason. When the real cause is known, it is not very difficult to abandon it. In fact, it is not difficult at all. When you see the kind of life you have built around yourself, you will laugh. You will see that you had become a pretender, and with that pretence you wanted to reach the truth. You wanted to reach God? Impossible!

For me, sannyas means knowing the web of delusion you have woven within you, eradicating it and living authentically and realistically. Whatever you are, if you are bad, be bad; if you have a temper, know it! Don't cover your faults with gold. If you try to cover your wounds with flowers, they will get worse. Simply say: "I am like this", whether I am good or bad. Don't offer any rationalisations or excuses for why you are the way you are. Do not look for good reasons for wrongdoing, for then evil cannot be eradicated.

When you are angry, you always justify your anger by looking for some cause; so how will the anger go away? So you feed your anger and make it look good. You have decorated your prison with flowers to make it look like your house. Now you are satisfied. If you consider sickness as health, how will you get rid of it?

When a man begins to awaken, he begins to realise that his wakefulness is false, that his dreams are the result of a twisted mind, that his very sleep is full of restlessness. In all three states there is a restlessness, an uneasiness, a sense of being haunted. As his perception sharpens, he is able to recognise the lies he has been carrying and abandon them. More light penetrates and his awareness grows in strength and intensity.

The state you are currently in is something like this.

One night there was an earthquake. There was thunder and lightning and the house shook. The woman woke her husband, who had fallen asleep. She said, "Wake up, it's an earthquake.

I think the house is going to fall down".

"Don't worry," said the husband. "Go back to sleep. It's not our house, we just rented it".

You do not understand that, though the house is not yours, when it falls, it is you who will die. The pseudo-truths you have built around you may not necessarily be your own creation, for some you have learned from the gurus, some you have gleaned from the scriptures, and some you have obtained from your religion; but when they fall it will be you who will be the loser. You will be the one who dies.

You have surrounded yourself with lies that seem useful; they help you keep up a good facade so that you always appear casual and charming. Inside you there is suffering and pain, but there is always a smile on your face. The suffering is real, the smile is fake. It is better to cry. Let the tears fall and wash the paint off your face. Let your genuine face be exposed, for only the authentic and genuine leads to truth.

As you wash your consciousness with wakefulness, all the paint runs off; this is what is known as sannyas. As you become more and more authentic to yourself, you will find that it is not so difficult to get rid of your problems. A genuine disease is curable, a pseudo-disease can never be cured.

Suppose you have cancer, but you are too scared to accept the fact. Instead, you insist that you have a chronic cold and keep treating your cold. How will this cure your cancer? How long can you fool yourself?

Gurdjieff always told his disciples that it is imperative for a seeker to know from the beginning what his problems really are. All seekers try to hide them. The one who hides the real disease cannot be diagnosed, and up to that point you go on trying to cure the pseudo-disease. You will die during the cure because that was not the real disease.

People come to me and tell me they are searching for God, searching for their soul. Their faces give no indication of their search. Their search is misnamed; they are looking for something quite different under the cover of God and soul.

A friend came up to me - he was an old man - and told me that he had been looking for God for thirty years. "That's a long time!" I exclaimed, "You should have found him by now. God seems to be avoiding you. If so, even thirty births won't be enough. Or it may be that you are not looking in the right direction, that you have not taken the path to his house. Either he is avoiding you or you are avoiding him. Tell me exactly what you are looking for.

"I have already told you. I am searching for God," he said. "I do my practices and meditation regularly, but I have no results to show."

"What results do you want to achieve?" I asked.

"I want to achieve some occult powers.

Now this man does not seek God; he seeks power in the name of God. It is not only in the bazaar that we find a name on the label and something very different inside the package. It is also in the temples.

A husband was looking for salt in the kitchen. When his wife thought he was taking too long, she shouted at him: "What happened, can't you find the salt?

"No, I can't.

"It's right in front of your eyes, in the can labelled 'Turmeric'," he said.

That's what every search is like. You are not sure what you are seeking, or why. As the waking water enters your life, it will acquire a direction. The useless will fall away and only the useful will remain. The day when only the useful remains, the goal will not be far away.

As your delight in the fourth state increases, as this drunkenness spreads in your life... but drunkenness is something else altogether. We have to use words to describe it; that is why we call it drunkenness, but it is not the drunkenness of a drunkard, but the opposite! When a man is drunk, he staggers and stumbles about aimlessly; he loses touch with his senses, cannot see what he is doing and commits all sorts of excesses. In the drunkenness of turiya it is just the opposite.

You don't wobble here! Your feet are firmly planted. Here you are full of self-remembering. You have full command of your senses. In the intoxication of the drunkard you can make all kinds of mistakes and go astray! In the intoxication of turiya it is impossible for a person to do wrong.

Akbar went out one day on his elephant for a ride around his capital. As he passed through the streets, a man on a rooftop began to insult him. He was immediately captured and brought before Akbar the next morning.

Akbar asked the man, "What made you behave so badly last night, you fool?".

"Your Majesty, I was drunk. I was not there. It was the wine that abused you, not me! I was very sorry when I came to myself. I beg you to forgive me, for I was not there at all."

Akbar understood this, for he himself sought the fourth estate. He was a wise king. He realised that it was useless to punish a man who was not in his right mind. True, he had behaved badly, but if he had done anything right in that state it would have been a miracle.

When you do something right it's a miracle; you always do something wrong. It is natural, because you are not conscious. Gurdjieff would say: "God will not punish you for your sins, because they were committed in unconsciousness. Even a court forgives a man who is not in his right mind. If a man commits a murder under the influence of drink, he is pardoned with a lighter sentence. God will not punish you for your sins. He is at least as wise as the courts.

Your sins were committed in unconsciousness, so were your good deeds! So there is hardly any difference between your good deeds and your bad deeds; the quality is the same. It doesn't matter whether you are a householder or a sannyasin, because you are unconscious. You are unconscious in your shop; you are unconscious in your temple; you are unconscious in your office; you are unconscious in your monastery. It makes no difference whether you put on your clothes or get rid of them; you are still unconscious. The real question is to break this unconsciousness, not to change the way you act, for that is very easy. If you are unconscious in one form of action, you will be unconscious in another.

*Thus bathed, it enters the state of self-consciousness.*

*Whoever experiences the divine energy that permeates all things, considers all things to be equal.*

As soon as a person enters self-awareness, he or she experiences prana, the life force, for the first time.

Through this experience he sees how everything around him is permeated with the emanations of divine energy; he attains dispassion and equality of vision. And as soon as a person knows his own being, he immediately comes to know that the same flame burns in each of us.

As long as you have not seen and experienced your own self, the other will always remain alien to you. As long as you have not recognised your own self, the other will remain the enemy. As soon as you witness your own self, you will see the light of the flame within the clay walls of all; you will attain equality of vision. Then there will be neither friend nor foe. No one is yours, no one is a stranger. Then it is really you who pervades all; then there is only one.

In this sutra, Shiva says that you now receive the news that there is only one life force everywhere. All lamps carry the same flame. All drops contain the same ocean. The lamps are different. Some are light, some are dark, some are brown, some are yellow; the shapes are different and the names are different, but the inner flame has no shape and no name. He who has known his own self, knows his own self in others.

In the first appearance of the fourth state you know your own state, but simultaneously even the second takes place: you know God. On the one hand, you become aware of the soul, and on the other, God, the supreme soul, reveals Himself.

Do not seek God directly, for then He will only be a figment of your imagination and nothing more. You may imagine Krishna playing the flute, but this will not reveal God to you, for it is only a dream. It is a pleasant dream, but a dream after all; it is no different from any other dream.

The mind imagines. You can imagine that you have a vision of Mahavir, Buddha or Rama. Many people do that. All they do is dream. They are religious dreams, but all dreams are dreams.

There is no way to seek God directly, for you yourself are the door. Unless and until you pass through this door, His door will remain closed to you. The soul is the door to God. Here you know yourself and here God reveals Himself. Then you see him and him alone everywhere: in the trees and in the stones, in the rocks and in the streams. It is him and him alone. Somewhere he is asleep, somewhere he is awake, somewhere he is dreaming, but it is him and only him!

Shiva refers to this experience of the One as *"experiencing divine energy"*. This is his greatest revelation. But it is attained only by one who knows his own self.

*One who experiences the divine energy that permeates all things, regards them as equal and attains Shivahood.*

When a person sees all things as equal, he becomes like Shiva. Then he becomes God himself.

You are the "I" as long as you do not know yourself. This seems very contradictory. You shout "I...

I..me" as long as you don't know yourself. The day you know yourself, the "I" falls, the "you" also falls, and you become like Shiva. You become God Himself. On that day the music of aham brahmasmi - I am God - will spontaneously arise in you. Then you will not repeat "Aham brahmasmi"; you will know it! You will not have to understand it, it will become your own existence, your own experience.

All around you, the air will vibrate with this music, the music of the one. As the drop loses itself and becomes one with the ocean, so all boundaries fall away and you become limitless: you attain Shivahood.

The efforts of Shiva and all those who have attained buddhahood are directed towards your becoming like them. What they have known, the supreme bliss, must also be your treasure, for it is also your possession. You are still a seed; they have blossomed into trees. These trees keep calling: "Become trees! Do not remain seeds! You will never attain peace until you attain Shivahood, for man cannot be content with less; his soul will not be fulfilled. Thirst will continue no matter how much you try to quench it with the waters of the world. It will be quenched only when you drink from the cup of God. Then the thirst is quenched forever; all desires, all ambitions, all rushes and races, all strivings and struggles are ended, for then you have become the highest, the supreme.

There is nothing higher.

Keep pouring the oil of the fourth state into the three states, that you may be so filled with delight that you enter into self-consciousness, that you may gain tidings of the life force, that you may know it to be that which resides in all, that you may attain the vision of equality, that you may become like Shiva himself.

# Right search, wrong address

*Katha japah.*
   *Danamatmagyanam.*
   *Yoavipastho oyahetushcha.*
   *Svashakti paschayoasya vishvam.*
   *Sthitilayau.*
   *Everything he pronounces is japa.*
   *Self-knowledge is your gift.*
   *He is the master of inner powers and the source of knowledge.*
   *The constant enjoyment of self-energies is his universe. Life and death are under his will.*

Prayer does not depend on what you say; rather, it depends on what you are. Worship does not depend on what you do, but on what you are. Religion is not about your actions, but about your existence. If love is at the centre of your being, there will be prayer at your periphery. If there is perpetual peace in your centre, there will be meditation in your periphery. If there is awareness at the centre, your life itself becomes an act of self-purification, but the reverse is not true.

By causing a change in the circumference you cannot change the centre, but a change in the centre automatically causes a change in the circumference, because the circumference is simply the shadow of the centre. By changing the shadow you cannot change yourself, the shadow changes accordingly.

This is very important to know, because most people waste their lives trying to change the periphery. They put everything on the line to bring about a change in their behaviour and conduct, but even if these are changed, nothing else changes along with them. No matter how much you change your behaviour, you will remain what you were: if you were a thief you will become a good man, if you loved wealth you will start giving to charity, but the inner you will remain the same. For you the value of money will not change. Money had a certain value for you when you were a thief, and it will remain the same when you become a philanthropist. Certainly, you do not consider it as dust, for who makes a gift of dust?

If wealth has turned to dust in your eyes, will you go around giving away your trash to others? And if someone accepts it, do you think you have done them a favour? Do you expect them to thank you?

In fact, if wealth is nothing but dust to you, you should be grateful to the person who accepts junk from you and does not disdain it, but a philanthropist never thinks in these terms. If he gives even a paisa, he expects some return.

A miserly marwari died. He went straight to the gates of heaven and knocked. He was confident that the gate would open for him, for had he not given alms? The gate opened and the sentry looked at him from head to toe. People are not recognised there by their actions, but by themselves. The sentry said, "I'm sorry, sir, but there has been a mistake. Perhaps you did not know that you had to knock at the other gate. Be so kind as to go there.

The marwari fumed. "How dare you!" he exclaimed. "Don't you know who I am, haven't you heard of my alms? Only yesterday I gave two paisa to an old beggar woman, and the day before yesterday I gave a paisa to a blind paperboy."

When he spoke of alms, the guard had to open his ledger. He scanned the page under the marwari's name, but except for these three paisa, the page was blank. He asked him, "What other alms have you given besides these?".

"Many, many," replied the marwari, "only right now I can't remember them". Imagine someone who can't forget a measly three paisa saying he can't remember them! And on the strength of those three paisa he knocks at the gates of heaven!

The guard consulted with his partner about what to do with the man. His partner said: "Give him his three paisa and tell him to go to hell!

Can money open the gates of heaven? Whether you cling to wealth or let it slip away, it is of equal value in your eyes. Whether you live in the world or run away from it, its hold on you is total. It makes no difference whether your face is turned towards these things or away from them; unless you bring about a radical change in the centre, the path remains more or less the same.

An inner transformation is necessary, not a change in the pattern of your behaviour. As soon as an inner change takes place, everything changes with it. These sutras are for inner transformation. Try to listen to each sutra very carefully. If there is even a fraction of dry powder inside you, it is bound to explode; but if the powder is not dry, the sparks will fall, but they will be extinguished immediately.

The problem with you is not that you don't have a chance to hear the truth, but that you are an expert at stifling it. Your gunpowder is not dry. It's soaked. How did you get your gunpowder wet? The more knowledge you have, the wetter the gunpowder gets. The more you think you know, the wetter your gunpowder becomes; it is because of this knowledge that you stifle every spark of wisdom. Your knowledge prevents the sparks of wisdom from igniting you. Your knowledge stands like a sentinel preventing all entry.

You are unconscious in your knowledge. Remember that there is no more potent intoxicant than the arrogance of learning, for nowhere is the ego more subtle than here. Wealth does not feed the ego half as much. For wealth can be stolen, the government can change, communism can enter... anything can happen. You cannot rely completely on wealth, yet knowledge cannot be stolen or taken away from you. Even if they put you in jail, a man's knowledge goes with him. Therefore, a rich man is not half as arrogant as a learned man. It is this arrogance that dampens the dust within you. Remove this arrogance and your gunpowder will dry up and, when it is dry, a small spark will be enough to ignite it.

These sutras are like sparks. Put aside all your knowledge and try to understand them. If you try to understand them through your knowledge, you will never succeed.

The first sutra is:

***Everything he pronounces is japa.***

The last sutra spoke of the state of yesterday that the seeker attains. Whatever such a person says is japa, repetition of a mantra. Whatever he says is japa, whatever words he uses, because there is no more desire, no more darkness; the world is absent from his heart. His heart is a light in itself; everything that comes out of such a heart is japa. It cannot be anything but japa, for how can darkness come out of light, hatred out of love or anger out of compassion? Whatever comes out of it must be japa.

There is a well-known saying of Jesus The kingdom of heaven is not determined by what you put in your mouth, but by what comes out of it. What comes out of you indicates who you are. One who becomes like Shiva does not need to practice japa, for everything he does is japa.

Kabir said My very sitting and standing is an act of "going around the temple". Kabir was asked When do you pray? When do you worship? We never see you perform any sadhana. You are called a great devotee, but we never see you perform any devotion. All you do is weave your cloth and sell it in the market. There is no sign of worship or meditation or going to the temple.

Kabir would reply All I do is "going round the temple"; all I say is japa, and my very being is my meditation.

What do you do when you are interested in meditation? You give meditation a little corner in your world of actions, but meditation is not an action, it is not an act. You take care of the shop, you take care of your work; you have to do it, it is necessary. Now you do your work and attend to the daily necessities of life. They form a procession on the periphery of your life, and you treat meditation in the same way. You say: Let me go to the temple before I go to the market.

Be aware of this distinction. You make meditation one more act to add to your daily activities. There are already a thousand activities in your life, and you add God as one more, but you will miss God, because God cannot be on the periphery. God has nothing to do with the market and the shops.

He is the very core of your being, where you really are. Where all work becomes rest, where you simply exist, where there is no doer, where there is only the witness - this is where He lives.

God does not occupy a part of you. He is immense. He is all-pervasive. You will only reach Him if you are not prepared to be completely enveloped by Him. If you devote only a part of your time and attention to Him, you will go astray. The day you give yourself completely to Him....

This does not mean that you abandon all your activities, but that you will do your work better, more effectively. The remembrance of God will permeate your whole being, it will be your very breath. When you work, when you are engaged in your activities, you do not stop breathing! Breathing continues in spite of you, it is not a voluntary process. In the same way, the remembrance of God must become an involuntary function within you. You will be going about your worldly duties and the stream of remembrance will continue to flow incessantly within you.

There is no competition or rivalry here, for this is not part of your mundane world.

Actions form the worldly world; therefore, as long as a person is involved in actions, he remains attached to the world of objects, samsara. When he attains non-action, he attains God. Non-action means your existence, where there is no doing, where there is you and you alone, your being alone. There you are united with yourself.

Whatever is said by someone who resembles Shiva becomes a remembrance, a japa. You won't find him praying, because he doesn't need to spend time in prayer. You won't find him worshipping, because that is no longer part of his "actions"; he himself is worship. If you observe such a person closely, you will see that everything he does is worship; when he breathes, it is remembrance, it is japa. When he moves his hand, it is also worship. When he sits or stands up, he is performing the ritual of going around the temple.

All acts of the Shiva-like person are acts of devotion. He does not need to observe any specific practice.

That would be unnatural. If something has to be practised, it is normal that sometimes we get tired of it.

So, when we are tired, we are forced to relax, and relaxing means moving to the opposite.

If you have practised holiness, you will be diligent for six days, but on the seventh day you will have to relax. On that day you will become a non-saint. So, our so-called saints and sadhus have to take a holiday from their sainthood. The sadhu has to go on holiday. If he does not, tensions increase alarmingly.

Thus, the sadhu finds moments of worldliness within himself and the non-sadhu finds moments of holiness. There is no sinner without moments of virtue in his life and no saint without moments of sin in his. The one is tired of virtue, the other is tired of sin, so they have to relax and rest by doing the opposite, in order to remove the burden from the mind.

A saint is a person whose holiness has not been acquired by practice; it is the result of his nature. So it is not a question of resting. You don't need to take a rest from the breath. You don't need to take a rest from the moment the Shiva-like state penetrates deep into you, whatever you do will be superficial. It is like covering a stinking body with perfumes and fine clothes. You may succeed in deceiving others, but how will you hide it from yourself?

That is why we see our sadhus so depressed. There is no trace of joy in them.

To others they look like sadhus, but they themselves do not feel sadhus; there is no dance, no music in their lives. Their anger, their greed and their lust are the same, only repressed. Their outer garb may hide the fact from you, but how can they hide it from themselves? And this keeps pricking their conscience and makes them unhappily unhappy. As long as a sadhu does not laugh and dance spontaneously, you must know that his holiness is cultivated; and cultivated holiness is false. The only true holiness is spontaneous holiness; that is why Kabir says again and again: Spontaneous samadhi is the best, my friend.

Spontaneous samadhi is that which needs no care, but this will only happen when the state of Shiva becomes the core of your being, when you become like Shiva. Remember that this is not an ideal to be achieved in the future; if you understand it, it can happen right now.

Actions need time, and this is not an action; this is a leap. This is knowledge, you just have to recognise it. It is as if a man has a diamond in his pocket but he is in the market begging.

Suddenly, someone reminds him: "Why are you begging? He reaches into his pocket and is surprised to see that he has always had a diamond in his pocket.

The Shivahood lives within you. It is your eternal treasure. There is no need to postpone its attainment:

You just have to turn your eyes inward. If it had been somewhere in the future, you might have needed time - perhaps several births - to reach it. But Shiva-ness is not to be attained, it is to be discovered. It has to be unfolded. Just as you peel an onion layer by layer until at the end you find the mere emptiness, so also man has to uncover himself layer by layer.

Shiva-ness is like emptiness. Let us understand the different layers so that it becomes easy for you to unfold them, so that your life becomes like Shiva and your every word is a remembrance, a japa.

What is the first layer? The first layer is the body. Most people build their identity on their body and consider themselves as nothing more than the body. It's like spending your life on the steps of the palace gate, considering it the palace. You have no idea that it is only the staircase leading to the palace. You drink and eat, get married and start a family, all on the outside porch.

Your children know nothing of the palace, for they were born on the steps; for them, the steps are their home. They will never knock at the gates. Perhaps the gates have rusted away or melted into the wall, so that now no one even knows where the gates were.

The first layer is the physical body, and you live there, totally within the body. You establish an identity with it, which makes you feel that you are the body. The body is mine, but it is not me. What is mine can never be me. What is mine is under my control, but it is not me. If you have a leg amputated, you don't feel diminished by it. If you lose your limbs or lose your eyes, or any other part or faculty of your body, you are still an integrated whole. The body is crippled, but you are a perfect whole.

That is why the ugliest man does not see himself as ugly, because inside each of us is beautiful.

And the worst of sinners is unwilling to call himself a sinner because he sees the good and generous aspects of himself. He will admit that a particular action was wrong, but he will insist that it was a mistake, for he is not a bad man. He calls the act wrong, but not himself. That is the way it should be, though he does not know why it is so.

People around you, in your family, in your neighbourhood, in your city, die; but you never feel that you are going to die too. It must be a deep, innate feeling, for isn't it amazing that you don't think of death for yourself when others are dying in front of you? You may philosophise outwardly, but deep within you is the ringing of bells proclaiming your immortality: Others may die, but I can never die! If it were not so, it would be difficult to live where death takes place at every moment.

All around you, death occurs with such persistence. Every man waits his turn in the queue, even you! And there you live with such nonchalance, as if life is eternal. There is an intrinsic reason, which is: what is inside can never die. However much you identify yourself with the body, you are not the body. The inner truth cannot be falsified by any means. You can drown yourself with intoxicants, but the sound of truth still reverberates within you.

One morning I found Mulla Nasruddin sitting in front of his house. He was laughing so loud and so long that I had to ask him what made him so happy. He said, "Something wonderful has happened, but you won't understand if I don't tell you everything".

"Please tell me the story," I asked.

"I had a twin brother," Mulla began. "We were so alike that it was hard to tell who was who.

This gave me a lot of problems. I would throw a stone at someone at school and they would catch me and punish me. I would steal something and they would punish me. I would start quarrelling in the street and the neighbours would catch me. It was the same at home. And if that wasn't enough, he ran away with my girl".

"So what is there to be happy about, Mulla," I asked.

"Seven days ago I took revenge on him," Nasruddin gloated.

"How is that possible? I asked, "I died, but he was buried!

No one can be that stupid! The Mulla was completely drunk. But you too have spent many lives just as drunk; yet you are never so drunk that your conscience is completely absent. It surfaces again and again. Somewhere within you you are aware of the immortality of your being.

All the facts point to one certainty - that you will die! And yet you still believe that you will never die.

The body belongs to you, but the body is not you. You are in the body, but you are not just the body.

It is the first layer, but you have identified with it through countless births. It has become, so to speak, your twin brother, and you find it difficult to distinguish one from the other. You cannot distinguish between the two faces. Moreover, the outside world knows you by your physical appearance, for it sees only the body. They consider the shape of your body to be your shape. Now, since you are only one in the collective opinion of everyone else, you are naturally influenced by them. If your body is ugly, they call you ugly. If your body is beautiful, they call you beautiful. If your body is old, they call you old. Now this collective opinion gives strength to your belief that you are the body, for no one can see the soul that is you.

There is a very ancient history of the Upanishads:

On a certain occasion, King Janak called a meeting of all the wise men of his kingdom. Invitations were sent out to all those who considered themselves versed in spiritual knowledge. The idea was that these luminaries would devote themselves to discussing spiritual matters with a view to discovering the supreme truth. Predictably, only the most eminent scholars were invited: those who had written scriptures, those who had participated in religious conferences, and those who were experts in the art of debating. There was one such person who was deliberately excluded. This was Ashtavakra. He was so called because his body was bent in eight places. His appearance was ugly and repulsive. How could such a distorted form belong to a man of spiritual knowledge? Nevertheless, his father was invited.

For some reason, Ashtavakra had to go to the Janak court to see his father. When he entered, he found a conference of sages in congress. As soon as he appeared, these people forgot their wisdom and burst into laughter at the sight of him. Indeed, he was a funny sight. The way he walked, the way he talked, everything about him evoked laughter. He should have been a circus clown. He was a caricature of a man. When Ashtavakra saw how those noble scholars laughed, he too burst into laughter. He laughed so loudly that all the others fell silent.

They could not understand why he was laughing like that. Finally Janak asked him, "I can understand why those people were laughing, Ashtavakra, but I can't understand why you were laughing".

"You have taken this conference for a conference of sages, but I see only skin and hide dealers gathered here," said Ashtavakra. "They can only see to the skin and not beyond. Their knowledge is limited to the body. Here am I, the most upright and straightest in this hall, but they see only my mutilated body. These are the mutilated people, O King! If you want to get knowledge from them, you are trying to get oil from the sand. If you want knowledge come to me.

Ashtavakra was absolutely right, for the physical eyes see only the external form.

You are also harassed by external eyes, for all around you there are eyes and eyes... looking at you. They decide for you whether you are ugly or beautiful. Their sin is so great, they are so noisy, that you are helpless. You are alone; the whole world is on the other side. If you give up it is no surprise. It is natural for you to believe "I am the body". It would be a wonder of wonders if you could turn away from the eyes around you and recognise the fact that you are not the body.

Freedom from society means only this. It does not mean fleeing to the Himalayas, it means freeing yourself from the eyes of the crowd around you. It is very difficult, for when a falsehood is repeated incessantly from everywhere, it also appears to be true. You may be a healthy person, but if the people around you decide to drum into you constantly: "You are sick, you are sick", you will soon feel sick. It won't take long. The hypnotic power of suggestion is hard to overcome.

All the world declares that you are the body. Not only men, but even stones and rocks, earth and sky seem to be in conspiracy to proclaim that you are the body. When a thorn pricks you, it pricks the body, not the soul. If someone throws a stone at you, the blood flows from the body, not the soul.

Everything - everyone - proclaims: "You are the body! You are the body!" When this constant repetition comes from everywhere, it is difficult to break it.

And you are alone! You are one against the whole world; for you alone are inside, and the rest of the world is outside. Moreover, they are not wrong, for they can only see your body. Your neighbour can only see the façade of your house, not the inside. He considers the façade to be your house, because it is the only thing he can see. The problem starts when you also start thinking that the façade is the house.

To free oneself from society is to free oneself from the influence of the external eyes. The one who is thus liberated begins to see clearly that he is inside the body, but that he is not the body.

Gradually begin to break through the first layer. Intensify this remembrance that you are not the body.

Experience it! Mere repetition is of no use. When a thorn pricks you, remember that it has pricked the foot; the pain is in the foot and you are only an observer. The thorn cannot prick you; the pain cannot reach you, for you are only the light it knows. That is why anaesthesia is used in surgery. Once you are unconscious you are not aware of what is happening to the body. This could not be so if you were the body. You are not the body, you are the consciousness. The surgeon simply cuts the connection between your body and your consciousness before he can start working on the body.

Those who have done intensive research in the field of life and death have experienced - and I subscribe to their statements - that when a person dies, he is not fully aware that he is dead until after three or four days! It normally takes three days for a person to realise that they are dead. The reason is that death takes place in unconsciousness, and the physical body falls; but a similar body - the mental body - remains within you. It takes three days or more for the person to realise that he is dead. Until then he wanders about the house, with his friends and family.

The soul wanders through the physical body and its earthly connections for three days, and is perplexed by what happens. No one seems to look at him or recognise him. He stands in the doorway and his wife continues to cry. She cannot understand the mystery, for she is the same as before: completely! With the loss of the body nothing is lost. It's like taking off your clothes. If you take off your clothes and remain naked you don't change in the slightest. You are the same with or without clothes. You will still be the same. There is an even more subtle body that remains with you. It has the same shape, the same feelings. It takes you a long time to realise that you are dead.

In Tibet there is a method called the Bardo. When a person is about to die, this process is initiated.

People sit around the dying man and give him suggestions: 'Look, you are about to drop your body.

Be filled with the thought that the body is disappearing. Be aware that very soon the body in which you find yourself will not be the physical body; it will be your subtle body. You have now left the body.

Now it's up to you to choose what kind of womb you want to enter". Such are the suggestions given.

Nowhere else in the world has death been investigated as much as in Tibet. A dying man is made to listen to the suggestions until his last breath. Even after his death, the instructions continue, for to the monk giving the instructions the man is not dead even though the body has been abandoned. The monk knows that death has made no difference to the dead man; he is still listening.

Now the monk influences and directs his next rebirth. This is a very good time to give directions, for the man who has just died can free himself from the attachments of his past life. At this time he can be reminded and made aware of the fact that he is not the physical body; otherwise this is very difficult to achieve. He can now clearly see that he is, while the body lies inert on the ground.

Now the monk says to him: 'Look, you are above while the body lies below. Look carefully! This is the same body with which you identified yourself. Now your loved ones, your friends, will carry the body to the burning ground. Follow them! See how the body burns, see how it is reduced to ashes; yet it has made no difference to you. Remember that this is your journey forward. Don't get involved with the body again.

In your next birth, remember from the first moment that you are not the body. Everyone will tell you that you are the body, but keep your remembrance alive; let no external suggestion drown it out.

If you can detach yourself from all external suggestions, spiritual knowledge will not be far away.

In this century no one equals Picasso as a painter, but people did not forgive him. There was no shortage of people who came to him with free advice. The truth is that only a sense gives unsolicited advice. The wise must be approached. You have to beg and plead with them for advice. You have to strive to get it. Only the fool gives free advice.

People came to Picasso, people who didn't even know the ABC of painting, and said:

Maybe a little more colour here would help" or "Maybe a different angle would have conveyed your meaning better". Picasso was fed up with them. He finally came up with a plan. It would be good if you also followed the same plan. He made a beautiful basket and printed on it the words "Suggestion Box". He instructed everyone who came to bring their suggestions on paper and put them in the box. People were delighted to think that he valued their opinion so highly, but there was one small drawback: the basket had no bottom. Instead there was a hole containing a rubbish bin. Every day his servants emptied the dustbin. You should do the same!

If you want to free yourself from society - and that is what sannyas means - free yourself from the opinions of others. They are outside you, and their opinions have to do with the outer world; they can only be an obstacle in the way of inner knowledge. Do not listen to them. If you want to hear the inner voice, exclude all outer sounds. Close all the doors through which they enter, because those sounds are so terrible, so sharp, that they will suffocate the soft wound within and you will not be able to hear it. This inner voice is always calling you, but you are lost in the sin of the marketplace.

The first layer is the body, and there is only one key to open it. It is a master key, because it opens all the locks. All locks are the same. The key is: become fully aware of the body. When you walk, be aware that it is the body that walks, not you. When you are hungry, know that the body is hungry, not you. When you are thirsty, know that the body is thirsty, not you. Let this awareness be with you always. Gradually you will discover that this awareness creates a chasm between you and the body. As the awareness increases, the distance between the body and you will become greater and greater. There is an infinite distance between the body and you. Remember! As your awareness deepens, the connecting links will begin to separate; then one day you will observe the profound fact that the body is nothing but a shell; you are life, the body is death;

you are consciousness, the body is matter, a set of atoms. You are not a collection of nothingness. You are consciousness - integrated consciousness - which always was, always is and always will be.

As soon as the first layer is peeled off, like the first layer of an onion, the second layer appears. This second layer is the mind. This disease is deeper, for the body is further away from you than the mind. If the body is a conglomerate of atoms, the mind is a conglomerate of thoughts. If the body is gross matter, the mind is subtle matter. Thoughts are subtle vibrations, and vibrations are matter. You are totally in the grip of thoughts. They are not like the body, which can be compared to the clothes you wear. Thoughts are more like the skin of the body; they don't come off as easily as clothes.

You have always had the illusion that thoughts are really 'yours'. You are always ready to defend your views, whether they are right or wrong. You are always afraid that if your point of view is wrong you are wrong. Your identification with your thoughts is much stronger than your identification with your body.

If someone is told: "Go to the doctor, your body is sick", he will not object; only the body is involved. Tell a person that he is sick and he will not be offended, but tell someone that his mind is sick and he should go to a psychiatrist and he will not like it at all. Tell him he is crazy and he will immediately jump down your throat. This is because there is a certain distance between you and the body, but your identification with the mind is more ingrained. Thoughts envelop you everywhere like smoke; as long as this smoke persists, your eyes will remain blind to this fact.

The second experiment - and it is a difficult practice - is to become aware of your thoughts, all thoughts. It doesn't matter what kind of thoughts - good, bad, right or wrong, whether they come from scripture, whether they are traditional or not - just know that "I am not these thoughts". All thoughts are borrowed. They are given to you by society; they come from others and you have learned them. You are what is within you: the unlearned. You are only the consciousness, not the thoughts. Thoughts are the surface ripples of a lake. They are like flotsam in a river. You are the river. You are the eternal current of consciousness.

Slowly, slowly, you must begin to peel away the layers of thoughts. Whenever a thought takes hold of you, remember immediately: It's not me! It is only the outer dust. As dust collects on a mirror, so thoughts have accumulated on you. Never consider a particular thought to be so much yours that you are willing to go to any lengths for it.

If people would break their connection with their thoughts there would be no more wars in the world.

All wars, all conflicts, all violence is caused by your identification with your thoughts. One is a Hindu, another is a Muslim; one is a communist, another is a socialist; this is nothing but identifying with thoughts. You are only God. You are neither Hindu, nor Muslim, nor Jain, nor Buddhist. Your purity is your Shivahood.

Unfortunately, you get caught up in what is cheap and worthless. You think it is more important to be a Hindu than to be God, or more important to be a Muslim than to be God. Whether you are Hindu or Muslim only causes temples to fight against mosques, and in the process you are depriving this land of religion. All religions cause fighting among themselves because all religions become mere ideas. Religion is only one: your Shivahood. You yourself are God. Religion is nothing but this; it cannot cause any fight, because how can there be fight when there are no thoughts? What kind of opposition can there be? What kind of support can there be?

The body separates you from others. Thoughts separate you even more. Understand one thing clearly, though it may seem contradictory: what disconnects you from your own self also disconnects you from others. The body has separated you from yourself; it has also separated you from others. Thoughts have further disconnected you from yourself, and from others. The day when you have peeled off the coverings of body and thought, and become established in your own nature, the day when you become pure existence without a shell, you will find that you have become one with all, for there are not two Gods. Then the God outside you and the God inside you merge into one. The space within the walls of the clay pot and the space outside it will become one. The vessel will break. The identification is the vessel.

As you continue to peel away the layers - and by layers I mean identification with things, which are not you! - you move towards meditation. Meditation is breaking the identifications. Meditation is the key. Gradually, all that remains is what you are. When you have removed all the layers of the onion, you will have nothing but emptiness in your hands. This emptiness, this very emptiness, is your divinity, your Shivahood.

Have you ever seen a Shivalingam? It is a phallic representation of Shiva, but its form is emptiness. It is intentionally made like that. It has no face of Shiva. There is no more beautiful statue or image of anyone, because it has no face. It is the form of emptiness. As you go deeper and deeper into yourself, this same form without emptiness will begin to appear within you, and you will come closer and closer to Shiva. The day you become an enlightened emptiness, a formless, nameless light, from then on everything you say will be japa, the mantra, the remembrance.

At this point, everything you say is a deception. Your religious actions are not religious. Right now you can't do anything else. You try to save yourself from one mistake and make a thousand more.

The best thing to do in these circumstances is to do nothing. Start tearing up your IDs.

Stay awake... and do nothing! Otherwise, in trying to correct one mistake you will find yourself trapped in another.

Mulla Nasruddin was sitting on the seashore, very calm. Next to him sat another man, who was very upset. Finally, with great anger in his voice, he said to the Mulla: "Excuse me, but is it your son who is throwing sand at me?

No," said the Mulla with a gentle smile. "That's my nephew. The one who just broke your umbrella and is busy filling your shoes with water is my son.

You try to correct one thing and something else goes wrong. The excuses you make for your mistakes turn out to be bigger mistakes. In ancient times, a king always had a fool in his court to always remind him of the fact that man's intelligence is no big deal.

A king had a jester in his court. One day, while the king was standing in front of a mirror, the jester suddenly appeared from behind and kicked him hard. The king fell to the ground and was badly bruised; the mirror fell and broke. When the king saw the jester, he couldn't believe his stupidity! "Unless you give me a plausible explanation for this, I'll have you hanged. I have seen many fools, but none to surpass you".

The jester replied: "I didn't know it was you, your majesty. I thought it was the queen.

The king had to let him go.

Wherever you are, you are in the dark. You make one mistake and, in your efforts to correct it, you invariably make another; thus a vicious circle is set up. You want to avoid going to your tent, so you go to the temple; but you turn the temple into a bigger tent. In essence, you are never able to get to the temple. You escape from one place and get stuck in another, and the reason is inside you, not outside. You are in darkness; wherever you go, you will create trouble.

Mulla Nasruddin was in prison. I went to see him. He is a former colleague of mine, so I had to visit him.

"You're very clever, Mulla," I said, "How did you get caught?"

"What can I say?" said the Mulla. "It is all a consequence of my own foolishness.

"Why?" I asked.

"For three months I tried hard to make friends with the dog in the house I was planning to rob, but, as luck would have it, I stumbled on the cat's tail as soon as I entered the house.

This is what you have done all your life. You strive to win the dog's friendship and you step on the cat! You have no eyes to see. You stumble here and there in the dark. The real problem is not searching: the real problem is the lack of light. Groping in the dark you get nowhere. If there is light, the door becomes visible and you can walk through it.

The one who cares to change his behavioural pattern gropes in the dark. Before he ate too much and now he fasts. What he did until yesterday, he does also today, but in reverse!

Whether you overeat or fast has no direction. Until now you were looking in one direction and now you are looking in the opposite direction; however, in both cases your eyes are closed. You go astray not because the direction is wrong, but because your eyes are closed. You have to open your eyes! And when I say "eyes" I mean your consciousness. Your unconsciousness must be broken and your awareness increased. Don't sleepwalk, wake up! As soon as you wake up you will become like Shiva.

*Everything he pronounces is japa.*
*Self-knowledge is your gift.*

He does not give wealth, because wealth is no better than rubbish. Giving wealth makes no sense to him.

What is the point of giving what he himself has given up? There is no point in giving what he considers useless. He does not render any service to his body. He gives only one thing, which in fact is the only thing worth giving: self-knowledge. This is his gift, but you don't take it into account. You have to look very carefully to see it.

Ask the Jainas, for they have kept a full account of how many horses and elephants and chariots, how many precious stones, etcetera, Mahavir gave in charity. He could not have had as many horses and elephants as the Jainas say. By their count, he would have had to be an emperor, not just a local king. The astronomical figures are totally wrong. He could not possibly have possessed so much, for his kingdom was very small, no bigger than a district, about the size of Sikkim today. In Mahavira's time there were about two thousand kingdoms in India. Mahavir would have been about the level of a modern-day tax collector.

Now, what is the reason for inflating the figures? The Jainas think that ordinary charity does not befit such a great tirthankara, so they inflated the figures to convey the greatness of his renunciation. Little do these blind people know that Mahavira's renunciation has nothing to do with this charity. The real diamond that Mahavir gave was self-knowledge, but this is never mentioned at all.

You only see what corresponds to your desires. You only see what interests you. Self-knowledge? The word doesn't sound very valuable. If I put the Kohinoor in one hand and self-knowledge in the other, tell me honestly which one you would choose. You will tell yourself:

Self-knowledge can be attained at any time, if not in this life, then in the next, but the Kohinoor, who knows if it will ever cross my path again? So you will invariably choose the Kohinoor. You are interested in useless things, because you are blind.

The contribution of a Shiva-like person is only one: self-knowledge. What he has attained, he distributes. What he has tasted he offers to you. He gives his own self. He does not give away possessions, but gives of himself. He makes you co-owner of his inner goods, because outer goods are worthless, worthless. It doesn't matter whether you die a prince or a pauper, whether you die of disease or heart failure. What really matters is that you live in full consciousness and die in full consciousness. Everything else depends on this. The fate of your life depends on it; it is this that decides the essence of your existence. Everything else is worthless.

***He is the master of inner powers and the source of knowledge.***

Only self-knowledge can make you master of your inner powers. Only self-knowledge fills your life with light, knowledge and splendour. The day you are able to awaken, or become aware, you will realise that you were always a king. You will marvel. You will laugh at your foolishness in considering yourself a beggar for so long! You will be shocked that you have 'remained in the nightmare of pain for so long; for that is life without consciousness.

Sometimes, while you are asleep, you put your hand on your chest; then you dream that someone is sitting on your chest, or that someone has placed a huge rock on you, or that you are being crushed by an avalanche. You will start sweating and your sleep will be interrupted. When you wake up, you will see that it is only your hand, your own hand - the dreams are so exaggerated that your own hand becomes a mountain! If your hand falls over the edge of the bed, you think you have fallen into an abyss!

Do some experiments. You can induce dreams in a sleeping person. Place a small fire at his feet. He will dream that he is in a desert, that his feet are burning in the sand and that he is dying of thirst.

Start sweating. Or touch his feet with ice; then he will dream that he is climbing Everest, that his feet are frozen and that he is freezing to death. Or put a pillow on his chest and he will see Satan riding on him; or put your hand around his neck and he will dream that he is being hanged. But all this can only be verified on waking. Dreams are many exaggerations. When he wakes up, he will burst out laughing. How much he has suffered, and for no reason! A slight gesture and the mind goes into action, the imagination runs wild!

You never suffer as much as you imagine you suffer. You never suffer the diseases you fear most or the miseries you dread. Ninety percent of your suffering is psychological; only ten percent is real. If ninety percent were eliminated, the imaginary evils, the real evils would be easily overcome. There is a way to overcome them. There is a way out of them and get rid of all the evils. It is you who magnify them so much that you become small; then you tremble and think you can do nothing.

As soon as the ray of knowledge is awakened and the inner flame is kindled, you become the master of all your energies, which is, in fact, the very source of your knowledge. Knowledge is the supreme event. Knowledge means the inner eye, the ability to see, the ability to see through and beyond.

Then life has no more sorrows, and there is bliss, and only bliss. All sufferings are caused by your own blindness. Your sleep turns your dreams into nightmares. Consciousness knows no evils; it knows bliss and only bliss.

***The constant enjoyment of one's own energies is his universe.***

He who attains knowledge and constantly enjoys his self-energies is in permanent bliss. The enjoyment of self-energy, the inner energy, gives rise to infinite pleasure. Bliss flows in a continuous stream, like a constantly flowing river. Infinite springs of bliss flow within you, but you have turned your back on them.

Remember, religion is not renunciation. Religion is supreme enjoyment. God is not someone who sits and cries. He is always dancing. Don't look for a God who weeps; you will never find him. And if you find him, he will not be God, but an impostor. God dances, always dances!

All life is a great festival of happiness. Life knows no suffering; it is only your imagination. You have created misery and pain; you have thought it all out and planned it. What else can a blind man do? Wherever he goes he is bound to hit something; yet he has the illusion that the whole world is ready to hit him. Why should anyone want to hit him? Does the wall or the door have any reason to knock him down? Wherever a blind man goes he is struck by a wall or a door, but he is always ready to find fault with the wall or the door. No one hits the one who has eyes.

Nobody wants to hit you. It is you who are to blame. It is you who are blind. The responsibility is entirely yours, but you put it on others.

The words of this sutra are worth understanding: *the constant enjoyment of the energies of the self is its universe; it* is bliss. When this state of knowledge is attained, bliss occurs at every instant. There are flowers, flowers everywhere, and not a trace of thorns. There flows the elixir of life, and death is nowhere to be found. Not a ray of suffering dares to enter.

There is a realm of supreme happiness within you, and that is what you seek; but you seek outside. Your search is right, but the direction is wrong. The wise man who knows himself gives you the direction and that is his contribution. He takes you in the direction he had taken.

The man of self-knowledge does not give explanations, because there is no way to explain. He just takes you by the hand and leads you there. But you are so timid and fearful; you are afraid even to take him by the hand! You cannot give up, you cannot have faith, you cannot believe anyone. You have been so frightened by your sufferings, so insecure, that you cannot trust even the one who offers to take you out of them. You feel that it will create new problems for you. You are so surrounded by problems that you see them everywhere.

If you do not reach out your hand, the man of self-knowledge cannot help you. How can he give you if your hands are closed; you will have to accept his gift. If you are not willing to open your hands, if you are not willing to accept his generosity, the man of self-knowledge will have to turn back without giving.

***The constant enjoyment of one's own energies is his universe.***

*There the pleasure is constant, while here the pain is constant.*
*To melt into the void or to remain behind is within their will.*

This is difficult to understand, as it can only be known through experience, but if you have some idea of it, it can sometimes be useful.

As soon as a person is able to know himself, he attains a unique energy, which is the greatest energy in this world and the greatest miracle. The miracle is: he can be when he wants and he can not be when he wants. It can come into existence whenever it pleases and it can lose itself in emptiness whenever it pleases. Now you sleep and you wake up, but not voluntarily. If you finish sleeping, you wake up and you cannot go back to sleep. Just as you do with sleep and waking, the one who knows himself disappears into the void and returns to existence at will.

There is a story in Buddha's life: When Buddha arrived in heaven and the guard opened the gate, Buddha turned his back to heaven. He said, "I will not enter until each and every person is liberated. When the last person enters, I will follow behind him".

This is a beautiful story. In this world there are two types of self-realised people, and all religions have known these two types. One attains self-realisation and becomes one with emptiness; the other type attains self-realisation but continues to exist to help others. The Jainas call the first type of the enlightened one, the one who has known ultimate solitude, the kaivalya. There have been many kaivalyas who have attained enlightenment and disappeared into emptiness. They have reached their destination. They enter and do not wait at the door.

The Jainas have given the name "tirthankaras" to twenty-four of these enlightened souls. These twenty-four waited at the gate. They are the ones who guided the others, who paved the way for them. Buddhists have also recognised these two types. One is the arhat, who attains self-realisation and merges into emptiness; the other is the bodhisattva, the one who waits for others.

So there are two kinds of self-realised souls. When you too reach this ultimate state, if the desire to help others remains in you - for the urge to help others is also a desire - you will wait. If it does not, you will merge with emptiness. That is why the true master tries to make bodhisattvas of those of his disciples who have the greatest capacity for compassion.

In the end there remain two elements: compassion and wisdom. Among you there are those who have a greater proportion of compassion or a greater proportion of wisdom. Those who have a greater proportion of wisdom will immediately melt into emptiness. They cannot be trained to be gurus. Those with a higher proportion of compassion are trained to become gurus, tirthankaras and bodhisattvas.

It is thus incumbent upon the guru to train his disciples. In those in whom he finds the element of love, compassion and service to a greater degree, he works so that the yearning for compassion remains in them to the end. When that disciple's knowledge matures, the element of compassion and love is still there. When their ship is ready to sail, one pole will still hold the line: the pole of compassion.

When there is smooth, dry knowledge inside, there is nothing to hold the boat. As soon as it is ready to set sail, it disappears into the void.

A person who has attained Shivahood remains or is absorbed, according to his own will; he may remain in existence to serve or disappear into emptiness. It all depends on his will.

Remember that only he has a will of his own, not you! You are not present in your being, so how can your actions be self-willed? You may say, "I wanted to do this and so I did it," but that is not right; everything you do is due to the pressure of some craving or desire.

What is free will? You can say you have free will if, when someone insults you, you don't get angry. You may not show it, but as soon as someone insults you, the anger is there. You have free will if, when someone insults you, you are as calm inside as if nothing had happened; or if, when someone praises you, you are as calm and unaffected by the praise as if it were directed at someone else. There must not be the slightest change within you; only then can you say that you are master of yourself. This mastery can only be decided at the final moment.

Accordingly, Buddhism has two main branches: Hinayana and Mahayana. Mahayana means the greater vehicle; it is the bodhisattva's "great boat". Even after sitting in his boat, he waits for others to join him. Hinayana is the lesser vehicle, the "small boat" that can carry only one person, and that is the arhat's boat. As soon as he is ready, he gets in and sets sail.

It is difficult to say who is right and who is wrong, the arhat or the bodhisattva. From this state it is difficult to judge; what suits a person's nature is best for him. Those with a feminine heart become bodhisattvas. Those with a masculine heart become arhats. There are these two types of heart and ultimately it is the heart that decides. Either you have a heart saturated with love and compassion, or you have the heart of a plain man and dry of knowledge; either you are a devotee or a sage.

This world is created by the combination of opposites: there is light and darkness, male and female, birth and death; and there is also knowledge and compassion. In the last moment, both elements are present on the shore; whichever is stronger becomes the deciding factor. Then you have to use your own free will, for a liberated person has no attachments. For the first time his free will emerges. Only a self-realised person, whose will is free, can really make a decision. Before that, everything a person does is determined by his desires; it flows only from his longings. He cannot really decide.

Someone once asked Gurdjieff: "Please tell me what I should do. Gurdjieff's reply was: "If you could do anything, I would have told you!

Right now you are incapable of doing anything. You just flow blindly. You are like a blade of straw in a rushing river. You go where the current takes you. Where are you?

Once someone told Buddha that he wanted to serve people. Buddha looked at him compassionately and said, "You are not yet one yourself, so how are you going to serve?

The decision is taken at the last moment. Only after Self-realisation do you attain the power to decide, for then you are like Shiva. Then you are no longer the creation, but the creator. Then you are no longer part of this universe; you are God Himself. Then the work is in your hands; then you are in control. Then, when the time comes to leave, it is for you to decide whether you stay behind and wait for others to get into your boat, and become a tirthankara; or you want to worry about them. You will say that every man must find his own way; every man has to follow his own path.

Who can guide whom, who will sit in whose boat? You will spread the sails and set sail.

It is necessary to remember this sutra: to ***melt into emptiness or to remain behind is within your will; for by paying attention to it*** you can begin to think of what you will choose at that last moment, if given the opportunity. This thought will invariably arise within you, and it is useful, for this very seed of a thought will grow into a tree when you come to the end of life's journey.

# Eternal spring

*Sukha-asukhavorbahirmananam tadvimuktastu kevali tadarorhapranitestatkshayaj jivasankshya bhootakanshuki tadavimukto bhuyah patisamah parah om shri Shivarpanam satu happiness and sadness are nothing but external states of mind, he knows this constantly.*

*Freed from them, he attains his solitude.*

*The yogi who is established in his solitude ceases to desire, and thus attains liberation from birth and death.*

*The liberated person, for whom body and mind are no more than garments, attains Shivahood.*

*Om! It is dedicated to Lord Shiva.*

Before going into the sutras....

I told you earlier that I would talk more about mantra, for I would like you to know how the right use of mantra can bring about a transformation in your life. The first thing is that, as I said before, your personality contains a series of layers like an onion. You have to peel away each layer in order to get to the centre which is hidden inside. The diamond is hidden. It is not lost, because you yourself are the diamond and you can never lose it. Only the centre is hidden under the different layers, but that's what a diamond is. A diamond is hidden under layers of stone; it also looks almost like a stone, but that does not alter its intrinsic quality as a diamond.

You may not know why diamonds are so valuable. Behind their value is man's search for the eternal. The diamond is the most stable object in the world. All things change, but a diamond dies unchanged. Thousands of years can pass and it will not deteriorate. In this ever-changing world, the diamond is the symbol of unchanging existence. Hence its value; otherwise it is nothing but a stone. Its value lies in its immutability, in its stability.

Your eternal nature is a diamond. Every sadhana is designed to remove the layers of dust that cover this diamond. Since the layers covering it are dust, they are easily removed. It is that which is constantly changing that covers the unchangeable, so it is not difficult to remove it. The mantra is a method of removing those layers.

Let me tell you a brief story:

Mulla Nasruddin met a friend whom he had not seen for many years. The friend asked the Mulla about his family. "What about your daughter, Nasruddin?

"Oh, my daughter," said the Mulla. "You won't believe this, but I have to tell you that she is happily married. Not only that, her husband is a famous doctor.

The friend knew Nasruddin, and could not believe a word of it. He said, "So give it to me, Mulla, but I find it hard to accept. Your daughter was not only... well, she wasn't beautiful, she was very ugly, really ugly. She had a body like a military tent. It's hard enough to believe that she married, but to a doctor? How could you wink at a doctor?

"Very good! All right!" replied the Mulla. "He may not be a great doctor.... He may not be a doctor at all, but he has relieved my headache, so for me he is the best doctor in the world".

The one who takes away your headache is a doctor; but the one who takes away your head is the mantra. The proverb says Without bamboo there can be no flute. But as long as the head remains there will be headache. There is a technique to remove the head. All your problems are caused by your head: your thoughts, your reasonings, your arguments, your obsessions and your questions. If the thoughts are lost, the head is lost; you will be, but not the mind! What kills the mind is the mantra. When the mind is gone, then the bridge between you and the body is broken. It is the mind that connects you to the body; if the bridge is broken, you are here and the body is ahead.

He who knows himself as separate from the body and without mind, attains Shivahood. He is the supreme "solitude".

Therefore, understand what mantra is. The definition of mantra is: that which destroys the head so that the mind no longer exists. There is a method to go through the layers of the body and the mind. It is very necessary to go step by step; you have to exercise the utmost patience. It is a method that demands immense patience. Impatient people will not only not benefit from the mantra, but will very possibly harm themselves. Understand this will. Do you have enough problems already?

The mantra will only be an added problem for you if you are impatient.

Once, during my travels, when the train stopped at a station, there was a man selling toys and he shouted until he was hoarse: "This toy is unbreakable. No child will be able to break it. He looked at the toy; it looked quite strong and it was very expensive. He immediately thought of Mulla Nasruddin's son. Mulla's wife always complained that he broke his toys before he got home, so I bought the toy, took it to Nasruddin's house and gave it to the boy.

A week later I went to visit them again. As soon as I walked in, Mulla's wife told me: "We are in terrible trouble.

"What happened," I asked, "Did your son break the toy?"

No," she replied. In trying to break it, he has broken all his other toys. Not only that, he has broken all the mirrors in the house with it, and now we have to do something to save ourselves from this deadly weapon."

As it is, you are already in a state of insanity. The mantra can destroy the madness, but there is also the danger of making it worse. As it is, you are already overburdened in life, and the mantra can be an additional burden. This offers an explanation for something very curious: people whom we generally consider religious often seem to be more troublesome than worldly men. The worldly man is burdened with his worldly problems. The religious man has the same worldly problems, but to these he has added another: his religion. His mind retains all its old activities and this becomes additional; he becomes even busier.

The mantra requires that you have the utmost patience; otherwise, do not dwell on it. It is to be used as a medicine. Don't consider drinking the whole bottle in one gulp. That will not cure anyone; it could kill him. The action of the mantra is very subtle, so it requires homeopathic doses. The first requirement is patience, a lot of patience. Don't expect quick results; the fruits of mantra ripen very slowly. It is not an annual plant that you can expect to flower soon after planting; it takes numerous births for the flowers to appear. Although it may seem difficult to understand, the more patient you are, the sooner the flowers will appear, and the more impatient you are, the longer the delay will be.

A man was walking down the street in great pain, as his shoes were too small for his feet. He cursed the shoes and was very upset. Nasruddin passed by. He said to him: "Where did you buy such narrow shoes? The man was already in a bad mood, and Nasruddin's question only made his blood boil.

"Where did I buy them, you ask? I plucked them from a tree.

"Well," said Nasruddin, "you should have waited a little and let the tree mature; then they would have fit your feet. You have broken off an unripe branch.

Never throw away an immature mantra or you will be in trouble. It is easy to throw away a shoe, but the mantra or you will be in trouble. It is easy to throw away a show, but it is not so easy to get rid of the mantra, for the shoe is external and the mantra is internal. If you get involved in the mantra by mistake, it is almost impossible to get rid of it. Many religious people go mad, and the reason is only this:

are in such a hurry that they pluck the fruit while it is still green. A ripe fruit is very sweet, while an unripe fruit is not only bitter, but sour and possibly poisonous.

The first layer is the body, so the mantra practice must begin in the body; you are in the body, so that is where the cure must begin. If you skip this layer, your disease will remain, and in due course you will find yourself with unripe fruit on your hands. Remember that you can only start from where you are; if you start elsewhere, you are only dreaming. Right now you think you are the body, so you have to start the mantra experience with the body.

Understand the technique. First, you have to sit quietly for ten minutes, but before you sit you have to purge yourself of all your restlessness by being totally active for five minutes; dance, jump, skip, hop, run, whatever it takes to satisfy your restlessness. It must be cleansed from every pore, from every part of the body; only then can you sit in silence for ten minutes. This catharsis is necessary before you begin to sit in silence; it will require five to ten minutes, according to the degree of your restlessness. Let your body become agitated, totally, completely, in every possible way, so that during those minutes it has no more desire to satisfy its craving for activity. Then sit down, so still that there is not a hint of movement. Keep your eyes half closed.

Do not try this practice in an open space. A closed room, preferably small and empty, is ideal.

There should be nothing inside the room. A church, temple or mosque is ideal because of its emptiness. If this is not possible, clear a corner of your room; let there be nothing in it. Remove all images of gods and goddesses, as they can also create problems.

Only emptiness is God. Everything else is a game of the mind, and the mind is so crazy! Look for yourself at the shrines people set up in their homes to worship. You will find pictures of gods and goddesses hanging all over the walls. They may be cut out of the newspaper or calendar pictures; it's all the same. The walls are full of them. By looking at their walls you can tell what goes on in people's minds.

When people worship their household gods, they rush into the shrine room, sprinkle a little on the entire collection of deities, fold their hands and believe they have satisfied each of them. Not one of them has been worshipped. If you try to satisfy them all, you have paid homage to none of them; but if you truly pay homage to one, they are all satisfied. Get one and you have got all; and the one is within, not without!

The emptier the place, the better; for the search is for that emptiness; the room will be the symbol of your inner emptiness. The room should be small; that helps the mantra. And it should also be empty; that also helps. Let the eyes be half-open; for when the eyes are wide open, you are standing in the doorway, with your back to the house and looking out into the world outside. You cannot make a complete turn, because a complete change is not easy. So keep your eyes half open and half closed; let them be half closed to the world and half open to yourself. Start here!

Remember that there is no hurry. When your eyes are half-open you experience a state of drowsiness.

Keep looking at the tip of your nose; keep your eyes open only up to that point. You should not concentrate. Observe the tip of the nose with a feeling of inner peace. Then start saying "Om" out loud. You are using the body, you start with the body, because that is where you are at this moment.

Repeat "Om" out loud, so that the sound hits the walls and bounces back to you. This is why an empty room is essential, for such resonance is only possible in a large room, and the greater the resonance, the better. Christian cathedrals were designed for mantra; it reverberates and resonates a thousand times everywhere. The Hindu temple is also built for meditation; the dome serves the same purpose. No vibration can escape from a circular place; the sound turns inwards.

Sit and repeat "Om" as loud as possible. Remember to use your body. Your whole body should be bathed in the vibrations of "Om". You must feel that you have spent all your vital energy in that "Om". Do not hold anything back; treat it as a matter of life and death. The mantra cannot be complete with anything less than this. If you repeat it quietly, half-heartedly, it is of no use. You have to say it with all your might, with all your being, as if your life depended on it; if you don't say "Om" with all your might, you will die. Stake all of you! Let "Om" roar like a lion from within you. Eyes squinted... half-open... and a strong repetition of "Om". Remember that vibrations are created like ripples in a pond when a stone is thrown. In the same way, your "Om" will create ripples and vibrations everywhere; it will hit the walls and come back to you.

Also, repeat the "Om" quickly, so that each repetition overlaps the previous one. Leave no interval between them, no space. Strive with all your might, until you are bathed in sweat. In a few days you will see that the whole room is full of "Om". You will see that the room helps you; all the sound will come back to you. If you can find a circular room, it will be very good; if you find a domed one, even better! The room should be absolutely empty, so that the vibrations rain down on you from all sides. Your whole body should be bathed in these vibrations. Then you will feel a wonderful freshness, unattainable even after bathing in water.

Scientists are conducting extensive research on vibrations. They have found that plants flower and bear fruit earlier when they have been exposed to music of a particular vibration. In Russia and America, music has been used in agriculture to promote earlier and more abundant harvests; the results have been quite satisfactory.

Ravi Shankar used his sitar in an experiment in Canada. He played the sitar when seeds of different plants were planted. When the plants grew, the most surprising thing was that they all leaned towards the place where Ravi Shankar had played. When they grew, they kept leaning in the same direction, just as a deaf person leans forward and brings his ear closer to hear better. All the plants have their ears oriented towards the sitar! And they grew twice as fast! A plant is a gross body in which everything is asleep, unconscious; but still, the body vibrates with sound and starts to sway.

When "Omkar" - the sound of "Om" - starts raining down on you from all sides, the vibrations will form a circle. You will find that every pore of your body will be filled with joy, and all bodily ailments will disappear; you will find a peace, a deep sense of well-being. You will be surprised how many bodily ailments will disappear by themselves, because it is a deep cleansing that penetrates you deeply.

The body is a concentration of vibrations, and there is no more wonderful vibration than "Omkar", the repetition of "Om". Repeat "Om" aloud for ten minutes, using the middle of the body to the fullest.

Then close your eyes. The tongue should touch the roof of your mouth, which should be completely closed. Now you should no longer use your tongue or lips.

The next step is to repeat "Om" inside, in your mind. Until now the room was outside, surrounding you on all four sides; now the body surrounds you on all four sides; now the body is the room. Let the mantra reverberate inside the body for the next ten minutes. You should not use the lips, the tongue or the throat at all. The mind should repeat "Om... Om... Om...", but you must keep the same fast rhythm, the same speed. Just as you have filled the room with omkar, fill the body also, letting it tremble with vibrations from head to toe. Leave no space between two oms, so that the mind has no opportunity to intrude. The mind cannot have two thoughts at the same time.

If your repetition is so fast and intense that there is no space between two repetitions, no thoughts will appear between them. If you relax your tranquillity the slightest, thoughts will appear. Therefore, repeat without gaps! Don't worry about overlapping repetitions. Let them pile up on top of each other like train cars in an accident. Remember that you must no longer use your body, so now the eyes must be closed. Now the body must be very still. The "Om" vibrations must strike the walls of the body from within and fall upon the mind, just as in the beginning they struck the walls of the room and then reflected back into the body, which purified the body, just as the inner vibrations cleanse the mind. As the vibrations become deeper, you will notice that the mind begins to fade. You begin to experience a deep silence that you have never tasted before.

Hold this posture for a few minutes; then lower your head until your chin touches your chest. For a few days you may feel a tension in the neck, but pay no attention to it and it will soon disappear. Then, in the third step you drop the chin on the chest, as if the neck is cut off, lifeless. Now, don't do any more repetitions, not even in the mind. Now just listen, as if the "Omkar" is reverberating within you and you are only the listener, not the doer. You can only come out of the mind completely when you give up all sense of the doer. Become only a witness. Put all your effort into it. Let your head hang down to your chest and try to listen to the "Om" resounding within you.

There is a famous verse by Galib:

*The beloved image is in the mirror of the heart.*
*Whenever I choose it, I just tilt my head to look at it.*

This inclination of the head is necessary. As soon as the neck is knotted, the image of the beloved appears before your eyes. But, unfortunately, you don't yet know how to knot the head. You strive to cultivate a stiff neck. When the question of tilting the head arises, you become even more rigid.

If you have so far failed to reach God, the only reason is that you are not prepared to bow your head; you are not prepared to surrender.

Bowing the head is nothing more than a symbol. Lower the head as if it were separated from the body; this is only so that you can bend down. As soon as the head is bent, it is easier to see; as soon as the neck is bent, it is more difficult to think.

Now try to listen. Until now you repeated the mantra, first with your body and then with your mind. Now try to become a witness of the mantra. You will be surprised; there is a very subtle sound of the mantra within you. It is exactly like "Om", although it is not "Om", because it is difficult to express it in any language. If you listen quietly, you will hear it for sure.

You are now separated from the body. The first step severed your connection with the body; the second severed your connection with the mind; now the third step is the attitude of witness, the feeling that "I am the witness".

No mantra is greater than "Om"; no mantra is more wonderful. Ram, Krishna, Mahavir, Buddha, they are all beautiful sounds, but they cannot take you beyond the mind, because they have an image, a form; whereas "Om" has no form. Besides, you have a relationship with Buddha, Krishna and Jesus; you have feelings of love, attachment, fondness, affection. These will not allow you to leave your mind. Om" has no meaning. It is unique. It has no meaning, no form, no image, not even an outline. And it is not part of the alphabet. It is the closest thing to the sound that actually resonates continuously within you, which is the very nature of your existence. Just as the stream does not babble, but its own flow causes the sound of babbling; just as when the wind passes through the branches and the leaves rustle, your being is such that "Om" resonates within you. It is the sound of your being.

Therefore, "Om" does not belong to any religion. It is neither Hindu, nor Jain, nor Christian, nor Buddhist, nor Muslim. It is a non-sectarian mantra. You may be surprised to know that Jains, Muslims and Christians all use this mantra, albeit with slight variations: Muslims say amin, Christians say amen. They are just modified forms of "Om". In the course of its journey from India to distant lands this mutation occurred. Om" is not related to any thought.

Whoever was observed in the state of non-thought, heard it.

In the first two steps you will pronounce the mantra, and in the third step you will just listen to it.

You will be the hearer, the witness. In the first two steps you are the doer, for the body and the mind are parts of the doer; the third is the witnessing state. In it you listen, you just listen. The body is cut off, the mind is cut off; the layers of the onion are peeled off and only pure existence remains, only you! And that is Shivahood!

And once you get a taste for it, you will thirst for more and more. The taste will draw you in, pull you in; it becomes a magnet. We are attracted to things that attract us and we naturally go towards them. The problem only arises when you don't get the taste; you meditate but you don't enjoy it. This is because you have not yet got the taste for meditation. Once you have got the taste for it, there is no difficulty, because then the mind floats by itself. Whenever you are free, even for a short time, your eyes will close, your head will lower and you will see the face of the beloved in the mirror of your heart. Then no matter where you are, in the house or in the market place, it is all the same.

Only the first step is very difficult. It is half the journey to hover around like a bee, always thirsting for more and more. The nature of the mind is to go again and again to the place of pleasure. Just because you have not yet enjoyed pleasure you have to find a way to direct the mind towards meditation.

Now your mind keeps saying: "Why not go to the market? Why waste time sitting here! You can do all that later when you have time; now it's time to go to the shop or to the office! The mind takes you to the place where it gets pleasure. Don't blame the mind for that. Once you have the taste inside you, you will find it more and more difficult to focus the mind outwards. first it was difficult to draw it inwards; now it is difficult to draw it outwards.

Sariputra, a disciple of Buddha, attained a taste for "Omkar". He attained the highest state of mantra; he listened to the supreme manta within.

When this happened, Buddha ordered him to go out and preach to the people.

He said to the Buddha, "Now I have no desire to go out".

Buddha replied, "That is precisely why I want you to leave. First you were trapped by the outside; that was a form of bondage. Now don't let the 'inside' bind you".

The perfect and enlightened soul is one that has no difficulty whatsoever. It comes in and goes out like a gust of wind. Now entering is no longer entering, and going out is no longer going out; they have become one. Just as you go in and out of your house easily, life is like your house; you should have no difficulty in going in and out of it. There are people attached to the world and people attached to the soul; both are enslaved. They have not yet attained the ultimate salvation. The knower is unattached, neither within nor without. He flows naturally inward and outward.

You should try to hold this third stage of the mantra for as long as possible. The first stage is to sit in silence. The prelude is to shake the body by dancing, jumping, writhing, for about ten minutes, to get rid of all the restlessness in the body. The body is full of restlessness; that is simply a scientific fact.

If you want to slap someone, the energy of your body immediately flows into your hand. That is why someone who is quite weak can give you a strong slap; his hand does not remain in the ordinary state, but is filled with energy. Suppose for some reason you cannot slap that person. There may be many reasons; life is very complex. Perhaps you are indebted to him, or perhaps you want to use him to get something, so you hold back; but the energy that has accumulated in his hand is blocked and has no way of returning.

Recent scientific research reports that there are ways to discharge energy from the body, but there is no way to draw the energy back into the body; therefore, if you don't hit someone or something, the energy will remain in the hand. It doesn't matter who you hit; even if you hit the empty space, you will discharge that energy; but there are no channels to draw that energy back to the centre. Thus, the energy is blocked in various parts of the body. In any twenty-four hour period, energy will be blocked in many different parts of the body, and that blocked energy is bound to hinder you. It is responsible for the feeling of numbness in your feet, or the sensation of ants crawling up your legs, or your back starting to ache, or your back suddenly itching. These things are not your imagination; they are really happening, but perhaps you never noticed them before because your energy was always busy and you never sat idle before. Now that you sit doing nothing, where the energy has been blocked, restlessness occurs.

Tell any small child to sit quietly for five minutes and you will feel how cruel you are being to him, how hard it is for him to sit quietly. Sometimes he lifts a foot, sometimes he clenches his hands, or moves his lips or twists his eyes; he will do anything to move. The energy flows everywhere. The legs want to run, the hands want to move, the eyes want to see, the ears want to hear. These are all old habits. This is how energy has always flowed.

That is why I always insist on catharsis before any meditation. It is very helpful. Punch, jump and jump for ten minutes to expel all the blocked energy, and then sit down to meditate. The peace that follows catharsis is the calm that follows the storm; the body becomes light, loses its restlessness.

These ten minutes are only a preparation, not an actual stage in the mantra meditation. It is the step out of your house. The real journey happens inside the house.

*First step, but the body: saying "om" - ten minutes Second step, but the mind: silent repetition of "om" - ten minutes.*

*Third step, listen silently to the resonance of "omkar" within - ten minutes.*

Repeating Rama, Krishna or Buddha will not be adequate for this journey, for they can only take you up to the second step; they cannot go beyond that, for on the third step the real resonance in the head is the sound of "Om". Sometimes, a person who repeats "Ram.... Ram... Ram... Ram...' can reach the third stage. It is like when you travel in a train, you hear the wheels saying whatever you feel like saying.

You may think they are saying "Ram-Ram-Ram" or "Allah-Allah-Allah", but the truth is that the sound of the wheels is actually "Chucka-Chucka-Chucka-Chucka".

Om" is that pure sound. If you repeat Ram you will also hear Ram, but this is only a superimposition, indicating that the mind is still alive and functioning to some extent. We should experience only what is. We should see only what is, without giving it our own colour. Hence the supreme mantra is "Omkar"; all others are secondary, inferior. They only take the seeker to the second step. In reality, they become an obstacle on the third step.

Use "Om" as I have specified. For at least three months, without worrying at all about the results. Don't even think about the results; just do the practice. Don't worry about whether you are making progress or not. Set a date; in exactly three months you can start thinking about results, not before! If you can muster that much patience, you will succeed.

A little boy digs a hole, puts in a mango seed and covers it up. After half an hour, his curiosity makes him dig it up to see if it has started to sprout. He is disappointed. He puts the seed back in the hole. After another half hour, his patience runs out again and he digs up the seed. Now he feels really unhappy, because nothing has happened. Now the seed will never sprout. Everything has its own timetable. A seed must remain in the dark soil for a certain time before it can sprout.

For this very reason, your meditation is not bearing fruit either. You are too impatient for results.

Jesus said: "Let not your left hand know what your right hand is doing". Act in the same way! Bury the mantra deep within you. That is why the mantra is spoken of as a seed. All it means is that you should not keep digging it up again and again to examine its progress. It has its own rhythm. It will sprout in its own time. Your impatience can only spoil things for you.

Take this supreme mantra with you and perform the experiment. If you do it with full patience for three months, you will be filled with a sweet nectar, and then it will be what Kabir calls the taste of "raw sugar for the dumb", which can never be spoken of. When you have tasted it, wherever you are you will be fine, whatever you do you will be fine. Then the world becomes a dream for you, and all life is but a drama; you become a witness and that in itself is Shivahood.

Now let us return to the sutras:

*Happiness and sadness are nothing more than external states of mind; this is a constant reminder.*

One who has attained Shivahood is constantly aware that happiness occurs outside, and also sorrow; neither penetrates inside you. But both disturb you. You cling to happiness, identify yourself with it and think that you are happy. In this way you have created sorrow. From this point the journey to suffering begins. In fact, it has already begun.

As soon as you say, "I am happy", you have sown the seed of unhappiness; now it will not be long in coming. Suffering means identifying yourself with your states of mind. So when suffering comes, you identify with that. Your problem is that you identify with what is presented to you. You are no longer the observer, but you become the reactor to what comes before you. If sadness comes, you beat your chest and tear your clothes; if happiness comes, you dance with joy. Both happiness and sorrow come from outside and have no way of entering you. It is you who identifies with them and suffers from them. As soon as a person goes beyond the mind, he begins to see that all this happens outside the temple, and that nothing enters inside.

*Happiness and sadness are external states of mind: this is a constant reminder.*

Here the word "constantly" is important. You also remember it sometimes, especially when you advise or counsel others; then you know it for sure. I wish you were as wise for yourself as you are for others. You are very wise when you advise others. It would be very good if you would apply the same understanding to the path of your life.

What is the reason for this deep understanding and wisdom towards others? If someone has big problems, you say, "Why are you so upset? That's life! That's the way the world is! Don't get so involved in it. When you find yourself in the same trouble, that same person may well return your good advice and say, "Don't worry, brother. Happiness and sadness are only external states".

What is the reason for this? It is simply that when suffering comes to others, you become a witness, so understanding arises in you. The pain has come to others, not to you; you are only the observer. To the extent that you become the observer, when the pain comes to you, this understanding will remain in you. Right now you have given away your understanding.

Mulla Nasruddin went to a psychologist and told him: "My wife's condition is very bad. You will have to do something.

The psychologist worked with her for a few weeks, and then told Mulla: "She has completely lost her mind. I am very sorry, Mulla.

I knew he would do it," Mulla exclaimed. "Every day he would tell me off and in the end it's all over.

You advise and counsel others. You give your wisdom to others, but you never use it for yourself.

The next time happiness comes to you, observe it as if it were happening to someone else.

Try to stand a little away from him and watch him. A little distance is enough. Don't stand so close to yourself. You are your neighbour; keep a little distance.

I once said to Nasruddin: "Mulla, the owner of the restaurant at the end of the street says he is a close relative of yours.

"Of course not!" replied the Mulla. "That is not correct. He is a distant relative of mine.

"How distant is the relationship?" I asked.

Well," said the Mulla, "we have the same father, but he is the first son and I am the twelfth. So that's it! We are far apart.

Whatever your neighbour is will be enough distance between the two of you. Don't stand so close to your neighbour. When there is no distance you lose perspective. Whatever you want to look at must be kept at a certain distance. If you bring a flower close to your eye, will you be able to see it? If you press your face to a mirror you will not be able to see your reflection. A little distance is necessary. A little distance from yourself, that is what sadhana is all about. As this distance increases, you will be surprised how insignificant all your problems were. Things were happening outside you, not to you!

Because of your closeness, they reflected back at you, the vibrations touched you and you took them in as if you were vibrating yourself. You allowed them to affect you.

A house caught fire. The owner was beating his chest and crying his eyes out. A man standing next to him said, "You are unnecessarily tormenting yourself. Only yesterday your son sold the house for a good sum.

The man could not believe his ears. He stopped lamenting. The house was still burning, but he looked on unconcerned. He kept his distance; he was no longer the owner of the house.

After a while, his son came running: "My God, how did the house catch fire? I made a deal for the house, but there is still no payment. Now who is going to pay for a ruined house?

The father started wailing again. The house was not affected. The happiness or sadness of its owners had no effect on it. It was burning before and it was still burning afterwards, but the owner's mood would have changed again if the buyer had come along and said he would honour the contract even if the house had burnt down.

Everything happens outside you, but you are too close; that's the problem. Keep your distance!

When happiness comes, step back a little and watch. When sadness comes, step back a little and watch.

But it starts with happiness, not grief. Generally, people try to dissociate from themselves in times of sadness in order to escape from it. That is a general tendency of the mind, and it gets you nowhere. Create distance when you are happy, because everyone wants to escape from sorrow. If you want to establish real detachment, it is not enough to run away from sorrow.

You need to do just the opposite. Your journey so far has only led you astray. You will have to turn back and retrace your steps. This turning back and doing the opposite is called pratikraman by Mahavira.

Patanjali used the word pratvahara, which literally means to recover or withdraw the sense organs from the object; it means to return to the source.

You must retrace your steps. When happiness comes, stand back; don't let your heart burst with joy, don't dance with rejoicing. Know that this too shall pass. Nothing is permanent; everything is transitory; nothing stops for you. Any mood is like a gust of wind that comes and goes. You are barely aware of its presence before it disappears. Stand aside, as an observer.

Why don't we act as witnesses to our happiness? What is the fear? There is a reason behind it. As soon as you relate to happiness as a witness, it no longer gives you joy; it is no longer happiness.

The closer you are to yourself, the more intense the happiness. The further you move away from yourself, the more you dissociate from yourself, the more you realise how transitory those moments of happiness are.

The more you associate with it and forget your intrinsic self, the more you will experience the joy of happiness. That is why no one wants to be an observer of happiness, but this is the only place from where the journey can begin.

When happiness comes, witness it. You will soon discover that, as you watch, happiness fades away and only you remain. Once you succeed with happiness, you will also succeed with sadness. Then the key is in your hand: come joy, come sorrow. A little effort will bring you success. All you have to do is to separate yourself a little from your body. There is already a great distance between you and the body. No two wings can be further apart, because that is the distance between matter and consciousness. Even the stars are not as distant from the earth as you are from the body. One is living and the other inanimate; one is made of clay and perishable and the other is spirit. They are the two extremes.

Start with happiness, and the word towards unhappiness, remembering only one thing all the time, you are involved! You will have to practice it again and again. Again and again there will be lapses; it will not be continuous at once. The remembrance can only be constant when you are established in the soul, when the mantra has succeeded in eliminating the mind. Until then you will have to practise it, to keep it as long as possible. This clears the way. The seed may not yet be sown, but at least the ground is clear. When you are ready to plant the seed, the soul will be ready. The memory will fade again and again, a slight unconsciousness and happiness will come back to you, but don't give up.

The yogi who has attained Shivahood is constantly aware that happiness and sorrow are external states. Constant means incessant, without a moment's pause. Only what is your own nature can be constant. What is not your nature cannot be constant. How long can you remain angry, for example?

Bodhidharma went to China, where the king who came to visit him said, "I am troubled by my anger.

What should I do?"

Bodhidharma replied: "How long can you be angry?

The king was surprised. "For an hour or two at most," he replied.

"What you can do for one or two hours is not your nature," Bodhidharma said. "Can you be angry for twenty-four hours a day?

"An hour or two of anger is a torment, and you ask me if I can be angry for twenty-four hours. I have not come to find out how to be angry all the time," said the king.

Bodhidharma said, "That is why I tell you that what you can do constantly is your nature. So why do you worry?".

What can you do constantly? Give it some thought. You cannot remain constantly happy.

You may find this hard to understand, but it is a fact. Think about it for a while: how long are you happy? After a while happiness declines and you begin to be unhappy; if nothing happens to disturb your happiness, you yourself begin to be bored with it. A palace to live in, plenty of food, a beautiful woman for a wife, and no trouble or bother.... what will you do then? Soon you will be fed up and long for a change.

It often happens that a man who has a very beautiful wife begins an affair with an ordinary servant girl. People wonder what he sees in such a plain Jane when he has such a beautiful wife. They wonder because they witness it. The man is just looking for a change. Even beauty bores him. How long can you keep looking at a beautiful face? How long can you listen to a beautiful melody? After a while, it hammers your ears and you want it to stop. If it continues, it becomes hell.

The mind cannot bear anything constantly; it cannot bear even happiness for too long. That is why, whenever happiness comes, the mind looks for ways to create unhappiness. The mind is constantly changing its taste; when there is happiness it wants sadness; when there is sadness it craves for joy. You cannot sit quietly for long; soon the mind becomes restless and bored with tranquillity.

Bertrand Russell wrote: "I would not choose liberation, for I have heard that the people of the kingdom have been sitting on the magic wish-fulfilling rock for eons. There is nothing to do there, for doing means the worldly world, samsara. What could Mahavira do sitting on this rock? Besides, who knows how long he will have to sit there? What can one do sitting there doing nothing? There are no newspapers to pass the time, and nothing ever happens there. Things only happen in the wrong places. In hell there must be a lot of news. Perhaps they produce twelve or more editions a day, for the news always involves murder, arson, looting, violence. In heaven nothing ever happens. It must be very boring.

Bertrand Russell says: "My mind dreads the thought of heaven. I would be better off without it. The mind speaks the truth. Bertrand

Russell does not know that there is no salvation as long as the mind exists.

Only he whose mind is annihilated, he who is constant, prefers salvation.

Is there anything you can endure continuously? Neither suffering nor happiness can be tolerated constantly because they cause tension. The only thing that is tolerable for any length of time is serenity; it contains no excitement. You can be serene constantly because it is a state between the two, and beyond the two.

One day I was having dinner at the Mulla's house. His son was sitting with us at the table. When he started eating, he ate with his left hand. Soon he switched to the right hand. After a while, he went back to eating with his left hand and then switched back to the right. Nasruddin said: "How many times have I told you, young man, to eat only with your right hand?

The boy said, "What difference does it make which hand I use, my mouth is in the way anyway?".

Only he can be constant who finds the point of balance between happiness and sorrow. The balance between righteousness lies exactly at the midpoint between happiness and sorrow. There are no extremes here. It is like the movement of the pointer on the scales; the stable point is right in the middle. Any slight weight and the needle swings towards sadness or happiness, and you will constantly tire of its weight and want to move it the other way.

When people carry a body to the burning ghats, they bear the weight of the coffin on one shoulder and soon tire and change shoulders; the weight does not diminish, but the shoulder is relieved.

Happiness and sadness are your two shoulders and the attitude of being the doer is your bier. You continuously change your shoulders. Sometimes you identify with happiness and sometimes with sadness. Be the witness - stay in the middle - then you can be constant.

Buddhahood can be constant, for it is a state of peace. There is bliss in it, but it is not like the sharp rays of the sun. It is cool and refreshing like the rays of the moon. Bliss is not like the fiery rays, but like a cool glow; there is no tension in it, no restlessness.

Have you noticed that often, when a man is happy, he suffers a heart attack? Suddenly, a man wins the lottery. He is extremely happy... and he drops dead!

A man won a lottery of ten lakh rupees. When he was told the news, he was not at home. His wife was very upset. She knew her husband, and if she found out that he had won two paise she might die of a heart attack. She ran to a nearby temple where she knew the priest was a wise man. She asked him for help. He told her not to worry and returned home with her, promising to tell her husband immediately.

When the husband cam the priest thought it would be better to start with a smaller amount, so he said, "I would like you to know that you have won one lakh rupees in the lottery".

The husband replied, "Really? If it is true, I will donate fifty thousand rupees to your temple".

The priest dropped dead of a heart attack. It never occurred to him that fifty thousand rupees would be too much for him.

Happiness can also kill. It is not only sadness that kills, for both contain a stimulant which causes excitement; and where there is excitement something breaks down. The only thing that can remain constant is your unexcited nature, and this need not be practised. It is always within you.

You cannot lose it, because it is your very nature.

Hence the quest of all religion is the quest for the basic nature of the individual. The search for the true nature of oneself is religion, because it is eternal; you can never be bored by it, because it is your true self. There is no way you can separate yourself from your nature; you cannot turn away from it and see it. If what you see bores you when you distance yourself from it, you must know that it is not your true nature.

When the mind is killed by the mantra, when the mantra causes the mind to commit suicide, the eternal spring arises within. When this eternal spring has arisen, the individual is freed from the external states of happiness and sadness, and attains ultimate solitude. Now he is alone!

Now he is drunk with himself; now he needs nothing; all his desires are dead, for happiness and sorrow are external. He does not long for happiness, nor does he want to be free from sorrow. All his external ties are broken. He is now stable and fixed within himself. He is constantly in bliss; he has no more desires. He is now absorbed in his own consciousness. His satchitananda, his truth-consciousness-bliss, is now constantly flowing. It is in every breath, in every footstep of his being.

*Freed from them, he attains his solitude.*

*The yogi who is established in his solitude ceases to desire, and thus attains liberation from birth and death.*

Then there is no birth; then there is no death. Birth and death are necessary when we travel in search of happiness. We desire happiness and happiness can only be achieved through the body; so we have no choice but to take a body. The happiness we desire decides the kind of body we take. The desire for happiness endures at the moment of death and becomes the seed of the next birth.

What does a tree do before it dies? It collects all its vital energy in its seeds. The seed is the tree's desire to exist after death. A seed is a marvellous phenomenon. The immense giant of a tree extracts its essence and deposits it in the seed, which it sends on the journey of life. Its own body will die, but the tree has already made preparations for a new body to live again. And this explains why, although the tree is born from a single seed, it produces millions of seeds in its lifetime. The tree takes no chances. It has to take many factors into account:

what if the seed falls on rocks or barren ground? What if it doesn't get water? It might be eaten by animals or crushed by someone else. The tree can't risk it, so it produces millions of seeds and, by various means, scatters them everywhere so that at least some of them will find a suitable place to grow.

In India there is the silk cotton tree. Nothing can grow under it, because its roots absorb all the water; so the tree has a wonderful way of spreading its seeds: it fills the pods with cotton so that they can fly away from the tree when the wind blows. It has arranged that the seeds do not fall on the ground, for that would be certain death for them.

It is not easy for a plant to grow under a bog tree, almost impossible, so all trees have devised their own ways of existing. Trees are clever and cunning in their own way; don't take them for simple and naive. In this world nothing and no one is simple and simple; no one can be simple and simple, for complexity and cunning are necessary prerequisites for existence. As soon as one becomes simple and clever, one has attained liberation.

Trees and plants have devised thousands of different ways to spread their seeds. The sweet nectar of flowers is only there for bees and butterflies. They alight on a flower for the nectar, thinking that it has been provided for them, unaware that as they suck the flower they collect hundreds of seeds on their legs in the form of pollen. The bees then transport the seed to distant places. When plants devise so many methods to survive, how many must you be inventing? Your cunning knows no bounds.

A man has enough sperm in his body to give birth to as many people as are alive in the world. A normal person, neither celibate nor libertine, has sexual intercourse at least four thousand times in his life. With each act he expels about one hundred million spermatozoa. Each sperm is capable of creating life, given the opportunity. Since a woman's ability to produce eggs is limited to one or two at a time, this is not possible, although one day it will be. That is why the kings of antiquity had so many wives.

Science now makes it possible for the sperm of a single individual to impregnate every woman in the world. This is a real possibility, for the discoveries of science can ultimately be put into practice, however dangerous they may be. Scientists to this day maintain that not everyone has the right to procreate: only people of the stature of an Einstein, for example. When we are so careful about the quality of plants, when we take so much trouble to improve the quality of flowers and animals, it is to be expected that we will begin to think the same of the human race; so in the near future scientists may decide which people should have the right to procreate. Various factors will be taken into account: health, intelligence, age, mental acuity, genius.

Those who are acceptable in these categories will be chosen and their seed will be used. Then it is possible that the sperm of one man can populate the whole world. There is also the desire for survival of each individual.

You will be surprised to know, and it has not yet been written in any book, that when a man reaches "loneliness", when he is beyond happiness and sorrow, his body stops producing semen; but the formation of sperm only stops when the desire for survival is completely extinguished. As long as the desire for survival remains, the body continues to produce sperm, whether in this body or in another.

Thus you keep the body alive on the one hand and your soul tormented by desire on the other, so that the soul will keep on searching for a new womb. You will wander as long as you identify yourself with happiness and sorrow, for then you will be longing for pleasure and more pleasure, and your dreams will lead you to new births.

Because all his desires have tone, the yogi who establishes himself in the state of "solitude" is completely freed from the cycle of birth and death. He is no longer born; and the unborn need not die. If you are born you must die. Death is the other side of birth. They are two sides of the same coin. He who wishes to be free from death must also be free from birth.

Everyone wants to be free from death, but not from birth. That is our difficulty. Everyone wants to be free from suffering and sorrow, but no one wants to give up joy and happiness. The day you seek freedom from joy, your life will undergo a transformation; on that day you will become religious.

Mulla Nasruddin set out on an ocean voyage with his wife. It was Mulla's first time at sea. He felt terribly ill; he could hardly lift his head. Moreover, the sea was very rough and that made things much worse for him. He called his wife and said, "Listen, I made a will before I went on this trip, and thank goodness I did. I've transferred everything to your name, and the will is in the bank with all the necessary papers. Bury me on the other shore, even if I'm not dead, because I'll never travel by sea again. You can go home and claim all my possessions.

The day when life seems worse than death - as it truly is - the day when life seems so horrible, grotesque and meaningless that under no circumstances will you undertake a new journey, on that day you will experience a transformation. At this moment, if you are interested in religion, it is only a part of your search for happiness, perhaps a new kind of happiness; and that is why you never attain religion.

Your search for religion will only be real when you are not ready to embark on another life journey.

You have seen it all and found it to be meaningless. You have experienced happiness and discovered that it is also filled with suffering and sorrow. You have seen pain and discovered that it is full of suffering. Sorrow is suffering, but even joy is not without suffering, but is another name for suffering. Everything that tastes sweet turns out to be poison. That which claims to be nectar is but another brand of poison. The day you recognise how useless and meaningless everything is, and also that everything is outside of you and has nothing to do with your intrinsic being, that day religion is born in you.

Remember to ask yourself if you are only interested in religion to achieve happiness.

Then you are not interested in religion at all. Dedication to religion is only true when you seek peace and serenity. Happiness is useless, suffering is useless; good riddance to both!

The yogi who establishes himself in his solitude is freed from all desires. Without desires, he no longer wants to embark on any new life journey. The journey itself no longer has any meaning for him. It is then that the cycle of birth and death is destroyed forever.

*The liberated person, for whom body and mind are no more than garments, attains Shivahood.*

He is Brahma! He is God, the supreme spirit that ever abides! The Sanskrit word for such a person is liberated, and refers to the five elements and the garment. It means that the five elements - earth, air, fire, water and ether - that make up the body are but garments for that person. The body and the mind are made of the five elements. The gross forms of the five elements form the body, and the subtle forms constitute the mind. When such a person recognises that the mind and body are but an outer garment, that his true self is hidden deep within the folds of his garment, he peels away the layers as one peels an onion and knows the Shivahood within. Such a liberated person becomes God Himself.

In our country we do not believe in a solitary God sitting somewhere high in the sky ruling the universe. No. In this country we believe that every life journey ends in God. It is through gradual flourishing that one becomes God. God is not an existential state. God is man's future possibility.

Try to understand it better. Judaism, Christianity and Islam are the three great religions born outside India. Hinduism, Buddhism and Jainism are the great religions born in India. There is a basic difference between the two. Islam, Judaism and Christianity place God at the beginning, as the primordial cause, the creator of the universe. We, in India, see God at the front, as the ultimate fruition. This makes a big difference. God is the future, not the past. God is the flower, not the seed. Hence we have placed our Buddhas on a flower, sitting on a lotus flower in full bloom, with its thousand petals.

If God is at the beginning of all things and is the creator, then he is the only one. Then this world is a dictatorship. Then there could be no liberation, for where can there be independence once you have been created? A created thing has no freedom of its own, for the creator can create and destroy as he pleases. Then you are mere playthings and puppets. Then your soul, your freedom, is meaningless. Hence in India we do not see God as the creator; we see him as the ultimate culmination, the ultimate completion. He is your ultimate development.

God is not the first step in your evolution, but the final peak. He is the Gourishankar, the Mount Everest. He is the sacred Mount Kailash, where all consciousness ultimately arrives. Everyone is heading for this very place. Sooner or later everyone has to get there. Every day you are becoming God, evolving into God. God is not a one-time event. God is a constantly flowing stream. God is happening every moment. He is growing inside you; you are His womb.

Hence this Shiva sutra ends with this last event. All scriptures end here. They start from you and end in God. What you are now is the first step. What you will finally be is the last and final step. Right now you are like the seed; that is your wandering. When you fully develop your wholeness, like a tree in full blossom, that will be your ultimate culmination, your fullness.

When the flowers bloom, the life of the tree is complete; in its blossoming, the tree has attained the full fragrance of its life. That for which it was born has been fulfilled. With the blossoming, the tree is filled with ecstasy. It is filled with dance. Every pore of its being thrills, for it has not lived in vain. Its purpose has been fulfilled because it has blossomed to its fullest fragrance and beauty.

When a tree is so filled with joy at the blossoming of a flower - a flower that begins to wilt as soon as it opens, a flower that does not bloom for a single day - then much more ecstasy must be in the universe when a Vardhaman becomes Mahavira or a Gautam Siddhartha blossoms into a Buddha. We call Shivahood such a blossom that never withers, and that is God!

Use the mantra so that all that is useless and meaningless in you fades away, and all that has meaning and purpose is cleansed and purified. Use the mantra so that all that you are at this moment is shattered, and you are scattered on the ground to bring forth that which is your possibility.